Mathematical Power

Mathematical Power

Lessons from a Classroom

■ **Ruth E. Parker**

Heinemann
Portsmouth, NH

Heinemann
A division of Reed Elsevier Inc.
361 Hanover Street
Portsmouth, NH 03801-3912
Offices and agents throughout the world

Material from *Curriculum and Evaluation Standards for School Mathematics* reprinted by permission of the National Council of Teachers of Mathematics.

Every effort has been made to contact the copyright holders for permission to reprint borrowed material where necessary. We regret any oversights that may have occurred and would be happy to rectify them in future printings of this work.

Library of Congress Cataloging-in-Publication Data
Parker, Ruth E.
    Mathematical power : lessons from a classroom / Ruth E. Parker.
        p.   cm.
    Includes bibliographical references.
    ISBN 0-435-08339-2
    1. Mathematics—Study and teaching (Elementary)   I. Title.
QA135.5.P338   1993
372.7044—dc20   92-46283
                                                                      CIP

Cover design by Jenny Jensen Greenleaf
Front cover mathematical rendering by Matthew Simpson
Back cover mathematical renderings by Sarah Mealy
Interior design and prepress production services by
    Camden Type 'n Graphics

03 02 01 00   ML   6 7 8 9

▪ ▪ ▪ Contents _____

CONTENTS

■ ■ ■ Foreword _____

This book is the story of a year Ruth Parker spent with fifth-grade teacher Cathy Young and her students. It is an important book for three reasons. First, it deals with the subject of mathematics; success or failure in mathematics affects the future life of a student as few other subjects do. Second, it depicts what the teaching and learning of mathematics can be and does so not by presenting an idealized, oversimplified version of a classroom but by capturing both the complexities and the challenges facing us as teachers. It does not trivialize or romanticize, but it does show us the wonderful and awesome possibilities of simple reality as it plays out in the daily life of the classroom. Third, it presents what will be for many readers a new view of what the subject of mathematics is really about. By observing real children in a real classroom, we see that children can be taught mathematics in a way that helps them see it as a powerful tool for making sense of the world.

Ruth's deep respect for children has motivated her search for ways to make the study of mathematics a powerful and enhancing experience for them. Her respect for and need to understand more fully the challenges facing teachers motivated the doctoral study that resulted in the writing of this book. Many of us have devoted much time and energy searching for ways to make mathematics make sense for children. We buy activity books, we attend workshops and conferences. We are eager to try new ideas and approaches in our classrooms. But the classroom realities we run into often resemble brick walls. Things don't always work the way we expect; we aren't sure of the big picture, no one really tells us what to do when it doesn't work. It's just not as easy as it sounds. After many years as a classroom teacher and many years of working with preservice and in-service teachers, Ruth knew that what was missing for many was a depiction of how to make the goals of mathematics reform efforts really happen in a classroom. She wanted to deal with all the factors that impinge on a teacher trying to bring about real change.

I first became aware of the challenge Ruth had given herself when I traveled with her to present the proposal for her doctoral study to her dissertation committee. Committee members were in agreement that rather than try to capture the full complexity of teaching and learning mathematics, the reasonable thing would be to isolate a smaller issue. What she planned to do was too comprehensive. Ruth resisted the committee's suggestion that she simplify her task. She knew it would be much more meaningful and helpful to teachers if she could capture the whole complexity—and simplicity—of what it means to teach mathematics, the relationship between all the factors: setting goals, planning for the short and long term, meeting the range of needs, responding to needs as they come up. It is the myriad ongoing decision making that is the challenge, and Ruth felt she could not help teachers better understand the process by looking at a small piece of the whole.

I admit that I, too, wasn't sure whether what she wanted to do would be possible. But it certainly was. The real power of this book is that it helps us look at everything we are doing with children, tune in to the process that is at work—a process that applies to everyone involved in teaching and learning. It is not pie in the sky but a picture of everyday joy and struggle—a real human endeavor that speaks to us all. You will feel like you have walked into this classroom with Ruth and Cathy and the students. You will see the struggle, feel the triumphs. You will understand that it is possible to support all children, to unlock the potential in each of them to make sense of and with mathematics.

Ruth's story is powerful and exciting precisely because it is real; real problems come up, real solutions are found, and real growth takes place. Because it is real, the story is necessarily unique. Still, it has much to teach us whatever our particular classroom situation. It gives us an idea of what can happen; it gives us tools to use. It shows us the process of teaching and learning mathematics. It answers real questions. *How do we really meet the range of needs within a classroom?* Meet Michael and Steven and see. *What mathematics is important and why?* Sit with Ruth and Cathy as they plan. See the power of patterns, the reality of children collecting data. Observe children starting out somewhat sillily, then digging into what really matters to them. Realize that although this doesn't happen instantly, it does happen. *What makes a lesson good?* Note the focus in this classroom on developing understanding over time: instruction is not organized around isolated lessons but rather children are immersed in multiday and multiweek units designed around important mathematical ideas. Applaud Ruth and Cathy as they revise their plans to respond to the interests and understanding the children reveal. *How can we possibly be accountable for our students' growth and work?* Watch as these teachers develop rubrics for investigations and use portfolios and learning logs to profile students' work. *We're told not to focus on written algorithms, but how can we make sure children develop the skills they need?* Read and see and understand this alternative to developing facility with number. *Where does cooperative or collaborative learning fit into the bigger picture?* Observe Cathy and Ruth as they bring collaborative learning alive in their classroom without using artificial or contrived models or methods. Learn from them as they deal with real problems in respectful, honest, and practical ways, not trying to prevent these problems but rather helping their students learn from them. *Where can we find an appropriate scope and sequence?* Look beyond scope and sequence in the traditional sense as Ruth and Cathy use purposeful planning around important mathematics as a process for working with children to develop mathematical thinking.

I'm confident that those of you who have been trying an activity-based approach only to feel sometimes lost and frustrated will find many answers to your questions here. Those of you who are reluctant to give up the textbook, concerned that your children will be cheated if you go along with those who are calling for major changes, will see how much more powerful the math experiences of these children are than anything you had imagined while doing pages of fractions. You will agree that Ruth is talking about raising expectations, not lowering them. Those of you who are excited by process writing and literature-based reading but have not been able to imagine how math can be that exciting or tap into the humanity of children will see what is possible.

For all of you who have been struggling alone to get your mathematics classroom to make sense, who know that sometimes what you are doing isn't working, here is the book to help you make those changes that will better serve your students. I know you will find it was worth waiting for.

—Kathy Richardson

■ ■ ■ Acknowledgments

I was so fortunate to spend a year in the classroom with Cathy Young, a remarkable teacher, and her twenty-eight fifth graders, who amazed me daily. I want to thank them for one of the best years of my professional career and for letting me tell their story.

This book would not have been written without the support and encouragement of the many people who have impacted my life and work. From the Makah children at Neah Bay, who taught me so much about teaching and learning, to the MSDs, in California, who stretched my understanding and continually prodded me to "hurry up and write," I am grateful for their lessons.

To Oscar Schaaf, who opened doors for me at the University of Oregon, and who never gave up on me, I extend deep appreciation. The study that resulted in this book would not have taken place without Oscar's ongoing encouragement.

To my teachers along the way, I am grateful. To Marilyn Burns, for all she has taught me and for those years when she pushed me to do things I knew I wasn't ready for, thank you. To my friend and colleague Margaret McCreary, I extend my gratitude for her encouragement and for all the work she did to support my work. A special thanks also to Kathy Richardson, whom I am fortunate to have as a close friend and colleague. And to Mary Bussanich, who has taught me so much about life and whose life continues to provide such inspiration, thank you seems inadequate. To the many others, too numerous to name, who have been my teachers, thank you all.

I dedicate this book to my parents, Don and Ellie Buckingham, whose remarkable life walk continues to impact my life profoundly. For so many reasons, this book would not have happened without their unwavering support and belief in me.

And finally, to Adonia, perhaps my greatest teacher and the inspiration for so much of my work, thank you for never hesitating to say, "Go for it, Mom."

▪ ▪ ▪ Preface _____

There is a growing consensus throughout the nation that what we have been doing to teach mathematics is not working for our children. Numerous reports have highlighted the shortcomings of mathematics education and have warned of the serious effects of such shortcomings on the health and future of our nation. Improving mathematics education is not a matter of adding a little spice to a dull subject or of making a few minor changes in content or approach. It requires no less than a redefinition of what mathematics is and an understanding that the goal of mathematics education must be the development of mathematical power in all students.

Making mathematics education meaningful and relevant requires a fundamental restructuring of nearly every aspect of mathematics instruction—curriculum content; learning environment; teacher role; and methods for assessing children's mathematical understanding.

Many organizations and individuals have worked diligently to define a new agenda for mathematics education. However, teachers faced with the realities of the classroom know that it is one thing to see the problem and call for reform and quite another to make it happen in the classroom. After years of working with teachers as they attempted to restructure their classrooms, I decided to return to the classroom in order to understand better how the theoretical ideas of the mathematics reform movement look through the eyes of the classroom teacher and to experience firsthand how these ideas play out in the classroom on a day-to-day basis.

This book is the result of my collaboration with Cathy Young, a fifth-grade teacher, as we worked to understand better what it means to teach toward the development of mathematical power in all children. We hope that our experiences will provide a picture of what happens when classroom-based instruction is aligned with mathematics reform goals.

For me this collaboration represents a return to the classroom after a twelve-year hiatus. During those twelve years, I was fortunate to work closely with many people involved in establishing a new national agenda for mathematics education. As a result, I had a solid theoretical understanding of the potential for mathematics education as defined by the professional mathematics community. As a classroom teacher in the 1970s, I had enjoyed teaching mathematics. I had had opportunities to work with several outstanding math educators. Manipulatives abounded in my classroom. I used place-value materials so that children would understand the algorithms I taught. I provided activities from the various strands of mathematics. My students, many of whom were "minorities" and/or "disadvantaged" and had previously been unsuccessful in school, learned to enjoy mathematics. But by the 1990s, the professional mathematics community was asking for more. For example, teachers were being asked to move away from isolated activities and toward multiday or multiweek investigations in which children interact with important ideas from diverse strands as they work to solve complex and relevant problems. Rather than teach standard algorithms, teachers were asked to encourage students to invent a variety of approaches and/or algorithms as they worked to solve problems.

Although I brought to this research study a clear understanding of the issues in mathematics reform and of what it means to "do" mathematics as outlined in current reform documents, I also brought curiosity and a spirit of inquiry. I hoped that this study would shed light on the complexities of what it means to teach for understanding in mathematics.

The Teacher

Cathy Young is forty-seven years old and has taught for nine years. This is her fourth year back in the classroom after leaving teaching for fourteen years to raise a family and pursue other interests. It is her seventh year of teaching at the fifth-grade level. She loves teaching.

Cathy does not have a mathematics background. In fact, she has learned to fear and dislike mathematics. Most of her math instruction to date has consisted of teaching from a textbook, although she has been dissatisfied with that approach and has occasionally moved away from the text and used problem-solving materials. Cathy has a sister-in-law who is very involved in mathematics reform efforts. They have talked extensively about the need for changes in how math is taught. Cathy has wanted to change her teaching, but has not had the confidence or support necessary to do so.

I first met her when she attended a course on collaborative learning in mathematics that I taught during the summer of 1991. When I mentioned that I was interested in going into a classroom to work with children, she invited me to work with her fifth-grade class. When I decided to conduct classroom-based research, I contacted Cathy. She was enthusiastic about our working together.

Although fearful of mathematics, Cathy is perhaps somewhat uncharacteristic in her willingness to risk being a learner herself and to collaborate in a fundamental restructuring of her mathematics program. She is not a timid person. She is an articulate and gently outspoken advocate for children, and her philosophical beliefs align with the goals of mathematics reform. She is recognized by administrative personnel at both the school and the district office as a dedicated and thoughtful teacher.

The Children

Cathy's fifth-grade class comprises nine girls and nineteen boys. One student has been in special education classes for the past several years, and two others would qualify for special services on the basis of low test scores. One child has participated in the district's "gifted" program, and a second has been referred to and tested for that program. The class is not ethnically diverse, reflecting the population in northwestern Washington. The only student of color is a Native American child, Steven, who has been in special education classes for several years. One student is on medication for hyperactivity. Nearly half of the students come from single-parent homes and/or are children of divorced parents. The students have diverse socioeconomic backgrounds. The school serves a low- to middle-income population. We anticipated that these students would have received traditional mathematics instruction before entering the fifth grade. Our expectations were confirmed when, on the second day of school, Cathy asked her fifth graders to write in their math learning logs about what it means to be good at mathematics:

> It means that you practise a lot. That you can do math fast. That you can do mathematics easily.—Paul, age 10

> You must be able to learn fast, think fast, and think clearly. It means to write fast and anserw qeastions corectly.—Zachary, age 10

It means being good at numbers thinking logicaly being smart and getting the right answer.—Bryan, age 10

Well I don't like math because its to hard but I have never liked math. I'm not a mathematichan because math is not my thing. it means you follow derections and alwas lisening.—Jed, age 10

It means to get good grades, and to be able to add and subtract. To think well and get correct answers. I think that I am pretty good at math because I'm in the ALPS program, I usually get 100%, I come from a smart family (except my brother) and I do well in many other subjects.—Rachael, age 10

I't means that you have to practice. I't means that you spend some time at school or at home go over math with other people or a parent. I don't feel perfect when I'm doing math because I'm not real good. I men I don't zip right threw the problems like some people do in math.—Timmy, age 10

The children's responses reveal much about their feelings about mathematics and their previous experiences with the subject. Clearly, they view speed and right answers as important aspects of doing mathematics. By fifth grade, some of these children have learned to like the subject, others have learned to dislike it. Their descriptions of what it means to be good at mathematics have little in common with what it means to be mathematically powerful.

The Study

I worked in Cathy's classroom from September through April. What follows is the story of our mathematics program as it played out in the life of a classroom. The study—and this book—is a picture of a meaningful fifth-grade mathematics program and of the effort and teacher decisions it took to implement such a program. It offers new information that can:

1. Help teacher educators better understand the day-to-day issues classroom teachers face in moving from a traditional to a restructured mathematics program.
2. Contribute to a better understanding of how the theoretical constructs of the mathematics reform movement play out day by day in the classroom.

3. Create a picture of a fifth-grade mathematics classroom that includes details of:
   a. Curriculum content.
   b. Practical steps for helping students work collaboratively and independently on mathematical problems.
   c. Issues and practices addressed by the teacher as she worked to change her role from imparter of information to facilitator of learning.
   d. Practices for making assessment indistinguishable from good instruction.

Our work with these fifth graders stretched my understanding of what a mathematics program can be. I am convinced we only scratched the surface of what children can do as mathematicians. My time back in the classroom left me with a profound respect for children as sense makers. It is my hope that their story leaves you with the same.

■ ■ ■ **Chapter One** _____

Issues in Mathematics Reform

This book is the story of children doing mathematics in a fifth-grade classroom. It is also the story of a teacher, Cathy Young, working to make her mathematics program more meaningful. This chapter discusses some of the important issues within the mathematics reform movement in order to place this story within the framework of mathematics reform.

One of the defining documents in current mathematics reform efforts is the *Curriculum and Evaluation Standards for School Mathematics* issued by the National Council of Teachers of Mathematics (NCTM) (1989). The *Standards* grew out of work in several states and in various mathematics arenas. With its publication of the *Standards,* the NCTM set a national agenda and established a direction for mathematics reform that has as its goal a thinking mathematics curriculum for all students. The first four standards describe instructional practices that vary substantially from typical mathematics instruction in schools throughout the country.

Standard 1: Mathematics As Problem Solving suggests that students should "use, with increasing confidence, problem-solving approaches to investigate and understand mathematical content" (p. 137). Standard 2:

Mathematics As Communication promotes the development of students who can "discuss mathematical ideas and make conjectures and convincing arguments, . . . reflect on and clarify their own thinking about mathematical ideas and situations" (p. 78), and "formulate mathematical definitions and express generalizations discovered through investigations" (p. 140). Standard 3: Mathematics As Reasoning describes students who can "make and evaluate mathematical conjectures and arguments, validate their own thinking" (p. 81), "judge the validity of arguments" (pp. 81, 143), and "appreciate the pervasive use and power of reasoning as part of mathematics" (p. 143). Standard 4: Mathematical Connections calls for instruction that helps students "see mathematics as an integrated whole, explore problems and describe results using graphical, numerical, physical, algebraic, and verbal mathematical models or representations" (p. 84), "recognize the equivalent representations of the same concept, . . . use and value the connections among mathematical topics" (p. 146), and "value the role of mathematics in our culture and society" (p. 84).

These four standards offer a vision of mathematics classrooms where students work both collaboratively and independently on challenging mathematical problems, discussing their ideas and considering diverse viewpoints and approaches as they use mathematics to make sense of situations; where students are expected to validate and explain their thinking and to communicate their findings rather than rely on the answer book; where students are encouraged to make connections between their experiences and mathematical ideas they have encountered previously.

What Is

Mathematics instruction throughout this country continues to present a quite different picture. Textbooks that focus on isolated skills and paper-and-pencil drill continue to be the primary source of the curriculum (Dossey et al. 1988). Mathematics is viewed as a fixed subject consisting of a collection of abstract skills or concepts to be mastered (Brown, Collins, and Duguid 1989). Students spend nearly all their school mathematics careers learning rote skills that are performed in the real world by inexpensive tools. They are taught, erroneously, that being good at mathematics means memorizing formulas and knowing when to apply them (Davis 1987; Schoenfeld 1989). In short, teachers continue to teach mathematics the way they themselves were taught.

Instruction based on this view of mathematics has produced large numbers of students unable to use math skills to solve even simple problems (Dossey et al. 1988). Numerous documents warn of the effect such instruction has on students and on society. In a summary of the National Assessment of Educational Progress (NAEP) in mathematics, Dossey warns:

> The skills and expertise of a country's workforce are the foundation of its economic success. Lately, in our country, this foundation appears too fragile to withstand the challenges of the 21st century. . . . Too many students leave high school without the mathematical understanding that will allow them to participate fully as workers and citizens in contemporary society. (pp. 8–9)

Large numbers of students are dropping out of mathematics after the tenth grade (Stein 1989). Given the increasingly technological workplace of the 1990s, more and more careers are closed to these students. This problem is particularly critical for minority and female students (Oakes 1985; Secada 1988). The National Research Council (NRC) (1989) suggests:

> More than any other subject, mathematics filters students out of programs leading to scientific and professional careers. . . . America is moving backward—not forward—in its efforts to achieve the full participation of minority citizens in the life and prosperity of the nation. . . . We are at risk of becoming a nation divided both economically and racially by knowledge of mathematics. (pp. 7, 13)

Many children are currently being labeled and ability grouped as early as six years of age based on their success, or lack thereof, with a curriculum that asks them to memorize facts rather than see relationships—a curriculum that has little to nothing in common with what it means to do mathematics. This practice of labeling children continues even in light of a substantial body of research that suggests that once children are labeled they have very little chance of ever moving beyond the boundaries of their label. Not surprisingly, many children decide early on that mathematics is not their game.

In his book *Innumeracy,* John Paulos (1988) warns that America has become a mathematically illiterate population unable to make sense of information presented numerically or to knowledgeably interpret statistical information, skills essential to an informed citizenry. No longer can we as a nation afford to have large numbers of our students leave school without the necessary mathematical skills to participate successfully in today's work force and without the skills to knowledgeably interpret information essential to full participation as an informed citizen. No longer can we afford to have a privileged few pursue the mathematics needed to enter expanding scientific fields (Stein 1989). No longer can we afford to have mathematics act as a filter that pushes many students, largely minorities, out of school (National Research Council 1989).

What Must Be: Mathematics for All Children

There are well-ingrained myths in this country about who can and who can't learn math. These myths are being challenged by proponents of mathematics reform. At the heart of mathematics reform efforts is a belief that mathematics is for *all* children. All children have the right to a mathematics education that engages them with important mathematical ideas, requires thinking, and develops understanding. The NCTM *Standards* call for restructured mathematics classrooms that will allow *all* students to experience the power and beauty of mathematics. If mathematical power for all students is the goal, then math classrooms must be restructured so that students' work in mathematics more closely resembles the work of mathematicians in the field.

Examining the differences between the culture of school mathematics and the culture of mathematics in the real world leads to the inescapable conclusion that school mathematics is unlikely to result in mathematically powerful students. In many ways the culture of school mathematics is the antithesis of the culture of mathematics as a discipline (Davis 1989; Dienes 1987; Goldenberg 1989). These differences are illustrated in Figure 1–1.

The goal of mathematics reform efforts is to develop students who are challenged by messy, ill-defined situations or complex problems; who are curious and have developed "thoughtful habits of inquiry" (Wiggins 1989a); who are able to use important mathematical ideas to make sense of information, events, and situations in the world; and who understand the power of mathematics as a way to reveal significant patterns and relationships that surround them. Meeting this goal will require a comprehensive restructuring of the content of mathematics courses, of the learning environment, of the role of the teacher, and of assessment practices.

THE CULTURE OF MATHEMATICS . . .	
In Schools	As a Discipline
Mathematics is neat and concise. It is about memorizing correct procedures or algorithms for solving well-defined problems.	Mathematics is messy. It involves a search for sense and order from complex, ill-defined situations.
Speed or getting answers quickly is important and emphasized.	Persistence and flexibility are essential to mathematical pursuits. Mathematicians often spend years of their lifetime trying to solve *a* single problem.
Right answers are emphasized. Answers are validated by the teacher or answer book.	There is no answer book. Often there are no best answers nor even a guarantee that an answer will be found. Problem resolution involves judgment calls. Justification of one's ideas and communication of one's findings are essential to mathematical endeavors.
Arithmetic and abstract manipulation of symbols form the core of the curriculum.	Important ideas and the interrelatedness of those ideas from diverse mathematical domains of geometry, patterns and functions, logic, number, measurement, probability, and data collection and analysis form the core of mathematics.
Calculators are to be used once basic skills are mastered. Computers and other technology are useful primarily for drill but also for enrichment.	Tools (e.g., manipulatives, computers, calculators) are continuously available and used to examine and represent ideas or extend thinking. Tedious computations are done by machines and thinking and reasoning by people.
Math is done in isolation, working quietly from a textbook or worksheet.	Math is used to make sense of information, events, or situations in the world. It is a collaborative endeavor with mathematicians and others working together, communicating their ideas and building on one another's ideas and experiences.

Figure 1.1. The culture of mathematics.

Restructuring Curriculum

While much of the mathematics used in the world today has been invented and/or extended within the past forty years (e.g., data analysis, photogrammetry, fractals and chaos, discrete mathematics), almost all of the mathematics that exists in schools is hundreds of years old. Course content must be restructured to reflect the dynamic, ever-expanding nature of mathematics, the availability of technology, and the study of mathematical topics relevant to the world of the 1990s. Tom Romberg, in an April 1991 address to the National Summit on Mathematics Education, addressed this issue as he described the vast discrepancy between our nation's goals for mathematics education and our current curriculum. He suggested that while we talk of America's having "world class" mathematics standards, we continue to offer a curriculum consisting of eight years of eighteenth-century arithmetic, three years of seventeenth-century algebra, and one year of third-century-B.C. geometry.

Several documents provide direction for restructuring the content of mathematics programs. *On the Shoulders of Giants* (National Research Council 1990a) explores the concepts of dimension, quantity, uncertainty, shape, and change. The NCTM *Standards* (1989) extends the call for curriculum based on important mathematical ideas and the interrelatedness of these ideas. The California Department of Education's *Mathematics Model Curriculum Guide* (1987) identifies "Essential Understandings," or important mathematical ideas within the strands of patterns and functions, logic, probability and statistics, number, geometry, and algebra. These documents are consistent in describing important mathematical ideas as ideas that develop in complexity over time. They are also consistent in their message that how math is taught is as important as what math is taught.

Restructuring the Learning Environment

Instructional practices that align with the NCTM *Standards* vary significantly from current beliefs and practices about teaching mathematics. In most classrooms throughout the country students sit at desks facing the front of the room. They spend the vast majority of their mathematics-instruction time listening to teachers explain new concepts or procedures and working silently at their desks, practicing mechanical procedures that consist primarily of paper-and-pencil skills. Students' understanding and their ability to use acquired knowledge and skills in new or unexpected situations receive relatively little instructional attention (NAEP 1983; Schoenfeld 1989). Even basic understandings of number and arithmetic are neglected. Children are asked to memorize algorithms and formulas without understanding, to accept answers without questioning. Talking is most often discouraged, and the asking of questions becomes increasingly rare as students move through the grades (Wiggins 1989a).

Mathematics classrooms that align with the NCTM *Standards* are alive with activity. Instruction is organized into coherent multiday and multiweek units of study around rich and important mathematical investigations. Students are often seated in small heterogeneous groups, using manipulatives and other tools and considering diverse viewpoints and approaches as they work together on complex tasks. Students rely on one another, on materials, and on experts in the field as well as on the teacher. There are frequent opportunities for students to make choices and to pursue individual areas of interest. Students have frequent opportunities to communicate their findings orally and through written or graphic displays. Animated discussions are the norm as students challenge one another's thinking and present diverse points of view. Often the teacher asks probing questions designed to help students make mathematical connections.

At the heart of mathematics reform efforts is a constructivist view of learning. This view is described in *Everybody Counts* (National Research Council 1989):

> Educational research offers compelling evidence that students learn mathematics well only when they construct their own mathematical understanding. To understand what they learn, they must enact for themselves verbs that permeate the mathematics curriculum: "examine," "represent," "transform," "solve," "apply," "prove," "communicate." This happens most readily when students work in groups, engage in discussion, make presentations, and in other ways take charge of their own learning. (pp. 58–59)

Mathematics instruction must be based on what is known about how learning occurs. Large bodies of research suggest that knowledge, if it is to be useful, must be constructed by the learner (Chaille and Brittain 1991; Kamii 1983b; Resnick 1987a). Classrooms should be restructured to provide children opportunities to construct mathematical understanding by encountering ideas in context, acting on physical objects, using appropriate tools, and talking about and reflecting on mathematical ideas and their relevance as they work to make sense of complex and engaging situations. Classrooms in which students listen to teachers impart knowledge, then work in isolation from a textbook or workbook, are inappropriate; we need instead mathematics classrooms in which students work in collaboration, talking about their learning, considering a variety of viewpoints, and justifying their thinking as they grapple to make sense of information, problems, and situations.

Although a constructivist view of learning permeates mathematics reform literature, much of current school structure, curriculum content, assessment methods, and resulting staff development is based on behaviorist or scientific management perspectives of learning. Romberg, Zarinnia, and Collins (1990) describe the three basic principles of this scientific management view: "specialization of work through the simplification of individual tasks, predetermined rules for coordinating the tasks, and detailed monitoring of performance" (p. 26). These principles, although challenged by a wide body of more-current research on learning, still permeate the predominant view of the role of the teacher in a mathematics classroom.

Restructuring the Role of the Teacher

In their efforts to improve instruction, school and district decision makers often turn to popular programs or models that have as their basis views about teaching and learning that differ fundamentally from the constructivist viewpoint supported in the NCTM *Standards.* For example, Madeline Hunter's (1976) "instructional theory into practice" approach teaches the importance of anticipatory sets, teacher modeling, monitored practice, and closure. The goal is clearly student mastery of identified concepts and skills. Many currently popular cooperative learning models emphasize teaching skills in isolation, correct answers, and mastery. Teachers are encouraged to control behavior and learning through external rewards for both social skills and academic tasks. Students bring their labels as high, middle, and low achievers to their cooperative groups. Step-by-step procedures or structures for teachers to implement in their classrooms are the primary focus of cooperative learning workshops. The works of David and Roger Johnson (1986) and Robert Slavin (1983), three of the most prolific writers and widely recognized leaders in the field of cooperative learning, are steeped in behaviorist assumptions about learning.

Attempts at educational reform often consist of the implementation of new techniques or procedures that rest on old paradigms of teaching and learning. This overlaying of new goals on old belief systems has all too often resulted in a loss of the intent and integrity of the goals of mathematics reform.

Isolating and simplifying skills and content will not produce students who are challenged by messy, ill-defined situations. Nor will it produce students who are able to see mathematics as an integrated whole. An emphasis on speed, right answers, and closure will not result in persistence and flexibility, dispositions essential to mathematical endeavors. An emphasis on mastery will not lead to a focus on the study of important mathematical ideas or to the development of students' understanding of these ideas and their interrelatedness over time. Teacher control of lessons, behaviors, and outcomes will not produce students who can take responsibility for their learning and actions, who make conjectures and then pursue ways of finding out, who can explain their reasoning and justify their own answers, who develop dispositions to seek and to understand. Labeling of students as high, middle, and low achievers works against the notion of *all* students as full participants in dynamic and relevant mathematics programs.

Old paradigms of teaching and learning will not result in mathematical power for teachers or students. We need new paradigms that support teachers as instructional decision makers and facilitators of learning, that recognize children as capable sense makers in control of constructing their new understandings.

Restructuring Assessment

Mathematics reform efforts based on new goals for mathematics education often meet an early demise because they fail to show significant gains on assessment measures that favor factual recall over thinking and reasoning, mastery of isolated skills over the integration of important mathematical ideas, speed over thoughtfulness. Peter Hilton (1981) highlights the limitations of current mathematics testing when he claims:

> [Current tests] . . . force students to answer artificial questions under artificial circumstances; they impose severe and artificial time constraints; they encourage the false view that mathematics can be separated out into tiny water-tight compartments; they teach the perverted doctrine that mathematical problems have a single right answer and that all other answers are equally wrong; they fail completely to take account of mathematical process, concentrating exclusively on the "answer." (p. 79)

It is widely recognized that norm-referenced standardized tests drive curriculum and instruction. The current movement toward developing performance-based assessment in mathematics is the result of growing recognition that both what is taught and how it is taught are directly impacted by the content and form of current assessment (Romberg et al. 1990). Assessment must be aligned with curriculum goals if restructuring efforts are to succeed. Short-answer and multiple-choice tests or norm-referenced standardized tests that measure primarily antiquated computation skills do not support the goals of the NCTM *Standards.* Indeed, such tests inhibit desired teaching practices. It is unfair to ask teachers to align their teaching with the NCTM *Standards* in order to provide mathematics instruction appropriate to the 1990s and then continue to hold them accountable for students' mastery of eighteenth-century skills. Current tests do little to reveal students' mathematical dispositions or their understanding of concepts. It is possible for students to provide right answers on worksheets or test items and yet have fundamental misunderstandings. Wiggins (1989b) addresses this issue when he poses the question, "Does a correct answer [on these types of tests] mask thoughtless recall? Does a wrong answer obscure thoughtful understanding?" (p. 708).

The impact of assessment on instruction is direct and all-encompassing. It is widely recognized that we get what we test, and that what we don't test disappears from the curriculum (Resnick and Resnick 1991). If we want important mathematics as the core of the curriculum, then we must find more authentic ways to measure how students can do mathematics.

District, state, and national efforts to develop and implement performance-based assessment must be an integral part of mathematics restructuring efforts. Many states are committed to the development of performance-based assessment alternatives. California, through the California Assessment Program (CAP), has been at the forefront of assessment reform through its development of alternative methods of assessment. CAP has developed, and is currently piloting, open-ended items, group investigations, and the use of portfolios as methods of assessing mathematics programs in schools throughout the state. The April 1991 National Summit on Mathematics Assessment had as its focus the need for authentic, performance-based assessment. The New Standards Project at the University of Pittsburgh, in conjunction with the Center for Education and the Economy, is currently spearheading a national effort to develop a performance-based assessment system in mathematics.

There is widespread recognition that the development and implementation of alternative forms of assessment better able to assess students' ability to do mathematics—to conjecture; to invent; to use mathematics to interpret information, solve problems, and make sense of and impact their world—is essential to mathematics restructuring efforts.

The NCTM *Standards* and other reform documents have provided a vision for mathematics education. The commitment it will take to realize that vision in classrooms throughout the country is substantial. Restructuring mathematics programs will be an emergent, sometimes messy process as we continue to respond to changes within the field of mathematics and to the changing needs of society. Yet the need for change is compelling. A population able to think and reason critically, able and willing to consider a variety of viewpoints, and able to use mathematics to make sense of complex situations is essential to the health and future of this nation.

Two Teachers: *Establishing Our Philosophical Base*

Cathy Young, a fifth-grade teacher, knew that inviting me into her classroom to work with mathematics meant that we would examine nearly every aspect of what went on in the classroom—the content of her curriculum, the learning environment, her role as a teacher, children as learners, and ways of assessing understanding. Although she was uncomfortable with mathematics, and somewhat apprehensive about what it would be like to have a researcher in her classroom, she believed the benefits (learning to provide meaningful mathematics instruction) outweighed the risks. Before the school year began, Cathy and I explored our philosophical beliefs about children and learning and examined our reasons for wanting to pursue this collaborative endeavor. We knew that as we worked to improve her mathematics program, our philosophical beliefs and goals would guide our decision making. It is important to make explicit some of the belief systems and goals that formed the basis of our efforts.

Philosophical Beliefs

1. *The goal of education is to promote the development of students as knowledgeable, responsible, and reflective decision makers.* Cathy and I agreed that we wanted children to understand that they can and do make a difference; that their knowledge and actions impact others; and that their responsibility is to become knowledgeable and reflective so that their influence on one another, their communities, and their world is a positive one.

If students are to be knowledgeable, then the content of what is taught is of primary importance. Our goal was to have mathematics instruction focus on relevant and essential mathematical ideas. We were not interested in students' mastery of skills that are of little value in the 1990s.

If children are to be responsible decisions makers, they need to participate in decision-making processes. If they are to become reflective, they need frequent opportunities and invitations to reflect on their ideas and actions.

2. *Mathematics classrooms must involve students in the investigation of important mathematical ideas across the domains of mathematics. It is essential that we teach mathematics, not just arithmetic.* The mathematics curriculum in this fifth-grade classroom involves students in the study of patterns and functional relationships, data collection and analysis, dimension and geometry, logic, measurement, quantification, size and growth, chance, prediction, number relationships, algorithmic thinking, and "number sense."

3. *The classroom should be a community of learners*. If we are to provide a classroom in which students are free to take risks, explore ideas, make conjectures, find out, challenge their own and one another's thinking, contribute to and build on one another's ideas and understandings, we must move beyond viewing the class either as a whole or as a collection of individuals to viewing the class as a community of learners. Lappan and Ferrini-Mundy (1992) present a rationale for promoting mathematics classrooms as communities of learners:

> We have ample evidence that learning in isolation from interaction with others is likely to result in students constructing mathematical worlds that have little fit with the accepted "truths" of the discipline.... The creation of a community in which one's private world is exposed has the potential to challenge the learner's currently held views and lead to the construction of more acceptable and powerful views. It is through the give and take, the back and forth of shared questions, ideas, and feelings

that community begins. . . . The acts of receiving help and being nurtured are important; of equal importance is the giving of help. However, herein lies one of the traps, especially for teachers—distinguishing between help given by telling, which results in dependent learners, and help given by questioning and collaborating, which results in the empowerment of the learner. (pp. 7–8)

Central to creating a community of learners is movement away from a view of the teacher as imparter of knowledge to a constructivist view of the child as actively involved in the construction of new understanding. It also involves movement away from a view of the teacher as validator of ideas or answers to a view of mathematical reasoning, logic, and mathematical evidence as verification. Mathematics can no longer be viewed as a fixed body of knowledge to be memorized. Individual and group sense making must be of primary importance. Our goal is for students as well as the teacher to take responsibility for keeping one another on the edge of their understanding, always pushing to extend the boundaries of what is known. Our goal is to produce students who do not rest content being asked to do things that don't make sense or that are not engaging or relevant.

4. *While algorithmic thinking and "number sense" are important to mathematical power, the teaching of standard U.S. algorithms is of little use other than for their historical value.* There is growing awareness within the professional mathematics community that the teaching of standard U.S. algorithms may serve little purpose in the technological world of the 1990s. Still, the teaching of such skills makes up the bulk of current instructional practice in this country. Furthermore, computation done in isolation is prominent on current standardized tests. Cathy and I decided to focus on having children invent algorithms rather than teaching standard paper-and-pencil algorithms. Would this inhibit their solving problems that necessitate computation or algorithmic understanding? We would explore alternatives to helping children develop facility with numbers and algorithmic proficiency.

5. *Tools are an important aspect of doing mathematics. Calculators, computers, and a variety of manipulatives should be continually available for use.* The National Council of Teachers of Mathematics (1989, 1991b) has taken the stand that calculators should be continuously available in class, during homework, and on tests. This remains a hotly debated issue at the school level. Many educators fear that students who have continual access to calculators will not be able to use algorithms to solve problems. Some worry that students will become lazy, lacking the discipline that practicing algorithms provides.

Standardized tests for the most part do not allow for limited let alone unlimited use of calculators (although there have been gains in this direction). Cathy and I had questions about how children would do on such tests if they had not been taught standard U.S. algorithms. We hoped this study would contribute to an understanding of what occurs when calculators and other tools are allowed to be used freely.

6. *How we teach mathematics is every bit as important as what mathematics we teach.* It is essential to restructure learning environments so that children are encouraged to "do" mathematics—to conjecture, invent, probe, search for relationships, value diversity, communicate and represent their ideas and findings as they work collaboratively and independently to resolve complex problems.

The California State Department of Education suggests a list of "Guiding Principles" for teaching mathematics. Cathy and I used these principles to guide our decision making throughout the year. The list below is reprinted, by permission, from the *Mathematics Model Curriculum Guide, Kindergarten Through Grade Eight,* copyright 1987, California State Department of Education, P. O. Box 271, Sacramento, CA 95812-0271:

Teaching for Understanding: Guiding Principles

1. Our top priority should be the development of students' thinking and understanding. Whenever possible, we should engage the students' thinking and teach the mathematical ideas through posing a problem, setting up a situation, or asking a question.

2. We must know that understanding is achieved through direct, personal experiences. Students need to verify their thinking for themselves rather than to depend on an outside authority to tell them if they are right or wrong. We must see our job as setting up appropriate situations, asking questions, listening to children, and focusing the attention of students on important elements rather than trying to teach a concept through explanations.

3. We must know that the understandings we seek to help the students gain are developed, elaborated, deepened, and made more complete over time. We must provide a variety of opportunities to explore and confront any mathematical idea many times.

4. We will not expect all students to get the same thing out of the same experience. What students learn from any particular activity depends in large part on their past experiences and cognitive maturity. We should try to provide activities that have the potential for being understood at many different levels.

5. To maximize the opportunities for meaningful learning, we should encourage students to work together in small groups. Students learn not only from adults but also from each other.

6. We must recognize that partially grasped ideas and periods of confusion are a natural part of the process of developing understanding. When a student does not reach the anticipated conclusion, we must resist giving an explanation and try to ask a question or pose a new problem that will give the student the opportunity to contemplate evidence not previously considered.

7. We must be interested in what students are really thinking and understanding. Students may be able to answer correctly but still have fundamental misunderstandings. It is through the probing of the students' thinking that we get the information we need to provide appropriate learning experiences.

8. We must be clear about the particular idea or concept we wish students to consider when we present activities or use concrete models. It is not the activities or the models by themselves that are important. What is important is the students' thinking about and reflection on those particular ideas dealt with in the activities or represented by the models.

9. We need to recognize that students' thinking can often be stimulated by questions, whether directed by the teacher or other students. We should foster a questioning attitude in our students.

10. We need to help students develop persistence in solving problems. Only in a learning environment in which mistakes and confusion are considered to be a natural part of the learning process can students believe they do not have to come up with quick, right answers.

11. We need to recognize the importance of verbalization. Putting thoughts into words requires students to organize their thinking and to confront their incomplete understanding. Listening to others affords them the opportunity to contemplate the thinking of others and to consider the implications for their own understanding.

12. We must value the development of mathematical language. Language should serve to internalize and clarify thinking and to communicate ideas and not be an end in itself. Memorizing definitions without understanding interferes with thinking. The emphasis is on developing a concept first, establishing the need for precise language, and then labeling the concept accurately. (pp. 13–14)

These guiding principles illustrate several areas in which new ways of thinking about the teaching and learning of mathematics are necessary. Cathy and I tried to keep these principles clearly in mind as we made instructional decisions, and in our day-to-day interactions with children. There were numerous instances throughout the study when

Cathy felt caught between old and new paradigms of what it means to teach mathematics. The guiding principles influenced our thinking in those instances.

Questions We Hoped to Explore

We were particularly interested in researching the following issues and questions:

1. How would decisions be made about what mathematics to teach and how and when to teach it? In particular, how would mathematics strands and domains such as data collection and analysis, geometry, and patterns and functional relationships be integrated into the mathematics curriculum?
2. What kinds of decisions must a teacher make day by day in order to teach in ways responsive to the understandings and interests children reveal?
3. How can the needs of all students (including gifted and special-needs children) be addressed in a self-contained mathematics program?
4. What classroom practices align with mathematics reform efforts?
5. What traditional beliefs about teaching and learning mathematics inhibit our implementation of the goals of mathematics reform?
6. How can performance-based assessment (e.g., portfolios, open-ended items, investigations, rubric scoring) be integrated with instruction?

In studying these issues and writing about the process, we hoped to provide a bridge of understanding between the professional mathematics community responsible for articulating mathematics goals and the classroom teacher responsible for translating those goals into practice. A clear understanding, gleaned from the professional mathematics community and reform documents, that current mathematics programs fail to meet the needs of children and of society gave us the courage to risk new practices.

## Chapter Three

Planning for Mathematics Instruction

Developing an Overview of the Year

During our initial planning session, Cathy and I created an overview of mathematics instruction for the year and outlined the first three or four weeks of instruction. We wanted to make preliminary decisions about when and how to address all the strands of mathematics during the course of the year. In the past Cathy had used her textbook as a guide. She was not altogether comfortable with this approach, however, and the previous year she had occasionally ventured away from the textbook, using ideas from Marilyn Burns's *Math Solutions* in-service workshops. She still felt responsible for focusing primarily on computation skills and fractions, prominent ideas in her fifth-grade text.

Cathy readily admitted not knowing how to think about planning. She knew it was important to emphasize the strands but didn't know the important ideas within the strands and didn't know how to think about an overview of the year. I suggested that many of our decisions about what to teach when would be arbitrary. At the same time, there were purposeful reasons for some of our timing decisions:

1. Since we wanted children to bring a disposition to search for patterns and relationships to all of their work in mathematics, a study of patterns and relationships seemed appropriate for early in the year. It was important to immerse the children in a study of patterns for several weeks, giving them an opportunity to begin to develop understandings within the strand. We would continue to emphasize the search for patterns throughout the year and would revisit the big ideas often.

2. Data collection and analysis were also useful as a focus early in the year. As students gather data about themselves, they get to know each other better and start to build a sense of themselves as a community of learners. We might want to focus on collecting and analyzing data in September and then conduct a several-weeks-long study of data collection and analysis later in the year when students could be engaged in statistical investigations on topics of importance or relevance to their world.

3. A sense of number and the ability to use mental computation and estimation were skills we wanted children to develop throughout the year. Rather than provide practice in a concentrated unit of study, we should disperse multiple opportunities to practice mental computation and estimation frequently throughout the year, along with multiple opportunities to use numbers in the context of solving problems. We might want to spend a week investigating multiplication, including primes, factors, composites, and multiples. This could be done early in the year when we briefly introduced children to all the strands. We might want to spend several weeks immersing the students in a study of fractions since it is a topic traditionally emphasized in fifth grade. Rather than studying fractions in isolation, we might use the curriculum replacement unit *Seeing Fractions* (California Department of Education 1991). This unit integrates the study of fractions with mathematical ideas from other strands.

4. Decisions about when to teach the remaining strands of probability, logic, measurement, and geometry seemed much more arbitrary. We might focus on each area for two- to six-week units of study, but our main goal would need to be helping children understand the interrelatedness of big ideas within and among the strands. As such, we needed to look for rich investigations that allowed children to work from their diverse areas of strength and that provided the potential for children to make connections between important ideas and related experiences.

5. It was easy to imagine immersing children in the study of probability, patterns and functions, measurement, and geometry for several weeks at a time. Logic, on the other hand, seemed to lend itself to shorter investigations dispersed throughout the year. Because of the level of concentration needed, logic would perhaps lead to burnout for many students if concentrated in large doses.

At the end of a two-hour planning session, Cathy and I had an overall plan for mathematics for the year:

September through early October   Establish a collaborative environment, allow self-directed exploration, find out about our students through data collection and analysis, and offer a new look at mathematics through coming attractions.

To introduce children to the world of mathematics and help them work collaboratively, we will intersperse self-directed exploration time with collaborative group lessons from each of the strands. During these group tasks we will focus on helping children learn to work together collaboratively. In addition, we will let children experience lessons from across the strands of mathematics. We will ask the students to reflect on their interests and skills in the various domains of mathematics and to explore the relevance of mathematics to the real world.

In addition, we will offer ongoing opportunities for students to participate in data collection and analysis. Graphs designed to gather information about the class will be posted most mornings. Entering information on and interpreting graphs will provide opportunities for children to (1) learn about each other; (2) ask questions and collect and analyze data in order to answer those questions; (3) make conjectures and pursue these conjectures by asking new questions; and (d) learn different ways to record information (e.g., ven-diagrams, two-variable graphs, histograms).

Early to mid-October through early November   A four-week unit on patterns and functions. This multiweek unit will immerse children in the study of patterns and functions and provide them opportunities over time to develop an understanding of the mathematics involved and a disposition to search for patterns and relationships. Although children will be surrounded with these concepts for several weeks, we will continue to emphasize the search for pattern throughout the year.

Mid-November through mid-December   Immersion in a unit on fractions using *Seeing Fractions* (CDE 1991), a fifth-grade replacement unit commissioned by the California State Department of Education and developed at the Technical Education Research Centers and Lesley College. This timing is largely to reassure students and parents. They may be getting nervous about when we are going to do "real math."

Mid- through late December A two-week unit on geometry. Again, somewhat arbitrary timing to provide a change of pace from the focus on numbers and a playful yet challenging focus to take us into the holidays. Many children will find geometry both challenging and inviting, a topic that will keep them highly engaged right up to winter break.

January A second two-week immersion in the *Seeing Fractions* unit. Having concentrated on fractions for an initial period in November, we will disperse the remainder of the unit throughout the year.

Mid-January through February A five- to six-week unit on data collection and analysis, primarily using *Used Numbers: The Shape of the Data*, developed by Susan Jo Russel and Rebecca Corwin (1989) at the Technical Education Research Centers and Lesley College. Although children will have numerous opportunities for graphing and data analysis early in the year, this unit will allow them to design and carry out investigations of interest to them and to study issues related to data collection and analysis (e.g., sampling, dealing with sensitive data, data displays).

March A three- to four-week unit on size. This unit will focus primarily on measurement. It will also provide a context for developing number concepts and number sense and for exploring ratio and proportion. The unit will integrate ideas from the geometry strand.

Early to mid-April A two-week focus on chance. Children will be involved in investigations and games designed to develop their understanding of probability.

Mid-April through May Long-term mathematical investigations (lasting from two to six weeks) that integrate ideas from diverse mathematical strands. Students will be involved in selecting and designing these investigations. We hope that we will be able to integrate mathematics with other curriculum areas. Ideas for investigations: when and where kids start to smoke; the amount of paper wasted by our class; the water pollution situation in Whatcom County; etc.

Getting Started: Planning the First Few Weeks of Mathematics Instruction

Once we had a general sense of the flow of the year, and had satisfied a need to articulate and clarify our goals for the children and ourselves, our thoughts turned to the practical: how to get started in September. We had multiple goals for the first several weeks of school:

1. Help children develop a different understanding of what mathematics is.
2. Help them learn to take responsibility for and act responsibly in their learning environment.
3. Help them begin to assess their individual areas of mathematical strength and interest.
4. Learn about the children, their work habits, interests, social interactions, and mathematical strengths and needs.

To accomplish these goals, we decided to emphasize four major areas during the beginning of the school year: self-directed exploration; a new look at mathematics; data collection and analysis; and assessment.

■ Self-Directed Exploration

Cathy confessed that although she realized free exploration was supposed to be important, she wasn't sure why and didn't really know how to go about it. I prefer to call it self-directed exploration because "free" may imply to both children and parents that it is a time when "anything goes." Although children are making choices and pursuing their own interests during this time, their work should be purposeful. Self-directed exploration gives students an opportunity to explore the materials they will be using in mathematics. Children are encouraged to make choices about what manipulatives they want to explore, where they want to work, and with whom they will work. This provides a context for addressing such issues as initiating the use of mathematical tools, returning materials when finished with them, respecting others' work, behaving responsibly and honestly when mistakes are made, working together as a community of learners, and pursuing individual interests.

Self-directed exploration also provides a context for us to learn about our students: whether they can make choices, whether they tend to be loners or prefer to work with others, how they interact with other students when things are going well and when accidents or disappointments happen, whether they give themselves challenging tasks, whether they work persistently or flit from one material to another.

Finally, self-directed exploration provides a context for establishing the parameters of the learning environment. When materials are misused (e.g., when the first rubber band is shot), we can talk about using materials appropriately and the consequences for those who choose to misuse them. When a tower someone has worked on for thirty minutes is accidentally knocked over, we can deal with reciprocity: saying we're sorry, offering to help rebuild the tower, in general making amends. When materials are left out or when someone spills hundreds of pattern blocks from a baggie that hasn't been properly zip-locked, we can discuss the consequences of not taking care of the materials. There are many opportunities to turn responsibility for the environment and interactions with one another over to the students. In many ways self-directed exploration supports our goal of developing children who are autonomous learners.

■ Learning About What It Means to Do Mathematics

Since the students would most likely have experienced only traditional arithmetic instruction, we thought we should begin the year by introducing students to the various strands of mathematics, helping them recognize their own mathematical strengths and interests and see that mathematics is relevant to their lives. We decided to spend the first several weeks of school interspersing self-directed exploration with problem-solving lessons from various strands of mathematics; observing children work and noting their strengths and interests; and prompting them to examine where the mathematics from each strand is used in the real world.

Many of the tasks selected for the first few weeks were collaborative group tasks, in order to (1) support the notion of the classroom as a community of learners; (2) provide a safe environment for the exploration of mathematics; and (3) help students learn both the value of collaborative efforts and the skills needed to make work done in collaboration as productive as possible. A productive collaborative learning environment does not develop naturally, and we knew we would have to work hard at this aspect of the program. Our students would have experienced at least four years of working within a competitive, individually focused learning environment.

Geometry would be the first strand of mathematics that the children would explore. Pentominoes, a math problem that asks them to find all the possible arrangements for five square tiles placed so that any two squares share a complete side, would be the initial collaborative group task. There were three main reasons for this decision: (1) the task is engaging and groups are likely to be challenged yet experience success; (2) there is a clearly defined group focus and task to be accomplished; and (3) geometry has the potential to level the playing field. Students who have previously excelled at arithmetic and developed reputations for being good at mathematics will not necessarily be the most confident on spatial relationship tasks. On the other hand, some students who have never felt confident in math will discover that they are good at solving spatial problems.

■ Graphing: Opportunities for Data Collection and Analysis

Every morning during the first several weeks of school we would post a graph on which the children would be asked to record information when they entered the classroom. The graphs would help us get a sense of who we were as a class. Children would be expected to figure out how to record on each graph posted. We anticipated some confusion, but through class discussions the children should be able to work their way through the confusion.

■ Planning for Assessment

Our initial assessments would come primarily through (1) observing self-directed exploration; (2) observing both the process and product of collaborative group work on diverse mathematical tasks; and (3) observing ongoing work and reflective writings in math learning logs kept by all students.

I have already discussed the opportunities for assessment as students engage in self-directed exploration. Students' work in collaborative groups on mathematics tasks tells us not only how they work with others but also their confidence and interest in the diverse domains of mathematics. By providing messy, complex-yet-inviting, intellectually challenging tasks and encouraging children to work together and talk about their thinking, we can observe students' mathematical thinking as well as their collaborative skills. Anecdotal notes made during these mathematics tasks help us retain what we find out about our students' interests, understandings, and social needs.

As a third means of gathering information about the children, and helping them gather information about themselves, we would ask students to keep a learning log. Much of their mathematical thinking would be recorded in these individual logs. Students would also be asked to write reflectively on such topics as, What does it mean to be good at mathematics? or How do I feel about myself as a mathematician? In addition to helping children focus on their thinking, these journals shed light on their developing mathematical understanding and their changing view of mathematics over time.

Cathy and I were convinced of the limitations and negative effects of traditional assessment methods and wanted to align our efforts with current efforts in the mathematics community to move toward performance-based assessment. We searched for ways in which assessment could concurrently promote children's learning of mathematics and reveal their developing understanding. A major purpose of assessment is to help us respond to our students' revealed knowledge and interests. Ongoing assessment is essential if we are to meet our goal of keeping children on the edge of their understanding, engaged and wanting to discover more. Assessment plays an important role in helping students and us reflect on our growth over time.

We planned to develop and pilot a variety of assessment approaches: (1) observe students at work; (2) analyze math learning logs; (3) develop rubrics for assessing both individual and group mathematical investigations; and (4) use student-selected mathematics portfolios. Although we had given this area considerable thought, we knew it would involve much more thought, further development, many false starts, a lot of reflection, and frequent revision. We hoped to examine our past practices in light of our current goals and to invent, pilot, and reinvent an assessment process that supports rather than limits or interferes with our students' learning.

Establishing the Learning Environment: *The First Four Months of School*

When children entered the classroom the first morning of school we asked them to make an entry on the graph we had posted, then draw a card and find a desk at the cluster that was labeled the same as their card. The cards ensured that children would be seated in random groups. Although much of the literature on cooperative learning groups suggests that four-student groups should consist of a high, a low, and two middle achievers (Johnson and Johnson 1986; Slavin 1983), we were interested in removing labels from children and helping them learn to work collaboratively in a variety of settings. Children would draw cards and switch to a new group about every two weeks.

Directions displayed on an overhead transparency encouraged children to start activities listed on a white board at the back of the room. Most children found their desks and began working before the bell rang. Checking the white board for directions would become a morning routine.

A Look at Self-Directed Exploration

Cathy decided to provide time for self-directed exploration that first day, since children would need to become familiar with the materials before using them for specific math problems. The school day began at 9:00. Math was scheduled for after recess, from 11:00 till 12:15. By recess the first day, both Cathy and I felt the kids had spent too much time listening and needed an engaging and challenging math problem. We shifted plans and decided to do the pentominoes problem after recess. The group task was to cut out one complete set of pentominoes from grid paper, then predict which shapes would fold into a box without a top.

But first we allotted fifteen minutes for self-directed exploration of color tiles (one-inch-square plastic tiles in four colors), since before we could ask them to use the tiles in a math problem they would need to have explored the tiles. Fifteen minutes seemed adequate. After all, how interesting could plastic squares be to fifth graders? Cathy gave these instructions for the self-directed exploration:

1. We expect that you will be working hard during this time. You need to discover all you can about the materials.
2. We expect that you will treat the materials and one another with respect. Please return materials when you have finished with them, and ask permission before dismantling anything that someone else has built.
3. You can choose whether to work alone or with others and are free to change your mind at any time.
4. You can choose where in the room you want to work.

How interesting could plastic tiles be to fifth graders indeed! What followed surprised us. Students immediately went to work exploring the tiles. Some kids sat at their desks working alone building towers with tiles stacked on edge. Some began arranging the tiles like dominoes to be knocked over. Before long, groups of children seated together began combining their tiles to make more elaborate domino designs.

Cathy and I wandered around the room, observing the children, who were for the most part oblivious to our presence. I posed a question here and there; I was curious, not really caring whether the students accepted my challenges. Nathan was working at his desk and had built a tower about eighteen inches high. I asked how tall he thought it was. He looked at the tower, shrugged his shoulders and said, "a little more than a foot." I asked, "How stable do you think it is? Do you think there is a point on the tower where you could blow it over? About where would that point be?" Nathan said, "It might blow over at the top." I moved on, but shortly Nathan was beside me asking, "Can I go to the lunch room and get some straws?" He and Bo wanted to investigate the problem I had posed.

Josh, working alone, had built a domino design on his desk, placed a tile on the floor, and was trying to make the design fall so that the last tile on the desk would knock over the tile on the floor. He worked hard to find the right spot to place the tile on the floor. I noticed that he was only looking from one perspective when placing the floor tile. I suggested that he might need to try out several perspectives in aligning the tiles. I knew Josh would only use my suggestion if it made sense to him. He got down on the floor and checked from several perspectives. His next attempt just missed the target. He began assembling his next try. I jotted a note about Josh's persistence for my anecdotal records.

Eight students (two groups of four) had gathered at the large table in the back of the room. They had pooled all their tiles and were involved in setting up an elaborate domino design that covered the six-foot by four-foot table. It was interesting to watch Jonathan and Joseph take charge of the group of eight. Some kids seemed content to watch, others were placing tiles. Before long a third group of four students joined them.

Cathy and I compared notes periodically as the students worked. When the noise level seemed too high, she blinked the lights and asked kids to bring their voices down. They did. It was apparent that students were highly engaged and that fifteen minutes would not be enough time. We extended the self-directed exploration. Pentominoes could wait until tomorrow. Only fifteen minutes into our first math lesson of the year, and we were changing plans for the second time! Would this happen often as we tried to teach in ways responsive to children's understandings and interests?

This time of self-directed exploration seemed valuable to the children and supported our goal of developing a community of learners. When problems arose (e.g., someone accidentally bumping the table and knocking the tiles over), children had to work them out. When they came to Cathy or me to complain, we sent them back to resolve the problems among themselves and made notes about their interactions.

After about forty minutes of self-directed exploration, Cathy asked students to put away the tiles and go back to their desks. Most students were not ready to stop, but did so with a little encouragement (or prodding). Cathy wanted to process the experience. She asked the class how they felt about self-directed exploration. Kids commented that they loved it and wanted to know when they could do it again. When asked what problems they ran into, kids mentioned several. Bryan said he'd been frustrated when someone knocked over his tiles. The children then discussed what could be done when this happened. John complained that some people had taken too many tiles and there weren't enough for others. The children were asked to think about solutions to this problem. Cathy also asked for solutions to keeping the noise level under control. She asked students to look at the supply shelf. Had materials been put away carefully? The class found that some baggies had been left open and the shelves looked disorganized and messy. They agreed that more care would have to be taken in putting away materials. Cathy asked for volunteers willing to share what they had done and what they had learned about the materials during this time. About twenty minutes were devoted to processing the experience. This processing was important to establishing a purposeful work ethic and helping students take responsibility for materials, the environment, and their actions and interactions with each other.

Three days later we planned a second self-directed exploration. This time we let the students choose the math manipulatives they wanted to explore. We were surprised, once again, when students fought (literally!) to get to the color tiles. Other materials with more interesting attributes (e.g., pattern blocks, Cuisenaire™ rods, interlocking cubes) sat on the shelves unnoticed as students grappled to "load up" on tiles. There was such a mad dash that Cathy asked the students to go back to their desks until they could come up with a plan to distribute the tiles in an orderly and equitable way. The class discussed the problem and decided to divide the tiles into separate baggies, each baggie containing approximately equal amounts. That way each group would get about the same number of tiles and could then decide how to share them. Cathy also suggested that students might find some of the other materials more interesting. After the discussion, children proceeded to get materials in a more orderly process, but still very few chose materials other than the tiles. One student who did, Sean, provided an opportunity for an estimation and data analysis lesson the following day.

Sean had spent his time exploring geoboards and rubberbands. Before we began to clean up, I noticed Sean's geoboard and asked whether he had any idea how many rubberbands were on it. He didn't know, but thought maybe fifty. I asked him not to take the bands off so that we could use his board for a graphing activity the next day. When children came to school the next day Sean's geoboard design was at the front board along with a sign asking them to estimate how many rubber-bands were on the board and record their estimate on a Post-It™ note. Later that morning, students were asked to put their Post-Its™ on a graph. We looked at the range of the estimates (fifteen to two hundred), and asked the children to describe the data:

JOHN: The lowest guess is fifteen and the highest was two hundred.
RUTH: Yes. That's what we call the range, from fifteen to two hundred.
TONYA: Lots of people guessed in the forties, fifties, and sixties.
RUTH: There is a cluster of guesses around forty, fifty, and sixty.
JONATHAN: The most guesses were twenty and forty-two.
RUTH: Statisticians call that the mode, or the most frequent response. In this case our data is bimodal, with one mode being twenty and the other forty-two.

Although I didn't expect children to remember these terms, I wanted to introduce them to the language of mathematics in context whenever possible. They would have opportunities to develop an understanding of these ideas over time.

After the data was analyzed, Sean counted the rubberbands on the board. When he told the class there were thirty-nine, there was a chorus of "No way." A second count confirmed the number: thirty-nine. Most of the class were surprised. Using children's work, ideas, and questions as the basis for lessons was something we hoped to do more of throughout the year. This would help the students understand that opportunities for mathematical reasoning are everywhere.

On the fifth day we gave students a third experience with self-directed exploration. I had (conveniently) borrowed many of the tiles for an adult math class I was teaching. Since few tiles were available students began to explore other materials. Patterns of student behavior were becoming more evident. By this time most children chose to spend their time working collaboratively with others. Some sat side by side with friends, doing similar tasks on their own but socializing as they worked. Others continued to work alone. Ray always took materials into the coat closet where he could work by himself building elaborate designs (usually with pattern blocks). He rarely interacted with others, and when he did the interchange was often combative. We noted that we would need to find ways to encourage Ray to work with others. Josh, who often tuned out during the day, consistently undertook challenging tasks during self-directed exploration. We wondered whether he might be a bright but unchallenged student who has learned that school isn't really his game. Heidi and Tonya often took materials and went off together during free explorations. Best friends, this was a time when they could choose to be together and they took advantage of the opportunity. Joseph, bright and social, seemed often able to take subtle command of situations and students. Bryan, cheerful and outgoing, couldn't get enough of this type of activity and continually asked, "When do we get more self-directed exploration time?" Molly always approached this time with gusto. She seemed to prefer building structures to making designs, and worked comfortably with both boys and girls. Shelli and Mari often approached these sessions in ways that tapped their artistic interests, usually making designs with the materials. John often moved from one material to another, rarely aware of what was going on around him and seemingly oblivious to the fact that he was destroying materials (e.g., chewing color tiles; walking over someone's geoboard, nail side up, without noticing; taking apart calculators and numerous fountain pens). Cathy and I conferred frequently about how to help John act responsibly. He seemed completely unaware that his behavior was inappropriate. J.R., the class comic, seemed equally content working with others or spending the entire period working alone. Steven, labeled "special ed," seemed to enjoy this time, and often worked alongside others.

Self-directed exploration provided rich opportunities both to learn about our students and to engage students in finding solutions to real problems. When calculators began to turn up damaged, the class had a problem they needed to solve. After much discussion, they decided they'd like to bring calculators from home so that they would have different models available. Classroom calculators would be numbered and assigned to those students who were unable to bring one from home.

When materials were not put away with care, students discussed things like the need to make sure bags were zip-locked carefully and materials returned to their proper place. They invented a plan for each group of four to have specific responsibilities that would help keep the classroom running efficiently.

The class discussed ways of resolving problems when someone intentionally or unintentionally disturbed another's work. Children's suggestions were sometimes vindictive. They viewed punishment as the route to restitution. This did not support our notion of logical or natural consequences as appropriate means for helping children take responsibility for their actions. Although Cathy was attempting to turn responsibility for decision making over to her students, she was also aware of the importance of her role as a mediator or questioner. Self-directed exploration was an important vehicle for getting the children to understand that we were a community of learners and that they were expected to be responsible problem solvers and to take responsibility for their learning.

Gradually we shifted from self-directed explorations to guided explorations by introducing new materials and mathematical challenges such as reproducing geoblock structures from bird's-eye-view photographs. It was interesting to note who accepted the challenges and who continued self-directed exploration. Children also brought the mathematical ideas they had been exploring to self-directed exploration. For example, they talked about the fractional relationships in the pattern blocks and were able to talk about lines of symmetry in their designs. Patterns of interactions also changed over time. Four weeks into the school year Ray no longer always chose to work alone. He still frequently worked in the coat room but most often with a few friends. Several children now chose to work with classmates whom they had not worked with earlier in the year.

Collaborative Mathematics Tasks: Learning to Work Together

It was important that we help children learn to work together collaboratively. We knew that this would not just happen naturally. We provided collaborative group lessons several times a week early in the school year. As problems were encountered during collaborative tasks, we involved the children in finding ways to resolve those problems. Collaborative group lessons from each of the strands were interspersed with self-directed exploration. The first strand we focused on was geometry. At the beginning of math period on the second day of school, Cathy introduced children to the guidelines for collaborative group work, which were posted at the front of the room:

Groups-of-Four Guidelines
1. Each person in the group is responsible for his or her own behavior and learning.
2. Each member of the group should be willing to help any other group member who asks for help.

3. You can only ask the teacher for help when all four members of the group have the same question.

4. There is always a challenge. When the group completes the task all four members should raise their hands and ask for the challenge.

Students were given the pentominoes task. As groups began the task, most children became actively involved. Not everyone participated fully, however. In some groups, one or two people took over the task and the others just watched. At the end of the session, Cathy took time to process the lesson with the class, focusing on both the mathematics and the group process. Although much of the literature on cooperative learning suggests that it is important to teach social skills before asking children to work on academic tasks in collaborative groups, we chose not to do so. We took the position that it is rarely desirable to teach any skill removed from the context of its use. We felt that the most appropriate time to help the children learn a new skill would be when they had a need for the skill. We believed this to be true for both academic and social skills. Cathy told the class that they would be assessing how their groups functioned, emphasizing that they would be talking about problems that occurred in the groups without placing individual blame or complaining about individuals. She acknowledged that working together would not always be easy but that it would be an essential part of how they were expected to function this year and during the rest of their schooling, and also later when they had jobs, and that the class would work together to find solutions to any problems that came up.

To encourage students to address real problems, Cathy asked them to write, anonymously, about any problems they had encountered in their groups. The next morning children were given another opportunity to do a collaborative geometry task. Before introducing the task, Cathy shared a problem from their writing the day before. One student had written, "When I tried to say somthing nobody paid atencion to me." Cathy asked the class to work on solutions to the problem of some people doing most of the work and not listening to or involving all the group members. Students generated a list of things group members could do or say if that situation recurred. Their suggestions, which follow, were posted in the room:

Collaborative Group Tasks
Things We Can Say or Do to Make Sure Everyone's Involved . . .
- "Can we make a plan so everybody has something to do?"
- "———has a good idea."

- "What do you think, ———?"
- "Does everybody agree with that?"
- "We need your help."
- "I don't think we heard ———'s idea."

Cathy asked students to be aware during the next task of whether or not everyone was involved and, if necessary, to try some of the ideas they had generated for involving everyone. She knew we would need to focus on this collaborative skill over time, and that there would be other problems to solve as children learned to work together collaboratively.

Groups were then given the "milk carton problem." They had saved milk cartons at lunch for two days and had cut the tops off the cartons. Each group was given fourteen cartons. They were asked to decide as a group how the cartons should be cut so that they would unfold into all the pentomino shapes that would fold into boxes without tops. After deciding how to cut the carton, groups were to mark the cut lines on the milk cartons and cut on the lines to test their predictions. Most children quickly engaged in the task, but some just watched. As the children worked, Cathy and I discussed the need to develop a rubric that would describe levels of performance for group work so that students would know what was expected.

During processing time, students were asked to discuss in their small groups whether or not all group members were involved and contributing to the task. They were asked to share examples of things they tried in order to ensure that everyone contributed. Students had opportunities to share their thinking with the class and were both honest and fairly accurate in their assessments of how they had worked as groups. Some still wanted to place individual blame, although they did not name names. For example, Mari said, "Someone in our group wouldn't cooperate no matter what we did." Cathy responded that the group might examine how they were asking that person to help. She said that she had noticed several groups work successfully to involve someone who was not participating. She asked Mari's group to consider how they were treating the student who wasn't participating, noting that "how you say something is every bit as important as what you say." Throughout the next few weeks, after each collaborative group task, students were asked to reflect on the quality of their group's collaborative efforts. Recurring problems were turned back to the class for resolution: What should be done about kids who don't pull their weight in the group? kids who don't feel their ideas are being listened to? How could a group decide who gets to do the recording? Etc.

A Broader View of Mathematics

Helping children learn to work together collaboratively was an important goal. We also wanted to expand their view of what it means to do mathematics. Most, if not all, of these children had experienced four years of textbook math that consisted primarily of arithmetic. We wanted to introduce them to the world of mathematics and help them understand that mathematics is something quite different from what they had previously experienced. Cathy also wanted children to see the relevance and importance of mathematics to their lives.

After spending three days doing geometry tasks, children were asked what the tasks had to do with mathematics. They gave such answers as, "Well, it's problem solving" and "You have to think hard to figure it out." It took a great deal of probing before Tonya suggested that it had something to do with shapes. Jonathan then said, "And how they fit together." Cathy asked, "Who needs geometry?" Children worked in small groups to generate a list of careers in which geometry is important (see Figure 4–1).

After a brief look at geometry we moved on to logic. When I entered the room the morning we planned the first logic task, Cathy said to me, "I'm not sure I have my head together to introduce 'poison' right away." I talked her through how I would do it.

After Cathy introduced the game, groups worked for forty-five minutes trying to find a winning strategy. (There are twelve objects that are the same and one that is different. Partners take turns taking away one or two objects. The goal is not to be left with the dissimilar object, which is "poison.") By the end of math time, several groups were able to "poison" me, and some were well on their way to finding a master strategy for any number of original objects, and any number that can be taken away on any one turn. This was further than I have seen most teachers take the task in a similar amount of time. Cathy wanted to assign homework that would support the mathematics being learned at school, so children were asked to play at least four games of "poison" with someone at home, and to try to find out more about winning strategies. Several students came in the next day and said they were ready to "poison" me with any number of objects.

After "poison," we moved to another logic problem, "rainbow logic," a game in which players ask questions to try to determine how color tiles are placed in a rectangular array. After doing these logic tasks, Cathy again asked students what these activities had to do with mathematics. They gave responses such as, "You have to think about it hard" and "You have to pay attention to what you know."

Geometry: Who Needs It?

- boat builders
- fishermen
- map makers
- architects
- carpenters
- anyone who wants to put things together using directions
- pilots
- shoemakers
- seamstresses
- interior designers
- basketball players
- football players
- cargo loaders
- bridge builders
- airplane designers
- mechanics

Logic: Who Needs It?

- video game programmers
- weathermen
- pilots
- power plant operators
- everybody—citizens
- chemists
- archaeologists
- doctors
- optometrists
- umpires
- people who make calculators
- policemen
- loggers
- lawyers
- managers
- "poison" players
- judges
- mayors

Figure 4.1.   Children's lists of careers for geometry and logic.

We asked groups to generate lists of careers in which logic is important. As they were working, Cathy and I talked about the difficulty they might have completing the assignment. We assumed that since the mathematics of logic was subtle and hard to grasp, they wouldn't be able to come up with many careers. Once again, we had underestimated the kids. Their list of careers requiring familiarity with logic is also shown in Figure 4–1. Notice the substantive difference between the geometry list and the logic list.

Following a three-day focus on logic, we moved to the number strand, selecting lessons on multiplication from *A Collection of Math Lessons* (Burns 1987). The students had experienced primarily a textbook approach to mathematics in the earlier grades and we wanted to provide experiences that would help them understand the concept of multiplication. Students used tiles and grid paper to lay out all the possible rectangles using from one to twenty-five tiles. They explored patterns of primes, composites, multiples, and square numbers. They used the rectangles to create multiplication tables and focused on patterns within the multiplication table. They colored in multiples of numbers and examined resulting patterns. They made predictions about how patterns would expand if the multiplication chart was extended, and on their own initiative created larger grids and extended the patterns.

Data Collection and Analysis

Most mornings Cathy posted a graph that asked a question about the students. Each graph was a challenge in that the children needed to figure out where their responses should go. At times we ended up with too many or too few data entries (mainly because children weren't sure how or where to record their responses), and the children decided we should do the graph again the next day. Each day the class processed the information from the graph. In addition to helping the students develop an understanding of statistical concepts, this processing activity often helped us see how children deal with numbers in context. For example, the third week of school the class interpreted the data they had collected about how they had gotten to school (see Figure 4–2).

Cathy asked the class what the data told us. Several students offered ideas: "More kids rode the bus than any other way of getting to school." "Only three kids got rides." When Cathy was through processing the graph with the children, I asked if I could ask another question. I wanted to find out how these children would use concepts that we hadn't taught yet this year, so I asked, "What fraction of the class rode the bus to school today?" There was silence. I waited about fifteen seconds and still no hands went up. Cathy was ready to move on, but I said to the class, "What, fifth graders don't do fractions?" They chuckled, but still no one responded.

Instead of assuming they didn't know how to solve the problem, I asked students to work in their small groups to come up with an answer to the question and to be prepared to explain why their answer made sense. Immediately, there was a lot of buzzing as children began to work on the problem. Cathy walked over to me and said, "I don't know if they can do this. In fact, I don't know if I know what to do." I noted her discomfort, but was willing to wait and see what would happen.

The children spent about five minutes working in their groups. When all the groups indicated that they were ready, I recorded their answers on the overhead. Two groups thought two fifths of the class rode the bus. One group thought it was three fifths. Two groups had come up with two thirds. One group thought it was five thirteenths, and

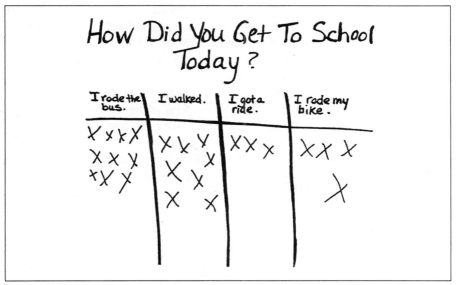

Figure 4.2. "How did you get to school today?" graph.

the last group said they didn't have an answer. I asked the groups how they had thought through the problem:

RUTH: Two groups thought it was two fifths. Would someone like to come up and explain to the rest of us how you got that?

J.R.: We thought since there were twenty-five people on the graph, that was five fives, and two of those fives rode the bus. So two fives out of five fives rode the bus and that's two fifths.

RUTH: That's an interesting way to think about it. Table 5, you also got two fifths. Did you think about it the same way?

MICHAEL: No. We thought ten people rode the bus and if that was half the class there would be twenty people in the class. And if that was a third of the class there would be thirty people in the class. But there were twenty-five people on the graph. So we thought it had to be between one half and one third but there wasn't any fraction there. So then we thought one half equals two fourths and one third equals two sixths, so our answer had to be between two fourths and two sixths, so we think it is two fifths.

[*This was one of many times when I was surprised by the sophistication of children's thinking. I was intrigued by this group's way of attempting to make sense of the situation and by the understanding of fractions their thinking revealed. I knew there was a flaw in their logic, that one fifth is not precisely in the middle between one fourth and one sixth, but I tucked this idea away as a task to bring back to them in the context of the fractions unit we would be starting in November. Cathy later told me she didn't have a clue whether their response made sense or was "off the wall." This raises the important issue of teachers' understanding of mathematics. In this case a teacher who was not comfortable with the mathematical ideas being discussed was unable either to follow her student's thinking or to pursue the mathematical ideas worth pursuing. The NCTM Standards (1989) describe a mathematics classroom in which diverse solutions are encouraged and instruction is responsive to children's understandings. It is difficult for a teacher to respond to children's ideas when she is unable to follow children's thinking. This issue will be discussed in Chapter 10.*]

RUTH: That's very interesting thinking. Several of you are talking with your groups right now. Table 5 must have triggered your thinking. Go ahead and discuss with your groups for a few minutes. (*The children continue their discussion*)

CATHY: (*Privately, to me*) What I like about teaching this way is that we don't have to pigeonhole everything. We do fractions a little bit, and I don't have to say, "Well, I'm doing that in Chapter 5." Instead there are lots of spontaneous opportunities to explore ideas in the context of investigations they're doing. And surprisingly, they seem to remember the ideas when we come back to them later. I love it. But the hardest part for me is figuring out what questions to ask, even when we're reading a story. I don't feel like I have the experience to know how to ask good questions that will stimulate their thinking. It's hard work for me!

[*This, too, is an important issue. How do we provide teachers opportunities as learners to experience and understand important ideas within disciplines, and how do we provide them ongoing support while they attempt to teach in a new way?*]

RUTH: (*After the buzzing dies down*) Table 3 (*They have their hands raised*), do you have a comment about table 5's ideas?

TONYA: No. It's about ours. We thought it was three fifths, but now we know our thinking was upside down.

RUTH: That's an interesting notion. Do you want to say anything more about it?

TONYA: No, but we agree with two fifths now.

RUTH: How about the table that thought it was two thirds, do you want to explain?

JONATHAN: We don't think we are right now, but we thought ten people rode the bus and fifteen people didn't ride the bus, and we divided those numbers by five and we got two thirds.

RUTH: Why don't you think your answer is right?

JONATHAN: Because we think tables 5 and 7 are right now. It would be ten people rode the bus, and twenty-five people all together.

[*This is an example of the kind of thing that happened frequently throughout the study. As children were asked to explain their thinking, others listened and often wanted to refine their own thinking because of new ideas that had been triggered.*]

RUTH: Okay. How about table 2? Do you still want to defend your answer of five thirteenths?

[*I was surprised when they said yes. I thought everyone was convinced that two fifths was the correct answer.*]

RUTH: Okay, table 2. You have an opportunity to do what mathematicians often have to do. You get a chance to convince some skeptics. Are there any skeptics in the room?

CLASS: What's a skeptic?

RUTH: If you were a skeptic, you could say to table 2, "We doubt it. We think it's two fifths. We don't think you're going to be able to convince us that it's five thirteenths." So do we have any skeptics in here? (*Cathy and many of the children raise their hands*)

RUTH: Okay, table 2, here's your chance to convince some skeptics.

HEIDI: Well, we think when the rest of you were working, you didn't notice that John came in late and he put his X on the graph. So there are actually twenty-six X's not twenty-five. So we said ten people rode the bus and twenty-six people are on the graph, so that's ten twenty-sixths, and we divided both numbers in half and that's five thirteenths!

RUTH: Well, you convinced this skeptic! Were any of the rest of you convinced? (*Lots of hands go up*)

It would have been easy to interpret the children's initial silence to mean they didn't know much about fractions. Yet by giving them a situation to make sense of, and a supportive environment in which to examine their thinking, these children revealed a lot of what they do know about fractions. Interpreting graphs often provided a context for exploring number relationships. This was just one of many opportunities we would have to observe what powerful sense makers children are.

Multiweek Units: In Search of a New Paradigm

■ Planning

After completing the multiplication exploration we were five weeks into the school year. Rather than continue with coming attractions, we decided to move into a multiweek unit on patterns and relationships. Cathy and I met for a planning session the weekend before we were to begin the patterns unit. Our conversation reveals Cathy's struggle to understand mathematics in a different way:

RUTH: What do you think about when planning a unit on patterns and functions?

CATHY: I know patterns and functions are important, but I don't know what I should have the kids do. Last year I did some things from *Math Solutions*, but I didn't know where I was going.

RUTH: We've talked a lot about wanting to focus on the big mathematical ideas. Do you have any thoughts about what the big ideas related to patterns and functions are?

CATHY: No, I guess I really don't.

RUTH: Where do you go to get ideas when you want to plan lessons?

CATHY: Well, in the past I mostly used the textbook but it hardly has anything on patterns. Last year I moved away from the textbook more. I used Marilyn Burns's books. They had lots of good ideas, but I guess my approach was mostly trying activities that looked fun. And I felt responsible for multiplication, division, and fractions so that's what we spent most of our time on. I haven't ever planned for a unit on other strands. I'm not sure where to go for ideas.

Like many teachers, Cathy knows it's important to include all the strands in mathematics instruction. Her responses to my questions about big ideas are typical of responses I hear from many classroom teachers when they are asked to identify the mathematical ideas they're teaching. Teachers can identify dozens of ideas within the number strand, yet commonly have no understanding of important ideas in other strands. For many teachers, planning often involves selecting isolated activities from teacher resource books to do as occasional diversions from the "real" work of number.

In planning together for a unit on patterns and functions there were several issues we needed to address: (1) the important mathematical ideas within this strand; (2) related skills that are important; (3) sequencing lessons; and (4) meeting the range of needs in the classroom.

The NCTM *Standards* and the *Mathematics Model Curriculum Guide: Kindergarten Through Grade Eight* (California Department of Education 1987) were the two main resources we used to help us identify the important mathematical ideas within the strands. Standard 8 from the grades-five-to-eight section of the *Standards* reads:

> In grades 5–8, the mathematics curriculum should include explorations of patterns and functions so that students can—
>
> - describe, extend, analyze, and create a wide variety of patterns;
> - describe and represent relationships with tables, graphs, and rules;
> - analyze functional relationships to explain how a change in one quantity results in a change in another;
> - use patterns and functions to represent and solve problems. (p. 98)

California's *Mathematics Model Curriculum Guide* identifies the following "Essential Understandings" within the patterns and functions strand:

1. Identifying a rule that could have been used to generate a pattern enables one to extend that pattern indefinitely.
2. When there is a functional relationship between two quantities, the value of the first quantity determines the corresponding value of the second.
3. The same patterns can emerge from a variety of settings. (pp. 35–38)

We selected lessons based on their potential to help children develop their understanding of these big ideas. As for related skills, we decided it was unlikely that children would come up with ideas like making a problem smaller, using tables, or looking for patterns. Since these are useful tools for solving problems, we would provide initial experiences that introduced the entire class to these ideas.

After initial whole-class experiences, we would provide some collaborative small-group tasks so that we could observe whether children were using the ideas and so that they would have a supportive environment in which to explore the ideas, talk about their learning, and learn from one another.

After students completed some group tasks we planned to introduce our first "menu" in order to surround children with concepts from the patterns and functions strand and provide multiple opportunities for them to develop their understanding of the mathematics involved. With the menu system, the teacher posts several tasks and children make choices about what to work on when, where they want to work, and whether to work alone or with others. They record their work in a menu booklet and are expected to allocate their time and complete the tasks by a due date.

■ Introducing the Unit

Cathy wanted me to introduce the first patterns and functions lesson because she was feeling both insecure with the mathematics and somewhat scattered. She wanted to watch the process before teaching it herself. Cathy had proven herself a risk taker since the school year began. Her reluctance here is an indication of her lack of confidence in her own understanding of the mathematical ideas within the patterns and functions strand and her lack of familiarity with the problems we wanted children to experience.

The first task we gave the class was "beans and ways." Students were asked to figure out how many ways a million beans could be put into two containers. I first asked the children to imagine a million beans on the table, and to do something to let me know what they were imagining. This was a quick check of their sense of a million. Several groups immediately began trying to figure out what space would be needed to contain a million beans. Their ideas ranged from "Our classroom would be filled" to "They would cover our desks to a height about four inches." Kids were challenged by this question, and I mentally tucked it away as a worthwhile problem to have them explore at another time.

I asked the kids to predict how many different ways there would be to put the beans into two containers. Their estimates ranged from 500,000 to billions of ways. I suggested we make the task easier by

# of Beans	# of Ways
1	2
2	3
3	4
4	5
●	●
●	●
●	●
1,000,000	1,000,001

Figure 4.3. *t* **table for beans and ways.**

keeping track of our information and looking for patterns. I put a *t* table on an overhead transparency and labeled it (see Figure 4–3).

We predicted, then tested, for one, two, three, and four beans. By the time we got to five beans all the kids were predicting six ways. I asked for patterns they saw in the table, then we looked at how to write the function ($B + 1 = W$). I chose this as an initial task because I knew children would be overwhelmed by the problem. But I also knew that once we made the problem simpler by using the *t* table and looking for patterns, the solution would be easy. I wanted children to experience firsthand the usefulness of these ideas for solving problems.

The following day the entire class did the "handshake problem": There are twenty-nine of us in the room. If everyone shakes hands with everyone else in the room, how many handshakes will occur? Children were first asked to predict. Several thought it would be twenty-eight. Others guessed twenty-nine. Some thought it would be twenty-nine times twenty-nine, and one child offered the prediction twenty-nine plus twenty-nine. I asked how we could make it a simpler problem. J.R. suggested we all get up and shake hands. I said I thought that might get kind of messy and hard to keep track of. Did they have any other ideas? Shelli said we could use fewer people. Again I drew a *t* table on the overhead (see Figure 4–4). We started with just one person in the room, then acted the problem out for two, three, four, five, six, and seven people. By this time most kids had discovered a pattern they could use to predict the next number of handshakes. I asked students to share the patterns they saw:

# of People	# of Handshakes
1	0
2	1
3	3
4	6
5	10
6	15
7	

Figure 4.4. *t* table for the handshake problem.

TONYA: The numbers . . . the handshakes go up by one more each time. There's a difference of one more each time.

J.R.: You can just add the people and the handshakes to get the next number of handshakes.

ZACHERY: For the odd numbers you could multiply by bigger numbers. Like, for one person times zero equals zero handshakes, three people times one equals three handshakes, five people times two equals ten handshakes.

SHELLI: To get the number of handshakes you add up all the numbers of people before. Like, to find the number of handshakes for six people, you could add five plus four plus three plus two plus one equals fifteen handshakes.

Each time students offered a pattern I asked whether it would help solve the problem and also whether it was a function. Students thought several patterns were functions, but when I had them test whether they could get the answer for twenty-nine people based on that pattern without figuring out all the remaining combinations, they realized they couldn't. Then Jonathan said, "You can multiply the number and the number before it and it's half." I asked how we would write that idea mathematically. I suggested we call the number of people in the room P. Jonathan said we had to multiply by one less person. I wrote $P \times (P - 1)$ and then asked, "How would we get half of that?" Sean said, "We can divide it by two." I wrote $P \times (P - 1) / 2$. We tested Jonathan's pattern on several numbers we had on the t table, and then Shelli said, "That's a function!" I had them test the procedure to see whether they could get answers for numbers of people we had not yet done. They quickly became convinced that Shelli was right. They had discovered a function.

I didn't want $1/2\ P\ (P - 1)$ to remain an abstraction so I asked students why the function worked and what each symbol in the function represented. They were able to determine that each person in the class shook hands with everyone but themselves giving us $P\ (P - 1)$, and that we only had half that number because every time one person shook hands with someone that someone was also shaking with them.

I knew that understanding the difference between a pattern and a function is a big idea and that the students would develop that understanding over time, but I wanted them to encounter the idea again and again in our unit, since some students would make the connections quickly and others wouldn't. My goal was not to get them to find the function but to get them to search for patterns that would make problems easier to solve. I also wanted them to see that many patterns can arise from a situation. These ten-year-olds generated as many patterns for the handshake problem as any group of teachers I've worked with. A few children were already identifying patterns as patterns and functions as functions.

■ Children Who Don't Understand

During the handshake problem Josh had tuned out. He was playing with materials in his desk, looking out the window, turned away from the action. Cathy kept him in from recess. She sat beside him to look at the problem we had done. After about fifteen minutes with Josh she came to me looking discouraged: "This isn't working. He doesn't even know what a t table is and he doesn't get any of it. I wonder how many other kids are in the same shape." I responded that I thought this was a case of old belief systems getting in the way of the new paradigm of mathematics and learning. Traditionally, a lesson was considered successful when all or most of the students got the anticipated and correct outcome. In the new paradigm, a lesson is successful when children's thinking and understanding are revealed. Confusion is seen as a natural part of the process of learning. I mentioned that the Guiding Principles in California's *Model Curriculum Guide* suggest that we should not expect all students to get the same thing from the same experience, that important mathematical ideas develop over time, and that children construct these understandings on their own time lines. We would need to surround children with many opportunities to construct new understandings about patterns and functions.

Cathy and I talked about her discouragement and my enthusiasm in watching the lesson and seeing the outcome. How much of her discomfort was rooted in her lack of confidence in her own understanding of the mathematics of patterns and functions? I was excited by the children's willingness to explore multiple patterns within problems and by their willingness to make predictions and build theories about why their predictions made sense. I knew that this was just the first day of a four- to six-week unit on patterns and functions and that children would have opportunities to develop their understanding. Cathy was uncomfortable with her own understanding and concerned that some kids weren't "getting it." Her old beliefs left her wanting to fix the problem for those who didn't yet understand rather than trusting that with numerous and diverse experiences children would have opportunities to "fix" their own understanding. We would come back to this issue often during the year.

The following day (a day I was absent), students were given two problems to work on in their small groups: the "ice cream cone problem" ("How many double-dip cones can you make with thirty-one different flavors of ice cream?") and the "rod stamping problem" ("Using the small [one centimeter] Cuisenaire™ rod as a stamp, how many times will you need to stamp each of the other rods [two through ten centimeters] to completely cover the rod?")

According to Cathy, few students used a *t* table initially in trying to solve the problem. They quickly became confused about what to do with the manipulatives. Cathy stopped the lesson and had several students demonstrate how they were using manipulatives to keep track of information. She also suggested they make the problem simpler and keep track of information on a table. She felt the lesson picked up afterward but wasn't sure whether she should have intervened. I told her I thought it was fine to give children a chance to examine different strategies and that we could be confident they would use a strategy only if it made sense to them. We would have opportunities to observe whether or not children used the ideas over time.

A Teacher's Perspective on Her Efforts to Change

That weekend Cathy and I went hiking. We were going to start our first menu on Monday and wanted to plan that as well as touch base without the interruptions ever-present in school. This excerpt from the transcripts of our conversation reveals Cathy's decision making as she tried to restructure her teaching, but I need to lead up to it with a bit of background.

The first week of school students were given an assignment using their *Scholastic Newspaper* (1991). We asked the students to read the newspaper individually and pick out the most important article. We did not define *important.*

We then asked them to share their thinking within their small groups and reach a consensus about which article was most important. They were to write a statement telling why the article they picked was most important. After all the groups had finished, each group read their statements to the class. Three groups picked an article on endangered species; two picked an article on drug use; and two picked an article on the Thomas nomination to the Supreme Court.

We next asked kids to go home and interview at least two adults, asking them these questions: What article do you think is most important? Why? Students had two evenings to gather this information.

Two days later, we had kids share what they'd been told in their interviews. After considering this new information, the groups had to decide whether to stay with their original selection or switch to another. In either case they were to defend their decision in writing. When students began to share with their small groups, it became obvious that some had taken the assignment seriously and others hadn't. Some kids had lengthy notes and were able to articulate positions taken by the adults they'd interviewed. Some had no notes. Some students had not done the assignment. One parent sent in a fairly long handwritten letter stating why each of the articles was extremely important, how the issues were interdependent, and why it was hard to isolate one as most important.

The groups with students who had conducted interviews and who had new information to share were engaged during the task. In groups where kids had not done the assignment or had not taken notes during the interviews, things quickly fell apart. Most of Cathy's and my attention was directed toward trying to engage the groups that weren't working. Because a large part of the class did not seem engaged, we decided to let the task go. We did a little processing, but did not come back to the task.

And now back to our conversation:

CATHY: I need some help with social studies. (*We both laugh: we have agreed to use this time to talk about mathematics*) I know we said we wouldn't talk about this, but because of what we're doing in math and what I'm now understanding, I'm having to reexamine everything I do. I'm still struggling to get a handle on what the big ideas are in social studies. I feel I have a handle on the writing process, and I feel fairly confident about the reading process, but I'm really struggling with social studies.

RUTH: Okay. I understand that. Since you brought it up, let me share some of my thinking about social studies. Some of the big ideas are related to what we're doing in math. I was thinking yesterday that we should reexamine the *Scholastic* task that we did for two days, got uncomfortable with, and left behind. When I think about big ideas in social studies, one of the things I want kids to understand is that most issues can be viewed from multiple perspectives. Being a knowledgeable decision maker involves taking into consideration various viewpoints and evaluating them based on your own research and understanding. I also want children to understand that decisions don't have to be irrevocable. If new evidence comes to light then we ought to be able to reconsider and say, "I made a decision that doesn't make a whole lot of sense based on this new information."

CATHY: So we know that part of decision making is knowing that some decisions we make are not right.

RUTH: Yes, judgment calls are involved. And if we apply that idea to us, we should perhaps reconsider our decision to drop the *Scholastic* lesson. If we think about the potential in the lesson, it asks kids to, one, read with a purpose; two, think about important issues that impact their lives; three, listen to other points of view presented by their classmates; four, attempt to reach a consensus; five, gather additional information and points of view by talking with their parents about issues of importance in the world; six, share that new information with their peers; seven, reconsider initial decisions; eight, research a relevant issue; and nine, write a defense of their decision. What seems most important to me is that we're asking children and their parents to look at current affairs and to think about the relevance of issues to their world and lives. These seem important issues in light of our goal of helping children develop into knowledgeable, responsible, and reflective decision makers.

CATHY: So maybe we should go back to that task.

RUTH: We don't want to leave a task behind because our kids are not competent at it or especially interested in it now. We want to develop in them the capacity to value this process, and to view themselves as decision makers. These understandings are going to develop over time. When we're a little uncomfortable with where a lesson is going ourselves, and some kids don't seem real engaged, our tendency is to say, "This isn't working. Let's go back to something we know better." This is really the same issue that we ran into with patterns and functions where we did a problem and kids were pretty engaged and discovered lots of different patterns (as many as any group of teachers I've ever worked with has) and yet when we came back to a pattern problem three days later, the patterns weren't there for kids; or like when Josh, at recess, reveals that he doesn't know how to use *t* tables or look for patterns, and they seem to have no recollection of the process they went through with us. That doesn't mean we give the whole thing up. We might instead say, "How silly of me to assume because I've had years of experience seeing the power of using a table and looking for patterns that kids are going to powerfully connect with those ideas and be able to use them to solve new problems in three days.

CATHY: You're right. When we did the first problems I felt like, gosh, maybe this is more than we can handle. But now I realize after we've done rod stamping and the ice cream cone problem, they're starting to get it!

RUTH: The feeling that this is more than they can handle is the danger I think. Because at that point, without adequate support, most teachers are going to give up. They're out of their own comfort zone and some kids are revealing to them that they don't get it.

CATHY: When the teacher isn't confident in her own understanding of the ideas, and can't see the light at the end of the tunnel, then it's so much easier to give up. You don't know what to expect. I'm lucky to have you there pushing on because you know what's at the end of the tunnel.

RUTH: I think this is one of those underlying paradigm-shifting ideas that both teachers and staff developers need to understand or they will continue to give up and go back to what's comfortable.

CATHY: But what it is, is that teachers have to recognize that they may have to be in the same process that the kids are, but they're still the teacher. I'm sometimes going to be dealing with ideas where I don't really understand where I'm going, but that's okay because that's where the kids are too.

RUTH: But that's such a shift from our typical role as a teacher. For so long we've believed that our job is to understand fully where we're going. I actually believe a teacher needs to understand, in terms of big ideas, where they're going. You have to have in your gut an understanding that a disposition to search for patterns is one of the most mathematically empowering traits there is. And you also have to understand that this will only develop over time. During the process kids are going to reveal what they do and don't understand. Instead of saying, "Oh my gosh, they don't get it, I better get out of this," we want to say, "Look at this, isn't it wonderful that we can see their different levels of understanding so that we can plan appropriate experiences."

CATHY: It hit me yesterday that there's a difference between the way you look at what's going on in the classroom and how I look at what's going on. I look at it as though, "Crud, I don't know what's happening here." And you're looking at it as, "Look at these wonderful things." You're getting goose bumps because of kids' responses and I'm going, "Really????" I'm thinking so and so's not getting it, this kid's not understanding, we're not getting any responses, what are we going to put in their portfolios, instead of relaxing and looking at all the things that are happening. I did write some notes the other day on the fact that Steven was finally seeming to participate more in the discussions, and listening more, and making predictions. His predictions were mostly wrong, but my gosh, he was making predictions. That's a huge step right there. And there were others. Mike is tuned in a little more. And Timmy, I went through his math log and he's written as much as anyone. And Rachael, she's making real progress and taking risks . . . Oh, you should have seen what happened Friday with John. We were having a class meeting about problems that need solving. We have six broken calculators and kids thought that was the most important issue for the class to discuss. They wanted to decide what to do about that. They all said it was happening because people are picking on the calculators. They didn't mention any names, but it was clear they all knew John was largely responsible. They came up with the solution of bringing calculators from home and assigning calculators to those who couldn't bring one. It was a good class discussion. Suddenly I look around and there's John, over at the supply center, he has his pen and he's using correction fluid to write on the pen, totally oblivious to what's going on. Or maybe not oblivious. Maybe this is his escape from what was being discussed. So that was frustrating. It really bothers me. Is he tuned out? Does he see his part in it?

RUTH: I think you should be able to ask John about that. Ask him what he was hearing during the class meeting. Ask if he was aware of his part in it. And ask how he was feeling. You don't know if he has accepted any responsibility, but you can try to find out directly.

CATHY: You know, these kinds of things become very important issues in the day. Sometimes they take over.

RUTH: And it's important that they get addressed when they do occur. That's part of what learning to be part of a community is all about.

CATHY: So back to the *Scholastic* issue. Do we try it again?

RUTH: I think so. But we understand that their initial reports will be somewhat unsatisfying, and that they will get better over time. Maybe we have to be clear with them about what we want initially. An outline might help if we ask questions like, What was your first opinion? What new evidence did you gather through your interviews? What ideas swayed you or didn't persuade you and why? Did new input affect your final decision? What article do you now think is most important and why? I'm not sure those are the questions, but maybe they need more guidance from us in writing their reports.

CATHY: Yes, I think you're right. Maybe then the other kids could have a rubric to look at when groups are giving their reports. They can provide feedback to each other that way and it gives them a purpose for listening. And we might keep these issues and reports in folders somewhere. We say to kids, "We're not leaving this issue, it's important," but we pull it from the forefront of what we're doing for awhile. We tell them, "If you run into more relevant information, be sure to bring it to class to share."

RUTH: Yes. And the same is true with patterns and functions. We're going to immerse them in patterns and functions for a few weeks, then it will move to the back burner in terms of emphasis, but we will continue to use the ideas all year, and when appropriate move it back up to the front burner.

By this time we were fifteen minutes into a two-hour hike and discussion.

Clearly, Cathy is a reflective teacher. She is not confident in her new understandings but is willing to struggle to understand because these new ideas match her philosophical beliefs and her goals for her children. The complexities of teaching are evident, as is the importance of providing support over time for teachers who are trying to take on new teaching practices.

Menus: Children Making Choices

On Monday we introduced the class to their first menu on patterns and functions. Four required tasks and four optional tasks were posted around the room. Each task was introduced, then Cathy presented a collaborative group task that was to be completed before children went on to the rest of the menu. After completing the group task, children were to make a menu book in which to keep their work. Then they were free to choose which tasks to work on first and whether they wanted to work alone, with their group, or with others. All required tasks were due at the end of math class on Wednesday. Students had three seventy-minute periods in which to complete the menu.

After Cathy gave directions, students got to work, or more accurately, some got to work. Several groups dallied, but eventually most completed their group task, and several groups got their menu books made. What happened next was somewhat discouraging. We watched as kids began working on the menu tasks. A few kids approached the work seriously; most used the time to socialize.

Those who did attempt the tasks rarely used a *t* table or made the problem simpler. Hadn't they learned anything from the four days spent in whole-group and small-group work? It would have been easy to conclude, "This obviously doesn't work." Cathy and I huddled, discussing what to do. I had lobbied for not putting examples of *t* tables on the menu tasks. Rather than structuring how kids did the task, I wanted to see whether they used the ideas we had been exploring as a class the previous three days. No one did.

When we gathered the class to talk about the menus, we mentioned that we hadn't observed anyone using the ideas we'd been studying. We recommended they include a table and make the problem easier on each of the menu tasks the next day. Cathy asked students how they felt they had used their time. She offered that she didn't think most of them had worked very productively.

We were willing not to intervene to get kids to complete their work on time, but we did want to have consequences for choosing not to work. Cathy and I developed a scoring guide to use for menus, and discussed it with the kids on Tuesday. We wanted them to know what their assessment would be based on. We hoped this would motivate kids to use their time productively. It didn't. About half the class didn't take the due date seriously until Wednesday, when they realized we weren't going to extend the due date and that they were going to have a difficult time completing the tasks. Most spent Wednesday scrambling to finish, frustrated because they weren't able to. If students had been using their time productively and were still unable to complete the tasks, Cathy would have extended the due date. Since almost all the students had wasted most of their menu time, she decided to let them live with the consequences.

We collected their menu books on Wednesday and scored them overnight. We planned to go directly into a second patterns and functions menu so that students would have another opportunity to learn to make responsible choices and to allocate their time better. We handed back their scores from the first menu on Thursday morning. Each required task was worth five points and optional tasks (which could not be done until the required tasks were completed) were each worth one point. Out of a possible score of twenty-four (five points each for four required tasks and one point each for four optional tasks), scores on this first menu ranged from seven to twenty and a half. Most students' scores were between seven and ten. (Student scores became the focus for a lesson on percents described in Chapter 6.)

When the kids learned their scores, not many were pleased. Cathy told them that she was much more interested in their growth than in where they were right now. They were going to go right into another menu, and if they did a much better job on their next menu it would be weighted more heavily than the first one. She hoped to see progress.

The transformation in the work ethic as students approached the second menu was dramatic. Everyone got right to work. A few (Ray included) chose to work alone, but most worked with others at desks or tables or spots on the floor. Although we hadn't mentioned *t* tables in introducing this second menu, almost all students approached the problems by making them simpler and setting up a table. Apparently they had experienced these ideas as useful in solving the problems they had initially grappled with unsuccessfully during the first menu. The conversation that took place during whole-class processing at the end of menu period went like this:

CATHY: How did you feel about menu time today?

J.R.: I got a lot done. I thought it went great.

JENNISE: It was really fun.

CATHY: What made it fun?

JENNISE: We got to choose what we wanted to do.

JONATHAN: I liked being able to choose who to work with.

BRYAN: We didn't have to stay in our desk. It was fun to move around.

J.R.: I liked having to think hard about the problems and then finding a pattern and it was easier.

CATHY: How did you feel about how you used your time?

PAUL: I think we got lots more done.

CATHY: I noticed people working much more productively. The only thing that bothers me just a little is that I worry that you're only working harder to get a better grade, and in my heart I want you to be working because you want to do your best at all times. (*Zachery's hand goes up*)

ZACHERY: I don't think that's fair. I think we're working better because we know more what's expected of us.

[*I suspect it might have been a little of both. Kids weren't happy with the scores they received on their first menus, but we also talked about the scoring guide as an attempt to help kids understand what their assessment was going to be based on.*]

After this discussion the children were dismissed for recess. Josh and John stayed in because they were in the middle of trying to figure out the "cubes pattern problem" when menu time was over. They hunched together at the back desk, talking animatedly, seemingly unconcerned that they were missing recess. Six other students also stayed inside to work on problems from their menu. Clearly, the scheduled routine of math followed by recess was not meeting their needs today. These kids were trying to solve challenging problems and were not ready to stop just because it was time for recess.

During menu time the next day, the children continued their active involvement in the tasks. Two minutes into the session, clusters of children were working collaboratively to complete tasks from the menu. Even Ray had joined other children. He was working at the front of the room with Steven, J.R., Tonya, Heidi, and Bo. They were all using geoboards to try to find the number of diagonals in any polygon. Steven was engaged in the task. This menu seemed to provide an opportunity for him to interact on a par with his classmates.

When I walked outside the classroom to see who was working in the hall, Josh and John were on the floor with pattern blocks. They had built a row of orange squares with green triangles attached to each square. Since this didn't look like anything on the menu, I said, "Are you two just playing? You were really working hard yesterday." John looked at me indignantly and replied, "We're not playing. We're trying to find the perimeter of a row of pentagons and there aren't any pentagons in the pattern blocks, so we made our own." I was chagrined, but told them I was impressed. I hadn't seen that solution before, and it was clever. I had certainly read their behavior incorrectly.

All of the class remained highly engaged during the hour devoted to the menu. Kids talked animatedly as they worked. Once again, almost all the children were trying to make the problems simpler by using *t* tables to search for patterns. At the end of this second session, Cathy once again took time to process the experience with the class:

CATHY: What were you able to accomplish today?
TONYA: Me and Heidi finished three things. We only have one more to go tomorrow.

SEAN: I'm on the optional problems now. I finished the rest.

CATHY: Are there any problems you're having trouble with?

J.R.: We're not having trouble, but we only finished two.

CATHY: Do you have any ideas about why some of you have completed the required tasks and are working on the optional tasks and others have only completed a couple of problems?

J.R.: Well, we're finding lots of patterns for each problem.

CATHY: How many of the rest of you are looking for several patterns in each problem? (*No one raises a hand*) Well I'm curious, J.R., why you and Jonathan would take the time to look for lots of patterns when other people are just finding a pattern, using it to solve the problem, and moving on.

J.R.: Well, we keep looking for the function. Sometimes we have six different patterns but they're not the function, so we search for another pattern. Sometimes we can just feel a function coming. So we look for another pattern, and then we find a pattern and discover it's a function!

J.R.'s description of what it is like to search for a functional relationship is as elegant as any I've heard. This was not only evidence that J.R. and Jonathan understood the difference between a pattern and a function, it was also evidence of their engagement and persistence as mathematicians.

Students clearly showed evidence of liking the menu approach to mathematics. Being able to make choices about what to work on when, being able to pursue their own thinking at their own pace, being able to walk away when frustrated with a problem and come back to it later, having choices about whom to work with and the freedom to move around the room, all no doubt contributed to their enjoyment. Cathy and I both wondered about the reasons for what seemed a startling turnaround in their engagement with the menu tasks. Whatever the reasons, the menu environment provided real opportunities for us to observe children in action.

We decided that our next menu would be longer; one to two weeks. Our goals in using menus were for children to become engaged in meaningful tasks while taking responsibility for themselves and their learning and to help them work independently of us. We wanted to use menu time to work with individual students or small groups of students. Menus would give Cathy time to work with children who needed extra assistance with some mathematical concept and to work with those who needed a challenge the rest of the class might not be ready for. It is important that we find ways to meet individual needs of students without labeling or tracking them into ability groups. Menus provide this opportunity.

Preparation for Parent Conferences

By the time we completed the second patterns and functions menu, it was the fourth week of October. Parent conferences and the first reporting period were two and a half weeks away. Before these conferences took place, Cathy wanted to focus on something that parents would recognize as mathematics. She had received few inquiries and no real complaints from parents, which was somewhat surprising since she hadn't sent any mathematics home that looked like the curriculum parents were used to. One parent had asked about long division, but seemed comfortable with Cathy's explanation that although she wanted children to understand division and know when to use it, performing the long-division algorithm with paper and pencil could no longer be considered an essential mathematical skill. Most other comments from parents had to do with their children's liking math this year or a general appreciation for Cathy's teaching and learning environment.

Cathy thought it might be helpful if we spent some time on the number strand before the end of the first trimester. Focusing on fractions would also provide an opportunity to try out a newly available fifth-grade curriculum replacement unit, *Seeing Fractions* (CDE 1991). These materials had received some national acclaim, and we were interested in trying the unit. We planned to spend the next four to six weeks on fractions.

Curriculum Replacement Units

Since the *Seeing Fractions* materials are widely available, I won't attempt to detail the unit here. Several issues that came up during the unit do deserve attention, however. The unit is designed to be used by classroom teachers who may or may not have had training consistent with the philosophy of mathematics presented. It may also be used by teachers who lack confidence in their own understanding of fractions. I therefore very much wanted to observe Cathy using the materials. She is quite convinced of the value of a problem-solving, manipulative-based approach to mathematics, but at the same time has expressed frustration with her own lack of understanding of fractions.

A second area of interest was whether or not we would use the materials as suggested, choose to augment them, and/or delete portions of the unit. My third concern was whether the materials could accommodate the range of needs in the classroom. Would they offer access to those students least confident in mathematics and would they prove challenging to those who were most successful academically? And finally, would they be consistent with notions that children's thinking should not be structured for them and that doing mathematics must be a sense-making process?

■ Initial Adaptation of the Unit

I was out of town at a conference for the first week and a half of the fractions unit. When I returned, students were sharing squares that they had divided into eighths. Prior to this day's session, students had divided the area of a geoboard in half and then in fourths in as many ways as they could and had transferred their solutions to dot paper. For this lesson, Cathy asked children to share their solutions with their groups. Then each group was to select four of their favorites to transfer to an overhead transparency to be shared with the whole class. As groups worked on the task, I was surprised to see how many groups wanted to make sure everyone had one of their solutions included.

During processing time, groups came up one at a time to share their solutions. Table 3 presented the solution shown in Figure 4–5.

RUTH: How do you know that figure *a* is an eighth?
JOSEPH: Because two squares make an eighth and you can just see that if you cut off the top triangle part it would fit into the top part on the eighth right below it.
RUTH: You can just see that it is the same?

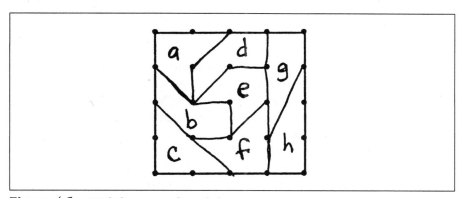

Figure 4.5. Eighths on geoboard dot paper.

JOSEPH: Yeah, if you cut off this part here it would fit over here.

RUTH: "You can just see" isn't really a convincing mathematical argument. Looks can be deceiving. Do you have a way to prove it?

JOSEPH: Well, you can just see.

RUTH: How else might you convince a skeptic like me? Can you prove it?

TONYA: (*Going over to her desk, getting the original design, and cutting the piece in question off and fitting it on the other space*) See, it works.

RUTH: I might be convinced, but they really don't fit on top of each other precisely. There's a little overlap here . . . .

TONYA: Well, that's because I didn't cut real carefully.

RUTH: So you think the difference might be because of imprecision in your cutting?

JOSEPH, TONYA, AND SEAN: Yeah.

RUTH: That might be. I'm not sure you've presented a mathematically convincing argument, though.

Several other groups shared their designs for eighths. Similar conversations took place. I was trying to emphasize that mathematicians couldn't just rely on how things looked, they needed to find other arguments to convince themselves and others that something is true. The use of mathematical reasoning, logic, and mathematical evidence to validate ideas is an important focus in mathematics reform efforts.

I suggested to Cathy that we give the class some experiences with finding areas on the geoboard. I thought this might help them use the notion of area to support their fractions solutions. It might also help them see other creative ways to divide regions in their fractions units.

The following morning Cathy asked if I would introduce "Area on the Geoboard" from *About Teaching Mathematics* (Burns 1992). On an overhead geoboard, I placed a rubberband that formed a rectangle and a second that formed a diagonal to the rectangle. I mentioned that the main idea the students needed to know was that a diagonal divides the rectangle in half. No sooner were the words out of my mouth than a chorus of "Prove it!" rang out. What a wonderful response. I turned the problem back to them, and they used scissors and other means to convince one another that my statement was true. We then passed out the worksheets and watched as students went to work finding the area of different shapes on the geoboard (see Figure 4–6). The class had two math periods to work on the task. They were then asked to complete the problem as homework and be ready to share their solutions in class the next day.

Cathy had made three overhead transparencies of the task, and let children choose which one they wanted to prove to the class. They had time to talk over their proofs in small groups before explaining their

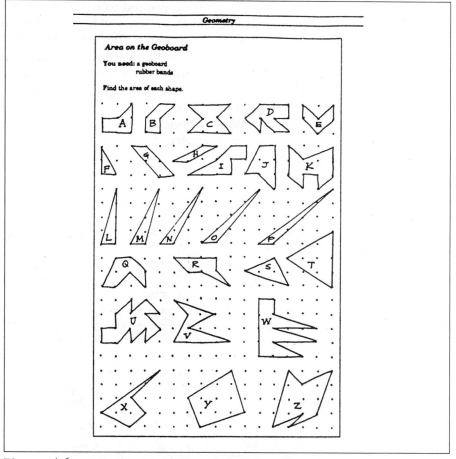

Figure 4.6. Area on the geoboard. Reprinted by permission from *About Teaching Mathematics: A K–8 Resource* **by Marilyn Burns (Math Solutions Publications, 1992).**

reasoning. During this time, I asked Steven whether he could prove *J* to me. When he was able to, I asked if he would be willing to share his proof with the class. He said, "No way. I can't. She might ask me to do one I don't know." I replied, "Sure you could. It might be scary, but you were able to convince me of your proof. I know Cathy would let you choose which one you want to prove. Would it help if you got to practice with me once more?" He said it might, so he explained his proof to me again. I told him I thought it would be great if he'd take a risk and share it with the class.

When Cathy asked if anyone wanted to share one of their proofs, Steven raised his hand. She called on him, and he solved the problem at the overhead, explaining his reasoning. This was a big risk for him to take. After Steven, several other children wanted to share their proofs. Most chose the more difficult problems to prove. Children challenged one another when they didn't think an adequate proof for the area of a shape had been presented. There was much discussion and sharing of ideas about how to make convincing proofs. Once again, these fifth graders had successfully completed a mathematics task I have seen many teachers drop out of.

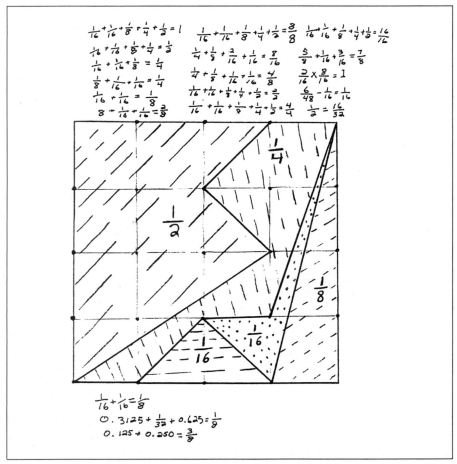

Figure 4.7. Michael's demonstration of fractions.

I wondered if their work with area on the geoboard would have any effect on their fractions designs. After doing "area on the geoboard," children were given an unmarked six-inch square and asked to divide it in a way that showed their understanding of fractions. They were to use at least three different fractions. Michael turned in the solution in Figure 4–7.

Soon children were challenging themselves and one another. Paul, an average student in math, came up with the solution in Figure 4–8. Michael also continued to stretch himself and us with solutions such as the one in Figure 4–9. Many of the children's solutions were so sophisticated that Cathy found herself spending hours at home trying to figure out whether the children's work was accurate so that she could respond appropriately.

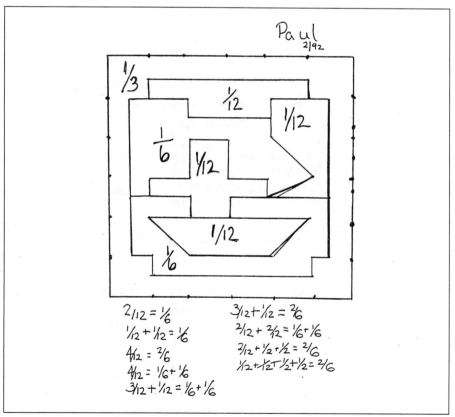

Figure 4.8.   Paul's fractions solution.

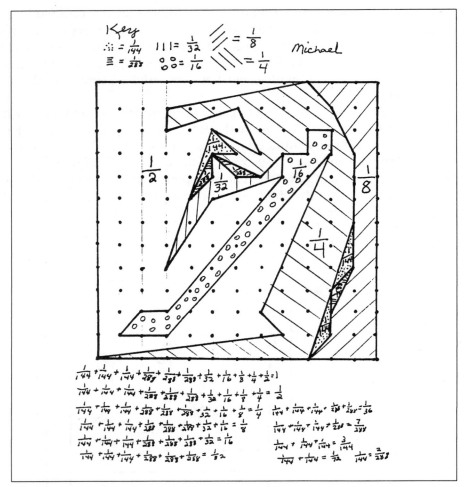

Figure 4.9. Michael's second fractions solution.

Once again, it was clear that it is difficult to teach mathematics in ways that are responsive to children if the teacher is not confident with her own understanding of mathematics. These children consistently took the mathematics to lengths we did not anticipate and would not have imagined.

After the square, children were given the task of dividing an equilateral triangle into fractional parts, again using at least three different fractions. Examples of the children's solutions are included in Figures 4–10 and 4–11.

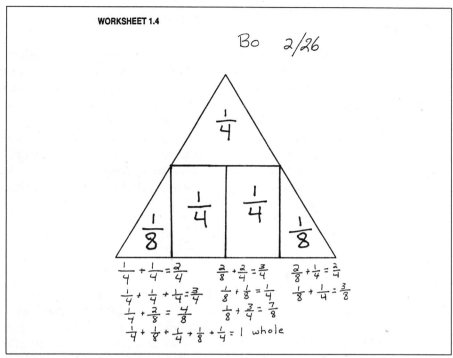

Figure 4.10. Bo's fractions triangle.

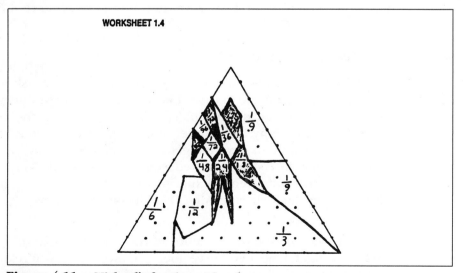

Figure 4.11. Michael's fractions triangle.

■ What About the Kids Who Don't Understand?

There were a few children who did not have a clear understanding of fractions at this point. Cathy and I talked about ways of supporting their learning without isolating them from meaningful math lessons. We decided to recycle some student work. By asking small groups to decide whether Paul's or Michael's solutions for dividing a square were accurate, we would provide a challenge for everyone and give Steven, Mike, and a few others the added support of hearing their groups' thinking. Recycling children's work became something we did often. In this way, children can be encouraged to stretch their thinking and challenge one another's ideas.

Geometry: A Change of Pace

The class spent another week working on the fractions unit, then Cathy thought they needed a change of pace. Since we had two and a half weeks until winter break, we decided it might be a good time to try a geometry menu. Cathy introduced the menu, then assigned the "toothpick problem" as a group task to be completed before children worked on the rest of the menu. For this problem groups were to place four toothpicks end to end, in as many ways as possible, so that any angle formed is either 90° or 180°. I was not in class to observe their work.

■ Substitute Teachers and Menus

The following morning Cathy was ill, and we decided I should be in class with her substitute in case children ran into any problems as they began their work on the menu. The substitute was in the classroom when I arrived. Cathy had left her a message saying I would be there, and she was happy to have me get the menu started. Several children wandered in before school started; some went to work on menu tasks, some worked on a science experiment they were doing, and others visited. When the bell rang, Mrs. O. addressed the class:

MRS. O: Okay. By the time I count to ten I want you all to be in your desks and quiet. One, two, three, four, put away what you're doing, and be ready to listen. Five, six, you're running out of time. S-e-v-e-n (*Con-*

tinuing her counting at a much slower pace), e-i-g-h-t, now I mean it. Get your things put away. N-i-n-e (*A long pause*), ten.

[*She introduced herself to the class and wrote her name on the board*.]

MRS. O: You need to know I expect you to work hard. I do give rewards at the end of the day for those of you who work hard all day. But if you don't, you'll lose your recess, and Mrs. Young will hear about it. I think we'll get along just fine.

What a change this was from Cathy's way of interacting with the children. I wondered what the students thought about this emphasis on rewards and punishment, and about the menacing sound of Mrs. O's count to ten. It was clear that Mrs. O. intended to be in control. Would the class notice the stark contrast? I'm sure Mrs. O. had been told that a good teacher establishes control quickly. I found myself wondering whether the class would feel insulted at being treated this way.

Mrs. O. then turned the lesson over to me. I told the class that I had noticed their work from the toothpick problem posted around the room, and asked if anyone could tell me what they had learned from the task.

J.R.: Well, we had to put four toothpicks together as many ways as we could.

RUTH: Could you put them any way you wanted to?

J.R.: No, they all had to be either ninety-degree or one-hundred-and-eighty-degree angles.

RUTH: Ah, can anyone explain to me what a ninety-degree angle is?

BO: (*Making the angle with his hands*) It's like the corner of the window or the door.

RUTH: And what about a one-hundred-and-eighty-degree angle?

TONYA: It makes a straight line. Like if you put two ninety-degree angles together it would make a straight line and it would be one hundred and eighty degrees.

RUTH: Was the toothpick problem easy or hard?

BRYAN: Well, it was sort of like the pentominoes problem, but there were more ways to put the toothpicks together. It was pretty fun.

RUTH: You also got started on the menu yesterday; were there any problems you didn't understand?

JOHN: I didn't really get spaghetti math. I'm not sure what to do.

RUTH: Did any of the rest of you have trouble with spaghetti math? (*Several children raise their hands*) Did any of you work on spaghetti math and think you understand it? (*Jonathan and Michael raise their* *hands*) Would you two be willing to help anyone who needs help on that one? Is it okay if kids come to you for help? (*They both agree*)

[*I wanted children to rely on one another while working on menus so that Cathy and I would be free to observe the learning and to work with small groups of children.*]

RUTH: Are there any other questions you have before you get started?

There weren't, so children were dismissed to work on their menus. Within a minute, everyone had gotten out their menu books and were busy working on geometry tasks. As I circulated, I wondered if the tasks we had chosen would be too difficult for fifth graders. I especially wondered if children like Steven would be able to access the tasks. Those concerns were not confirmed. Steven sat with Paul at the couch in the back of the room working to solve a cube problem for twenty minutes. A couple of times he held up his yet-to-be-completed cube for me to see, but he was challenged by the task and clearly enjoying what he was doing.

Sean walked up and showed me a finished cube. When I asked him how he did it, he sheepishly said, "I didn't. Jennise made it for me." I asked him to come with me to talk to Jennise. I knew it would be important to help both of them understand that Jennise's solving the problem for him was not helping Sean. They agreed, Sean gave me his cube, and he went to work trying to build one of his own.

The class worked on the menu for ninety minutes that day. The children were highly engaged. The tasks were very challenging, yet no one seemed to mind. I was impressed that they were willing to persist at solving the tasks for long periods. Cathy and I were both gone from school the next day, and a different substitute took the class. When she returned to school on Friday, Cathy received the messages shown in Figures 4–12 and 4–13.

The geometry menu was due the day before winter vacation. Students had consistently used their time productively during these two weeks. When we thought back to their first menu experience in October, it was clear the class as a whole had shown progress in their willingness to take responsibility for their learning and in making choices, allocating their time wisely, solving problems, and explaining their thinking and findings. It was also clear that the geometry menu had leveled the playing field. Children like Steven and Ray, who had struggled with the fractions unit, mental computation, and other number

Great kids!

We had a super day! The students were on task and worked hard during our "work times." There were no real discipline problems. — The class as a whole had a cooperative – helpful attitude. They earned an extra 6 min. of afternoon recess because of their great choices. —

Math: Great! All the students worked very well! A very manageable noise level, all students actively involved. — Some groups will need more time to finish up.

Figure 4.12.   Comments from first substitute.

Helpful students!

Hi Cathy,   We had a great day – no difficulties at all. I really do enjoy your class.

Math Menu:

A very productive time. Every student was involved the complete time. — I love all your ideas.   Would you mind if I got copies of your "menu items" and games? The students seem interested, challenged and busy in math exploration.

Figure 4.13.   Comments from second substitute.

concepts, found they were good at solving spatial relationship problems. The reverse was also true. Sean, who dealt with numbers easily, struggled with these geometry tasks, at times expressing his frustration at having to complete the tasks. Cathy found, once again, that when she opened up her mathematics program to include work in strands other than number, children were able to identify different areas of mathematics in which they felt confident.

After winter break, Cathy spent another week on the fractions unit, then began the unit on data collection and analysis that is the basis for Chapter 5.

Data Collection and Analysis:
A Closer Look at Instruction

This chapter details a multiweek curriculum unit on data collection and analysis. It discusses planning issues; recounts day-to-day life in the classroom; includes examples of student work; touches on assessment techniques; and offers some reflections on the unit's effectiveness.

Planning

In preparing for this unit Cathy and I again used resources to help us identify the essential mathematical understandings on which we wanted to focus. Standard 10: Statistics (NCTM 1989) states:

> In grades 5–8, the mathematics curriculum should include exploration of statistics in real-world situations so that students can—
>
> - systematically collect, organize, and describe data;
> - construct, read, and interpret tables, charts, and graphs;
> - make inferences and convincing arguments that are based on data analysis;

■ evaluate arguments that are based on data analysis;

■ develop an appreciation for statistical methods as powerful means for decision making. (p. 105)

The Essential Understandings for statistics as identified by the California Department of Education's *Mathematics Model Curriculum Guide* (1987) are:

1. When there is no direct observation that will answer a particular question, it is often possible to gather data which can be used to answer the question. Working with the data often generates additional questions.
2. You can gather data about every member of a group, or you can use a representational sample from that group.
3. Data can be organized, represented, and summarized in a variety of ways.
4. There are many reasons why an inference made from a set of data can be invalid. (pp. 40–44)

For our unit, we planned to use the *Used Numbers* materials developed under the auspices of the Technical Education Research Centers. These materials are highly regarded within the professional mathematics community, and Cathy felt they were fully consistent with her goals for children. The materials suggest beginning with *Used Numbers: The Shape of the Data* (Russell and Corwin 1989) at the fifth-grade level. This resource begins with several investigations involving fairly controlled data that provide contexts for children to learn to display and describe data. Sample questions to be investigated include: How many raisins are in a half-ounce box? How long can a fifth grader hold his or her breath? How much taller is a typical fifth grader than a typical first grader? Rather than begin with these questions, we decided to have children participate in a complete data collection and analysis cycle. We wanted to know how the children on their own would identify a question to investigate and then collect, analyze, and display their data. We knew that children were likely to run into problems as they collected data, and we thought it valuable to have them confront issues such as poorly formed questions, messy data, and data display options. We hoped that encountering these problems on their own would increase their interest in learning about methods of data collection and analysis that provide solutions to such problems. We believed opening up the lesson would also provide an opportunity to assess growth in the children's understanding of the data collection and analysis process.

A First Experience with Data Collection

The first day of the unit, Cathy introduced the initial investigation:

CATHY: Earlier in the year we collected data from you on graphs and we talked about and analyzed the data. It gave us a way to find out who you were. Do you remember some of the questions we asked?

JENNISE: Where were you born?

SEAN: How do you get to school?

TONYA: Did you read a good book this summer?

[*I was disappointed that Cathy referred to previous graphs while introducing this lesson. This can lead children to believe they should post their question on a predetermined graph and let everyone respond. Collecting data on a graph, although a typical school activity, is inconsistent with real-world uses of data collection and analysis. In the real world, data typically is first collected and then displayed in a variety of ways appropriate to the analysis. Collecting data directly onto a graph short-circuits the process of playing with the data to see what patterns emerge. By referring to previous graphs, Cathy may have eliminated some of the very explorations we had hoped to see.*]

CATHY: Today you're going to have an opportunity to figure out what you would like to know about those of us in the room. There are probably hundreds of things you would like to know. You and your partner will decide on something you want to find out. The first thing you'll have to do is formulate a question that you think will get you the information.

Cathy placed a transparency (see Figure 5–1) on the overhead projector and discussed the importance of each phase of the data collection cycle. She asked children to work as pairs or threesomes and told them they would have two days to complete their statistical investigation.

Some children began an eye-contact search for partners as soon as Cathy mentioned in her introduction that they would be working in pairs. Others looked for partners when she told them they could go to work. Three minutes into the lesson, everyone had found partners.

Data Collection and Analysis

1. Formulate a question.
2. Collect your data.
3. Organize and display the data. (You might want to do a sketch or rough draft of your display.)
4. Analyze the data thoughtfully. (What did you learn from the data?)
5. Make predictions or conjectures based on the data. (Include any new questions you now have as a result of your study.)

Figure 5.1.   Steps in data collection and analysis.

J.R. and Bryan immediately sat down at the back table and started writing. When I asked them if they knew their question already, Bryan replied, "No, we're brainstorming ideas first." About ten minutes later J.R. came over and asked, "If you could be anyone in history who would you want to be?" I thought for a minute then replied, "That's an interesting but hard question. I'm going to have to think about it and I'll get back to you." A few minutes later I noticed they were asking others this question and that when people hesitated they were offering suggestions. I made a mental note to talk about the importance of asking questions in a way that doesn't influence responses if you want to get real data.

Nathan and Chris were just sitting so I joined them:

RUTH: Are you two working together?

NATHAN: We don't know what to do.

RUTH: Can you tell me what you think you're supposed to do?

NATHAN: No.

RUTH: No idea? You're supposed to figure out something that you wish you knew about this group. Anything you want to know, here's your chance to ask. Then you have to come up with a question you think will get you the information you want. You'll need to find a way to get everyone to answer your question. That's called collecting your data. Then you have to figure out how to display your data on a graph so that it shows the rest of us what you found out. Bryan and J.R. are starting by brainstorming a list of things they might want to ask. Then they'll try to decide on just one question to ask. Does that help you get started?

NATHAN: Yes.

Jonathan and Michael were busy making a graph. I intervened, even though I knew it might not be a good idea for me to do so:

RUTH: What are you two working on?

JONATHAN: We're making a graph to put up.

RUTH: So you've decided on your question?

MICHAEL: Yes. We want to know what pets people have.

RUTH: Okay. Well, posting a graph is one way to find out. The choices you're offering might limit the information you get, though.

MICHAEL: Well, we have a category for other.

RUTH: A graph is one way to collect your data. Another way is to go around and ask people what pets they have and record their responses. Then you would have to decide what kind of a graph would best display the information you got.

[*I used to think it was important to ask the right question so that you could get a "good graph," but I now realize the important idea is that we can ask a question about what we want to find out, then determine how best to represent the information we get.*]

JONATHAN: Oh. I thought we had to put a graph up like we did before.

RUTH: No. You just have to decide the best way to get the information you want. Okay?

Several other groups were making graphs on which to have people record data. I struggled with whether to get out of the way and see what children would do with the task or intervene and try to alter the impression Cathy may have given that they were supposed to gather data through graphs as we had done earlier in the year. I finally did let them know they could determine what kind of graph best fit their data once they had their information, but I continue to be bothered by my decision. When to intervene as a teacher often poses a dilemma. I'm usually very comfortable watching as children struggle to make sense of messy situations. In this case I wanted to make the problem messier and at the same time was very aware that I was interfering with their processes.

Josh and John called me over. They had decided they wanted to find out how many seconds everybody in class had been alive. I mentioned that it might take a long time for everyone to figure that out before they could give an answer.

JOHN: Well, we're just going to ask how many years and months old people are. Then we'll figure out the seconds.

RUTH: Will you be able to tell how many seconds if you're asking about years and months?

JOSH: We're going to ask in years and months and then we'll find out at least how many seconds all together the class has been alive. It will be more than that but we'll be close.

JOHN: But we're not sure what to do here. We got 86,400 seconds in a day. Now would we plus 365?

RUTH: What will adding 365 tell you?

JOHN: Oh, it would be times. It would be 365 more times.

RUTH: You guys don't need my help to figure that out.

Josh and John began to gather their data. After about ten minutes John came over to us:

JOSH: Jed won't cooperate. He's not answering our question.

RUTH: What did you ask him?

JOHN: We asked him how old he is and he said, "None of your damn business."

CATHY: Why don't you just move on then?

JOSH: He's just being stubborn and stupid.

RUTH: Maybe not, Josh. You might be dealing with sensitive data. Maybe he got moved ahead a grade, or maybe he's older and doesn't want to tell you. Age could be an issue that some people might be sensitive about.

JOHN: He just doesn't want to tell.

Cathy and I agreed that we should deal with the issue of sensitive data during processing time.

After collecting their data Josh and John sat hunched over their desks, calculators in hand, talking animatedly. At one point Josh called me over and said, "We're getting numbers so big we don't know what they are." I sat down with them and we spent a couple of minutes reading numbers in the millions, billions, and trillions. Their interest was high, and they seemed comfortable with this new information, so I left them to deal with their data. When I told Cathy what they were working on she responded, "John always gives himself a challenge. He isn't always accurate, but he loves a challenge." I mentioned the importance of providing open-ended problems in which children can encounter the need for new skills. Josh and John wanted to figure out how to read numbers in the billions because that was the data they were generating.

Cathy told me that Steven and Timmy were asking people who the best mathematician was and that someone had answered, "Ruth." About ten minutes later I heard them ask Sean, "Who do you think is the best mathematician, Michael or Joseph?" I was sorry to hear their question had changed. It looked like this might turn into a popularity contest with the potential for hurt feelings. A few minutes later, Timmy asked Tonya the same question. When Tonya said, "Joseph," Timmy replied, "No, say Michael. Come on." I decided it was time to intervene and called Timmy and Steven over for a conversation about the importance of not influencing their data. I told them their data would not be believable if they were treating this as a vote or if they were trying to influence people. About fifteen minutes later they were on their third question. But this time they were just asking the question, and they had developed a system for keeping track of their information. They had a class list and as Timmy asked people their question, Steven recorded everyone's response.

Many children were beginning to run into messy problems in collecting data. We had anticipated this. Cathy and I were talking about what we were observing when Tonya walked over and asked Cathy what her favorite subject was. She answered, "Math," then turned to me and said, "I can't believe I said that. Last year it would have been my least favorite." She also commented that she thought we could just repeat this activity several more times and kids would get more sophisticated on their own as they kept running into problems they needed to solve. She may be right.

Seventy minutes into the lesson, most of the children were trying to decide how they were going to display their data. Ten minutes later Cathy asked the class to return to their desks and began a processing discussion:

CATHY: Please be sure you put your data in a safe place because you'll need it tomorrow. What kind of issues did you run into today while you were working?

BRYAN: Some people wouldn't say the answer and we had to keep coming back about ten times. (*Remember Bryan and J.R.'s question: "If you could be anyone in history, who would you want to be?"*)

CATHY: Why do you think that might have happened?

BRYAN: Lots of people wanted to be different people and they had to think.

CATHY: It was a hard question. Did anyone else run into any problems?

SEAN: Somebody asked the same question as us. We wanted to change our question, but then you said we only had ten more minutes.

CATHY: Why does that bother you?

SEAN: Because they're going to have the same stuff as us on their graph.

CATHY: So you think you'll both display your data the same?

SEAN: Yeah.

CATHY: I think it will be interesting to compare both of your results. We can compare whether or not the data is the same and if different displays give us different information about the data.

JOHN: We had a problem with someone not answering our question.

CATHY: Do you think it might have been because the information they would have to give out was personal?

JOHN: Not really.

CATHY: (*Turning to me*) Do we want to deal with that issue now? Would you talk about sensitive data?

RUTH: Some of you might be dealing with sensitive data. You might be asking people some questions that it would be hard for them to answer. One of the ideas we'll look at over the next couple of weeks is how to collect sensitive data. You may still want to collect data like how many fifth graders smoke or where do kids first encounter drugs or alcohol, but you won't get true data by going around and asking, "Zachary, have you ever smoked a cigarette?" If you want real data, then you have to learn to ask the question so that nobody (even the person collecting the data) knows who answered what. Even asking people about their age can be sensitive. My daughter was sick for five months during her sixth-grade year and she decided to spend another year in the sixth grade. If someone came up to her and asked, "How old are you?" and she had to say she was a year older than all her friends, that would be sensitive data to her. She wouldn't want to answer it because she might feel a little embarrassed about it. So if you're collecting sensitive data, one of the things we have to look at is how can you collect the data so that people can answer privately. Even a question that seems as easy as "How old are you?" can be sensitive for some people. Asking "How much do you weigh?" would be sensitive data for me. So if you want me to tell the truth, you can't come up and ask me. You have to find a way to collect the data sensitively.

TONYA: Mrs. Young, what question didn't you want to answer?

CATHY: They gave me the names of two people and asked me who was the best mathematician. I couldn't choose between the two and really didn't want to. Did anyone else run into any problems?

JOSEPH: Well, we didn't get all of our data collected.

CATHY: Do you have any idea why that happened?

JOSEPH: Well, we found out that I'm hard to work with, so I was collecting all the data.

CATHY: So you two need to work to come up with a plan so that both you and Zachary are using your time productively?

JOSEPH: Yes.

CATHY: Any other problems?

RACHAEL: It was hard to keep track of whether we had asked people our question. Sometimes they would say, "We already answered that," and sometimes they might answer again. We're not sure we asked everybody.

CATHY: Did anyone else run into that problem, and what did you do to solve it?

TIMMY: Steven and I got a class list and when we asked somebody, we checked their name off on the list.

CATHY: Okay, did anyone solve the problem differently?

MARCI: When we asked somebody, we wrote their name down on our list.

CATHY: Okay, those are a couple of good ways to keep track of your data collection. There may be other ways. You are going to have about thirty minutes tomorrow morning to finish displaying and analyzing your data, then we'll hear your reports. If that's not going to be enough time, you may have to find a time to work on your investigation before tomorrow morning. Part of what we'll be looking at is how statistics are used and also how they are misused. I just sent a letter home to your parents explaining this. I hope if you have a magazine or newspaper that you enjoy, you'll look through it and bring in statistics of interest to you. We'll take a look at the data and try to see how it is used. Okay, it's time for recess.

This first day of data collection and analysis, many of the problems and messy issues we had anticipated had indeed emerged. The children's work had provided a context for examining issues such as dealing with sensitive data; gathering information and then deciding on the best display; not influencing responses; dealing with messy data; and keeping track during data collection.

The second day of the unit, Cathy spent fifteen minutes on mental computation, then reviewed the phases of data collection and analysis children were expected to complete. She told them they would have forty minutes to finish analyzing and displaying their data.

Most children got right to work. Joseph and Zachary hadn't finished collecting their data, and I saw Joseph carrying a list and questioning people while Zachary tagged along, socializing as he went. I asked if they had spent any time trying to find a way to divide up the task. They hadn't. I said it wasn't a very efficient use of time for Zachary just to be following Joseph around and that they didn't have much time to complete the task. Then I left, wondering if they would come up with a solution.

Twenty minutes into the lesson, Cathy noticed that Timmy was now making the graph and Steven was sitting doing nothing. Since it was common for Timmy to volunteer for or take over recording tasks without conferring with his group to be sure everyone had something to do, she decided to pose the problem to the two boys. When she told them she noticed Timmy was busy working and Steven wasn't, Timmy replied, "Yes he is. I'm sending him out to get the last of our data while I'm making the graph." They didn't seem to be bothered that this left Steven with long periods of time with nothing to do.

At 10:30 the class processed the experience. Five groups had posted their results and others were still working to complete the task. Figures 5–2, 5–3, and 5–4 are samples of their data displays.

CATHY: Most of you have finished, but some of you are still working on your display. I'd like you to put away your work and listen to people's ideas now. Did anyone run into any problems today?
TIMMY: Steven would be asking the same kids who I already asked.
CATHY: So you were duplicating your efforts. Did anyone come up with a way to solve that problem?
TIMMY: Steven went out and asked people then brought their answers to me.
CATHY: So you came up with a system, and next time you'll know what to do better.
JOSEPH: We got off kind of slow 'cause one of us was doing it and the other one was just following him around, until I went and cut our sheet of names in half and I gave my partner the bottom half.
CATHY: You're talking about collecting your data? So you found a way to divide up that task. Did it seem to help?
JOSEPH: Yes. We could get it done faster that way.
J.R.: Bryan and I were collecting data and I just gave people some ideas to get their thinking going.

Cathy asked for volunteers willing to explain what they learned from their data collection. J.R. volunteered to explain their data display (Figure 5–2):

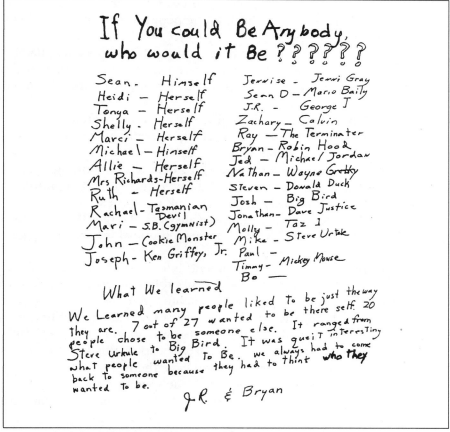

Figure 5.2. J.R. and Bryan's graph from their "Who would you be?" statistical survey.

J.R.: Our question was, "If you could be anybody who would you be, who would you like to be or you could be yourself." (*Their question had changed from the question they'd asked me earlier, "If you could be anyone in history, who would you want to be?"*) And five more people wanted to be somebody else, oh wait, um, a dozen people wanted to be themselves. Right. And there were only five more people who wanted to be somebody else than their self. Two people wanted to be the same thing, that was the Tasmanian Devil.

RUTH: Was there anything that surprised you about your data?

J.R.: Yeah, Cookie Monster and Big Bird. Also, most of the people didn't want to be someone else. We figured more people would want to be someone else. Also, I didn't think it was that hard a question, but some people would sit there for ten years trying to think of an answer. We usually had to come back to the people cause they couldn't think of an answer.

CATHY: Does anybody have any questions about this data?

SHELLI: You kind of have to give people time to think and come back for their answers. Plus everybody's working on their own work and it's hard to think.

CATHY: So do you think they have a valid comment?

SHELLI: Yeah, if they're working on something, it's okay to come back and ask them again.

RUTH: So one issue we need to deal with is finding a way to provide adequate time for people to answer questions thoughtfully.

CATHY: Do you think people took your question seriously?

J.R.: Well, obviously not with answers like Big Bird and Mickey Mouse.

CATHY: You had a very interesting question. Are you disappointed in the responses you got?

J.R.: Yeah, gee, some people didn't really care. I mean I really wanted to be George Jetson, 'cause he has this little power-drive, power-drafted machine and it turns into a machine gun.

RUTH: Well, I guess if you were serious about wanting to be George Jetson, it's possible someone else was serious about Big Bird. I'm curious about one thing. You two said earlier this morning that when you asked people the question you gave them some ideas to get their brain going. Do you remember any of the specific suggestions you gave them?

J.R.: Yeah, we said like maybe you want to be Superman or Spiderman or JFK or Bambi.

RUTH: When you're collecting data you're trying to get real answers to a question. You two came up with a good question, but you probably got different answers than you might have gotten because of the way you asked your question. From the suggestions you mentioned giving people, there was one person from history and three cartoon characters. Your suggestions may have caused people to give you silly answers that they might not have given if you had just asked everyone, "What one person in history would you most like to be?" The important thing to consider here is that if you are trying to get real data you have to be careful to ask the question in a way that doesn't lead people to a specific answer. Your job as a statistician is to be careful not to influence people's responses.

[I had looked forward to this unit on data collection and analysis because of its potential to help children learn that statistics is a powerful tool for finding information of importance to their lives and a vehicle for making

decisions that can impact their world. This first experience wasn't mea-
suring up. Watching children identify questions, then gather data, raised
several intriguing questions: Why did they stay with "safe" and mainly
trivial questions? Are cartoons, brands of tennis shoes, and favorite sports
figures most important to them at this stage of their life? Is it a reflection
of the culture of which they are a part? Has school become a place removed
from real issues and problems? Are they afraid to ask what they really
want to know? If we had begun the unit by presenting them with statistics
on issues relevant to their lives, would their questions have been dif-
ferent? Will the nature of their questions become more meaningful
over time?]

CATHY: Shelli and Rachael, you're waiting to share your results.

SHELLI: (*Coming with Rachael to the front of the room where their*
graph—Figure 5–3—is posted) Our question was, "Who do you like best
the Cougars or the Huskies?" Some people didn't care so we added
another column. Some people got confused so we added confused as
another column.

CATHY: And what did you learn from the data you collected?

SHELLI: The people who chose the Huskies probably did it because
they're a good team, and the people who chose the Cougars . . . well . . .
some people it was like their family members liked them, so . . .

BRYAN: But they put Bo for the Cougars and he has been absent.

SHELLI: Well, we asked his friend.

JOSEPH: When you came up to me you said, "Huskies, Cougars, don't
care, or confused." For a minute I was confused about the question, and
you just put me down as confused.

JOHN: That happened to me too. You said it real fast, and I tried to
figure the question out and you said, "Oh, you're confused."

CATHY: So some of you felt the question wasn't clear. You had to guess
at the question.

RUTH: Could you repeat the conclusions that you made from your
data? (*Shelli does*) When you're analyzing data it is important to be clear
about what you really know, and what you just think might be. Did you
ask people why they like the Huskies?

SHELLI AND RACHAEL: No.

RUTH: Then that wasn't the data you collected. You can offer your
thoughts as a conjecture, but you shouldn't present them as findings.
(*To the class*) What do you feel confident that you know from Shelli and
Rachael's data?

HEIDI: A lot of people in this class like the Huskies.

Which Team do you like the best? Cougars or Huskies

Huskies	Cougars	Don't care	Confused
Mari	John	Ray	Zachary
Joseph	Bo	Mrs Inglis	Mike
Jennise	Josh	Ruth	
Sean D	Molly		
J.R.			
Sean			
Bryan			
Heide			
Tonya			
Shelly			
Jed			
Nathan			
Steven			
Marci			
Jonathan			
Michael			
Allie			
Paul			
Timmy			
Rachael			
20	4	3	2

Total 29

The data tells us that the majority of the class likes the Huskies. Obvesly because The Huskie win. (most of the time)

Molly say's, "I don't know why I like them, I just do. So were not really sure why these 4 people like them

These 3 people probibly don't keep on Top of sports so they don't care.

Zachary and Mike couldn't make up there minds so we just put them in the confused section.

Rachael & Shelli

Figure 5.3. Shelli and Rachael's graph from their team-preference statistical survey.

J.R.: We can tell you don't like sports.

RUTH: Can you tell I don't like sports?

SEAN: No. All we can tell is you don't care about the Huskies or Cougars.

RUTH: In fact, it's not true that I don't like sports. I love swimming and tennis, and there are other sports I enjoy also. I'm a little concerned that people are going to feel bad or attacked because of things we are talking about. Shelli and Rachael, do you feel like we've been critical of your data analysis?

RACHAEL: It's okay.

CATHY: It's important to realize we're just starting to learn about data collection and analysis. You'll get a lot better as we learn more about it. When we're sharing ideas, it's important for us to try to do that in a way that doesn't hurt people's feelings. The rest of you will have time to share your findings tomorrow. Thanks to those of you who were willing to risk and go first. If you haven't finished your display and analysis, you will have to find time to do that before tomorrow.

During recess, Cathy and I talked about our concern that children might feel bad about the kinds of questions being raised about their data collection. We decided it would be important to talk with the class about this. The following day, at the beginning of the math lesson, Cathy addressed the issue:

CATHY: One of the things that occurred to Ruth and me yesterday was that we gave you a task of gathering statistics that was new to you, and when we were looking at your results people were sometimes critical of how you asked questions or how you interpreted the data. We hope you weren't discouraged by that. It's important to know we're just beginning a study of data collection and analysis. We don't expect you to know all about it yet. We'll be learning a lot more over the next several weeks. It was important for us to know where you are, and now that you've tried collecting data you'll be more aware of problems that have to be solved. We'll be challenging people's ideas, but we want to do it in a way that helps us all to learn more. Yesterday's challenges might have felt like we all got into putting people down and it shouldn't be done in that spirit. We're trying to learn some new things here.

Several groups then shared their findings with the class. When Michael and Jonathan shared their data on pets, they noted that results can be misleading. Their graph (see Figure 5–4) had a lot of fish. Michael noted that fish weren't the most popular pets though. Only seven people had fish as pets, but three people had a lot of fish. Joseph and Zachary shared their findings about what kind of car people wish they had. They noted that their question kept changing as they got more suggestions. Not everyone was asked the same question. We talked about

DOG	CAT	bird	fish	other	Total	Amount of Pets
2					2	Mari
2	2				4	John
					0	Joseph
				1	2	Jennise
1	1				2	Sean O
					0	J. R.
	2				2	Zachery
	.1		.		1	Sean
1		1		1	3	Bryan
1	1				2	Heidi
	.1				1	Tonya
	1	1			2	Shelli
2					2	Jed
2	1				3	Nathan
2					2	Steven
1				3	4	Josh
1					1	Marci
2			1		3	Jonathan
	2			1	3	Molly
1			3	4	8	Michael
1	2			3	6	Allie
1	3	5	15	2	26	Mike
2	4		5		11	Paul
1	1		2	1	5	Timmy
1	2				13	Rachael
	1		2	3	6	Bo
	3		7	4	14	Ray
25	38	7	35	23	128	

Michael
Jonathan

We did a project of the amount of pets everyone has and how many of each animal there is altogether. We learned that seventeen people had dogs and there are twenty four dogs together. There are also twenty five cats but only forteen people have them. Seven people have dogs and cats. Only three people in the class have birds. Two people have one bird and one person has five birds. Seven people have fish and altogether there are thirty five. There our 23 others and ten people have other. Altogether there are a 114 pets.

Figure 5.4. Michael and Jonathan's graph from their statistical survey on types and numbers of pets.

the need to ask more open questions rather than giving a limited choice. Cathy suggested that in the future they spend more time figuring out what they want to find out, thinking about how to form the questions, and getting a feeling for the kind of information they may get. They needed to understand that the way a question is formed can influence the responses.

After everyone had an opportunity to share their findings, I raised another issue:

RUTH: One of the things I've noticed is that people's names are listed on almost every graph that you've posted. On graphs that you see other places, names are rarely used. Why do you suppose that is?

JONATHAN: People won't want to give some responses if their name is there. They might want to say something they think is right.

RACHAEL: Well, like right now. People might have said something they thought was popular.

JENNISE: I think some people put their names by where their friends were.

TONYA: I think it's kind of weird to put people's names up. It makes it harder to answer how you really feel if your name will be up there.

CATHY: You mentioned several reasons why it might not be a good idea to include names on the graphs.

RUTH: It's a bigger issue than not including names on a graph. If you want people to answer honestly, then you might have to collect the data so that even you don't know who said what.

CATHY: What else would you do differently now? What would you do to display the same data without names?

MARI: We could use tally marks.

SEAN: We wanted to know if it was a boy or girl, so we might mark F and M so we can still make comparisons.

Cathy told the class she was sorry she had to cut off the discussion because there was wonderful participation in looking at issues, but it was time for recess. As the kids were going out, Rachael asked Cathy if they could do another survey. Cathy answered, "Yes, we'll do another one." Rachael replied, "Soon?" Cathy told her they could do another survey any time, so Rachael and Shelli spent the recess deciding on their next question. We had worried that Rachael and Shelli might have felt put down when they had shared their data earlier. If they had, it didn't appear to have dampened their enthusiasm for the task.

Data Collection: Raisins in a Box

The next day we moved into the *Used Numbers: The Shape of the Data* (Russell and Corwin 1989) materials. Several of these lessons are designed to help children learn different ways of displaying and describing data.

When I arrived at school at 8:45, Cathy was studying "raisins in a box." She appeared nervous as she reread and underlined parts of the lesson plan. Her tentativeness was understandable since this was her first attempt to teach something new in an area of mathematics in which she hadn't had enough time to develop her own confidence. This lesson has students open and count the number of raisins in half-ounce boxes. Data is displayed on a line plot, and children are asked to describe the data. We planned to adapt the lesson by having children collect data from a second sample after making predictions based on the first sample. This would provide a context for introducing the idea of random sampling and sample size.

At 9:10, the business of starting the day completed, Cathy addressed the class:

CATHY: We're going to be doing a statistical analysis today. (*Turning to me*) Is that the correct term? (*Back to the class*) I have some statistics that some of you brought in. (*She shares statistics about bicycle helmets, family size, and seatbelts and mentions that statistics are often used to answer important questions*) What we'll do today doesn't seem as important as wearing bicycle helmets or seat belts. We'll be looking at raisins, but you'll be learning new ways to organize and display data. First, would you open your boxes and without taking any raisins out, estimate how many raisins are in your box.

J.R.: Bryan and I thought about twenty to fiftyish. That just seems about right.

JOSEPH: We thought it was about thirty. I was thinking about the space that ten took up and it seems about thirty will fit in the box.

MICHAEL: One layer had seven, and I thought about four layers would fit in the box, so I guessed twenty-eight.

SHELLI: Seventeen, eighteen. I found where ten would be then put fifteen on the bottom 'cause they're smushed.

Cathy then had children open and count their raisins. She recorded their counts in a column on an overhead transparency: 30, 30, 28, 24, 32, 32, 31, 35, 29, 32, 31, 25. She asked the class if they had any ideas about how to organize the data better. Michael suggested putting them in order, and J.R. suggested clustering the twenties and thirties. Cathy assigned the task of finding a way to organize the information so that it would be easier to interpret. When she asked kids to go to work, most sat not knowing (or not being interested in) what to do. After about three minutes, she turned the lights off and on, her signal for every-one to pay attention. She commented that no one seemed to be working on the task. Since *Used Numbers* asks students to order the data and write three important things they can tell from the data, I asked Cathy if she left that part out on purpose. She had overlooked it, easy to do when a teacher is trying to do something new by following a suggested lesson plan rather than creating experiences based on mathematical ideas she herself wants to develop. I told Cathy I thought that having to write statements about the data might give students a purpose for ordering their data. I also suggested that having them do their work on transparencies might facilitate sharing time. Cathy agreed and passed out the transparencies. Kids seemed to get more engaged in the task when they knew they would be sharing their work on the overhead. We wandered about observing as the children organized their data. Cathy said excitedly, "I can see how this will really be important when they collect data later. They didn't do this step of organizing their data when they did their first surveys. It's going to be important."

After about fifteen minutes, Cathy pulled the group together, explaining that she knew everyone hadn't had time to finish, but that it was important for them to hear one another's ideas. Several groups shared their data displays on the overhead. They had invented a variety of ways to display the data (see Figures 5–5 through 5–7). The *Used Numbers* materials consistently have children invent their own ways to deal with data before introducing conventional practices.

Cathy introduced a line plot and had children help put the data from the raisin samples on the plot (see Figure 5–8). She then asked the children how they would describe the data.

JOHN: Thirty-five was the most.
SHELLI: Mainly twenty-eight, thirty-two.
HEIDI: They're clustered around thirty to thirty-two.
CATHY: (*Writing "clustered around 30 to 32" on the overhead transparency*) Statisticians talk about clusters too.
RUTH: Statisticians also talk about what John noticed, thirty-two was the most. They call it the mode. (*Cathy writes "mode" on the transparency*)

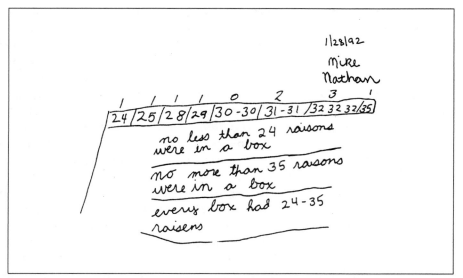

Figure 5.5. Mike and Nathan's invented display for raisins.

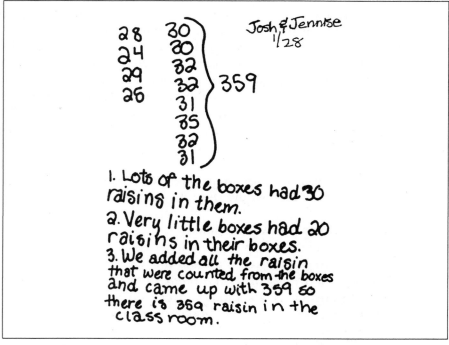

Figure 5.6. Josh and Jennise's invented display for raisins.

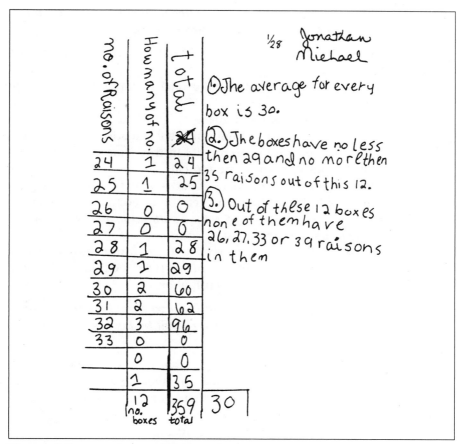

Figure 5.7. Jonathan and Michael's invented display for raisins.

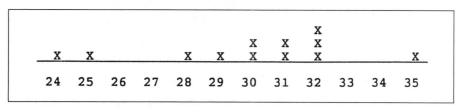

Figure 5.8. Line plot of first sample of raisins.

[I use the language of mathematics with children, but I don't focus on it or assume they know it from this one experience.]

PAUL: There are holes in the data at twenty-six and twenty-seven and thirty-three and thirty-four.

JOSEPH: If you spread out the data evenly, every box would have a number.

RAY: Thirty-five is the highest.

RUTH: Yes. Thirty-five might be what statisticians call an outlier. (*Cathy writes "outlier" on the overhead*) In this sample it's sitting out there by itself. It doesn't seem to be typical.

CATHY: Based on this data, what would be your best guess for how many would be in the next box you're going to open, and why?

SEAN: (*Using the idea of mode without using the term*) Thirty-two. Because that had the most last time.

JENNISE: Thirty-five to thirty-eight. Last time we guessed real low and it turned out to be higher. So this time we'll guess higher but it will probably turn out to be even higher.

[Jennise doesn't seem to think the next sample will have anything to do with the first. That idea is overridden by her surprise that there were so many in the first boxes.]

MICHAEL: (*Using the arithmetic mean as the most likely number*) Thirty. We found out that was the average number in the boxes.

SHELLI: Thirty-two because that is closest to the median.

RUTH: What is the median?

SHELLI: It's in the middle, the average.

[Shelli uses the right words for median, but 30.5 would be the median for the first sample.]

JOHN: Thirty or thirty-two. It's the most common.

JOSEPH: (*Appearing to rely on some notion of chance in making his prediction*) Twenty-seven. I felt them and one didn't feel as heavy. There was nothing [no twenty-sevens] before so the odds are there might be this time.

Cathy then had students open and count the raisins in their second boxes. Children talked animatedly this time. Having analyzed the data and made predictions, there was a higher level of interest in finding out. Cathy collected the data on a second line plot (see Figure 5–9). There were expressions of surprise at how different the two displays were. She then asked students to describe this second set of data.

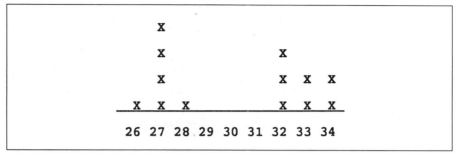

Figure 5.9. Line plot of second sample of raisins.

SHELLI: I think your lines should be spread out the same so we could compare. (*Cathy redraws the line plot for the second set of data*)

JOSEPH: This time twenty-seven was the most common. I said the odds were that twenty-seven would happen this time. That was my guess.

SHELLI: If everybody opened more boxes there'd be more in the twenties.

JOHN: Every number not on the top line is on the bottom line.

[*Cathy made repeated attempts to get them to describe the second set of data, but the kids seemed more interested in comparing the two sets, offering a range of naive to fairly sophisticated statistical ideas.*]

BRYAN: I think if we opened another box there would still be holes in the data.

SEVERAL KIDS: Yeah. Let's open another box.

Cathy told the class they had to move on. Although children had been able to work as partners until now, Cathy wanted to be able to assess each child's understanding of the ideas we had been studying. She therefore assigned them (as individuals) to make a line plot combining the data from both samples and write about the resulting display of data. (Two examples are included, as Figures 5–10 and 5–11.)

The lesson ran from 9:10 till 10:45. Cathy made a decision midstream to move readers workshop to the afternoon. When I asked how she felt about the length of the lesson, she said, "I like the things we added [the second box of raisins, the kids' recording on transparencies, asking them for a line plot that combines the data] and I don't mind adjusting the schedule. It would have been detrimental to the lesson to have closed it and gone on to something else."

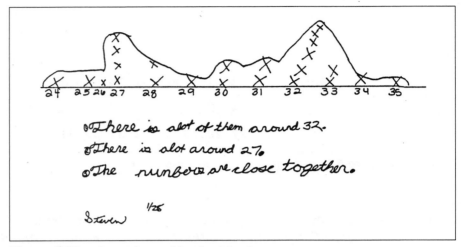

Figure 5.10.   **Steven's combined raisin data.**

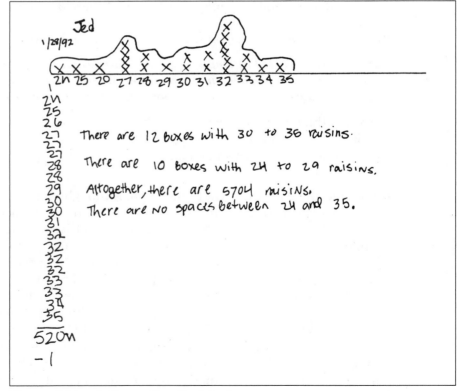

Figure 5.11.   **Jed's combined raisin data.**

An Experiment in Holding Your Breath

The next day, Cathy had children work together in their groups to find out how long a typical fifth grader could hold his or her breath. This lesson calls for collecting an initial data sample and then discussing the need for standardized procedures. She first asked the class for estimates (which ranged from twenty seconds to one and a half minutes), then had them time each other. Before collecting the resulting data, however, Cathy led a discussion about what the class might have to agree on in order to standardize the data collection. She was hoping they would come up with suggestions like taking two timings per person and averaging them, or having everyone hold their nose. She asked the question in a variety of ways and got very few responses. Cathy knew the goal was to look at the need to standardize data collection methods. She was trying to help them understand this issue, but students had not yet seen the need for themselves. After about fifteen deadly minutes, I asked Cathy if she was going to collect the data and introduce a stem-and-leaf plot. She responded, "No. That's not till tomorrow's lesson." I told her I thought it was part of this lesson, so she reread it, then said to the class, "Oh, I'm sorry. No wonder this part was so boring. This is all new to me. I was supposed to show you something new." Mari replied with surprise, "You mean you got this out of a book?" (I don't know where she thought our ideas were coming from.)

First, however, Cathy recorded their times on a line plot (see Figure 5–12). When John gave his time of 125 seconds, the class responded, "No way." He insisted it was true and offered to prove it by doing it again. Cathy moved on, asking the class to describe the data. Tonya said 125 was an outlier. Everyone agreed. Michael said the range of the data was from 35 seconds to 125 seconds. Shelli said most of the data was from 35 to 50 seconds. After taking a few more suggestions, Cathy asked the class if they had any ideas about why the data was so spread out.

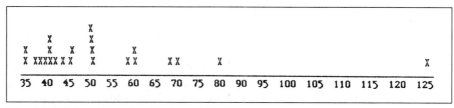

Figure 5.12. Line plot for breath-holding experiment.

ALLIE: Some people held their nose. Maybe they can hold their breath longer that way.

JOHN: Some people let air out gradually and counted that but not when they took another breath.

SEAN: Some people watched their time, maybe they tried hard to get a longer time.

CATHY: These are all ideas that you might want to consider if we want to come up with a standard procedure for collecting the data again tomorrow. Does anyone else have ideas about what we might want to consider?

SHELLI: I took mine two times, and the second time was longer. Maybe we should do two or three tries, then we can take the longest one.

CATHY: Will that tell us a typical time a fifth grader can hold his or her breath?

SHELLI: Well, maybe we could take an average.

This lively conversation shows that once the children had an opportunity to see how much variance there was in the data, they were eager to explore reasons for the differences and ways to standardize their data collection. Cathy then introduced the stem-and-leaf plot, drawing the stem and recording data on the leaf part of the plot as kids gave their times. She then rearranged the data in order (see Figure 5–13). She asked the class if any different patterns were evident on the stem-and-leaf plot.

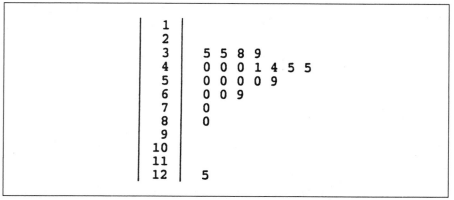

Figure 5.13. Stem-and-leaf plot for breath-holding experiment.

Kids thought the data looked much more clustered between 35 and 68, and that 125 still looked like an outlier. After discussing the stem-and-leaf chart, the class decided that the next day they would collect breath-holding data two ways—once with and once without everyone holding their nose.

The next math class was scheduled late the following afternoon. When the class came in from recess, Cathy introduced their task for the day. Working in groups of four, children were to take two measures of how long each person could hold his or her breath and record the data on a class chart. Then they were to (1) display the data in two different ways; (2) describe the data and write about what the data suggested; and (3) decide the typical time that fifth graders can hold their breath, and give reasons for this decision. (Midway through her discussion, two workers came into the classroom, excused themselves, and proceeded to climb noisily through the opening to the roof. Once on the roof they began hammering and scraping. This had been going on all day, and loud bangs continued to be heard through the roof for the remainder of the afternoon.)

Some groups worked well, others were slow to get started. Zachary immediately put his head down on his desk. Josh, J.R., and Chris were laughing about something other than math. In some groups one student worked while the other three watched. Cathy didn't appear to have the energy to do anything about it. She said, "I'm just going to let them go and see what they do. I don't know how we're expected to work in this." She let kids work until the end of the day, then had them turn in their work without any processing of the task. Every group but one displayed their data using a stem-and-leaf plot and a line plot, abandoning their invented methods of display for the formal methods to which they had been introduced.

The following Monday Cathy went back to the work the class had done on breath holding:

CATHY: Rachael, Nathan, and John, I noticed that your line plot is very long and divided into four sections. Can you hold that up for everyone to see? I noticed that it was hard to pick up patterns in the data when it was spread out on different pages. I think that is the reason for putting intervals on your line plot. I didn't model that very well last week. Do you think that might be useful?

RACHAEL: Well, it was hard to see patterns with everything so spread out.

CATHY: Does anyone else want to share their data?

JONATHAN: We found out that most people could hold their breath thirty-four seconds.

RUTH: Did most people respond thirty-four?

JONATHAN: I mean there were more thirty-fours than any other numbers.

BRYAN: Well, you could say that most people held their breath thirty-five seconds or longer.

JONATHAN: We also think seventeen is an outlier. That was a lot shorter than most people.

ALLIE: That was mine and somebody made me laugh.

CATHY: So our data still wasn't collected under standard conditions. Did you notice different patterns using the stem-and-leaf or the line plot?

JONATHAN: It was easier to see clusters with a line plot.

NATHAN: Outliers were easier to see too.

SHELLI: If you really look at your data on your stem-and-leaf you can figure out whether something is an outlier or not. It just isn't as easy to see.

CATHY: What other things did you notice about your data?

JOHN: It looks like seventeen and sixty-four are both outliers.

ZACHARY: I think seventeen's an outlier but not sixty-four, because there are some clustered around sixty-four and two people got sixty-four.

RUTH: Sixty-four is the upper limit of the range, but it doesn't seem unusual so I don't think we could call it an outlier. (*Moving on*) I read several papers where people said, "The lowest number is seventeen seconds and the highest number is sixty-four." Does anyone know the mathematical term we can use to describe that? (*When no one does*) That's the range of our data.

JOSEPH: That was on the tip of my tongue.

CATHY: I noticed that no one wrote about what they thought was the typical amount of time a fifth grader can hold his or her breath. I'm going to give you some time to discuss that now.

The groups used different ways of determining the typical time. Two groups said thirty-four seconds because it happened the most. One group said forty-three because there was a cluster around forty-three. Two groups said fifty seconds was typical because it was right in the middle. Rachael's group said forty-seven seconds because they added up all the seconds and divided by the number of kids in the room. The last group said they took seventeen and sixty-four and found the difference, which was forty-three. Groups had used all three traditional measures of central tendency—mean, median, and mode—although no one had mentioned the terms as such. They were also beginning to use the language of statistics in describing their data.

When the children had gone to recess, Cathy mentioned she was having a hard time staying interested and it seemed like the kids were too. I was feeling the same way. It might have been that the kids had done the task on Friday so it was no longer engaging now. Finding out how long they could hold their breath seemed to engage them the first time they clocked it, but there had also been a lessening of interest on Friday when they'd taken second timings and displayed and analyzed their data. They seemed to approach it more as a chore than a challenge.

Investigating Heights of Fifth and First Graders

The next *Used Numbers* lesson the class did was to find out how tall a typical fifth grader is. Cathy introduced the lesson:

CATHY: We're going to try to find out how much taller a fifth grader is than a first grader. Today you'll measure your own height and we'll talk about any problems you run into. You'll be working in threes. You'll need a large piece of paper, a yardstick, and a pencil. You'll use that same piece of paper when you measure first graders. Any questions?
RUTH: They suggest you have two groups measure so we can watch.
CATHY: That's right. (*Taping a sheet of paper on the door*) Jonathan, can you and two others measure someone for us?

Bryan and J.R. had Jonathan back up to the wall; then they made a pencil mark about an inch below Jonathan's actual height. Would the other children notice this? All three then worked to measure how far it was to the line. First they found the height of one yardstick, then rotated the stick. They decided the numbers weren't right so they measured again, sliding the yardstick up. They measured sixty-one inches.

Rachael and Allie then measured Shelli. Rachael laid a yardstick across Shelli's head, but kids told her it wasn't straight. They leveled the yardstick, made a mark at the top side of the stick, measured and recorded fifty-nine inches.

CATHY: Let's figure out whether you have any questions or not.

JOSEPH: Well, the mark on the paper shows Shelli is about two inches taller but the numbers say she's two inches shorter.

CATHY: Okay, what do you think are some of the problems here?

BRYAN: We measured where his hair was so that made him shorter.

JOHN: Well, the shoes make him a little taller and (*Slanting the pencil*) the pencil was going like that.

SHELLI: I think we should all measure by putting the stick on top of their head.

CATHY: If we want our data to be precise, what are the things we have to agree on before we go out and do our measuring?

MIKE: We should take our shoes off. They can make a big difference.

CATHY: Mike suggested we do something about the shoes. Anybody else think of anything else we should agree on so our data will be more accurate?

TONYA: We should agree on the yardstick.

RUTH: If you use a yardstick, where do you put the mark on the paper?

PAUL: On the bottom because that's the part that's touching the head.

[*No one but Joseph seemed bothered by the fact that the girls' measurement was a good two inches higher on the paper than the boys' and yet Shelli's height was listed at fifty-nine inches and Jonathan's at sixty-one. I decided to question it again.*]

RUTH: I'm still curious about how they got fifty-nine and sixty-one.

J.R.: Well the girls might have miscalculated.

CATHY: How might they have miscalculated?

J.R.: Possibly they could have used the wrong end of the yardstick.

SEAN: They were holding the yardstick crooked.

[*Sean's idea doesn't take into consideration that the girls' mark is higher on the wall. I'm surprised that no one picks up on the issue.*]

CATHY: Okay, we've agreed to use a yardstick, mark at the bottom of the stick, take our shoes off—anything else?

TONYA: Be sure the yardstick is straight.

CATHY: Okay, you can go ahead and get started measuring in the hall.

As we watched children measuring each other, it became obvious they didn't have a great need for precision. Some were not careful about marking where the yardstick ended, so its second use overlapped slightly with the first. Slanted yardsticks made a difference of about an inch in either direction. I walked over to Rachael, Shelli, and Molly.

RUTH: Rachael, I see your height is listed as forty-five inches. How tall would that be?

RACHAEL: (*Thinking*) Less than four feet.

RUTH: Does that seem about right?

RACHAEL: No.

RUTH: What do you think could have happened?

SHELLI: Maybe we used the wrong end of the yardstick. We better measure you again.

Again, no one in the group had noticed this on her own. I had imagined kids would be interested in how tall they were in feet and inches, but they appeared simply to be doing a task, not noticing whether the numbers they were getting made sense.

Cathy also noticed the kids were not being very precise. She asked what we should do. I suggested that we collect their data, then have kids stand back-to-back. When everyone had finished measuring, Cathy called the class back together.

CATHY: We need to talk about any problems that you might have encountered while you were trying to get accurate measurements. Did you encounter any problems?

BRYAN: Well two people got smack dab on the half. It was like fifty-eight and a half.

CATHY: So you didn't know whether to round it off or not. Did any of the rest of you encounter that problem?

SHELLI: Well it wasn't really a problem. When we measured, we just put fifty-nine and a half.

CATHY: This might be something everybody needs to pay attention to. Even if your measurement didn't include one-half today, it might tomorrow when you're measuring first graders.

JENNISE: I want to know my height in feet not inches.

CATHY: Do you know how to figure that out?

JENNISE: Yes.

SHELLI: We recorded ours in both.

[*Did they do this after they realized Rachael's didn't make sense?*]

CATHY: At one point I saw somebody who forgot to measure underneath the yardstick, but we got that cleared up.

RUTH: I saw some people measuring thirty-nine inches to the top of the meterstick instead of where thirty-nine inches is on the stick. So that's about a half-inch difference.

JOSEPH: I had a yardstick and I put the mark where the thirty-nine inches was.

RUTH: That's an interesting notion. If you had a yardstick would there be a mark for thirty-nine inches?

CATHY: How long is a yard?

SEAN: Three feet.

CATHY: How many inches?

[*Cathy is taking them through thinking about this question. I would have waited to see what they did with it.*]

J.R.: Thirty-six inches.

CATHY: So it couldn't have been a yardstick, it's a meterstick. I guess that's the difference between the two, isn't it?

SHELLI: So if we have the thirty-nine one, are we going to have to measure again with the other one?

RUTH: (*Surprised*) What do you think? Will it make a difference in your data?

JONATHAN: No it won't. An inch is the same length on the meterstick and the yardstick; you just have to keep track of the numbers.

[*A side conversation has been going on and Cathy asks the participants to share their discussion with the class.*]

ZACHARY: Something is wrong here because I got into the water slide where you have to be four feet, eight inches. That's fifty-six inches and they measured me as fifty-four inches.

J.R.: You have to be forty-eight inches tall for the water slide.

CATHY: So you're not so sure you have accurate measurements. Do you have any ideas what you might have done to make it so that the measurements are inaccurate?

ZACHARY: The door might not have been straight.

CATHY: I'm going to collect your data. You'll need to give me the data in inches. (*Recording the data and stopping with Josh's*) According to this, J.R. and Josh are the same height. Why don't you two stand up back-to-back and see if you're the same size. Pretty close.

[*Cathy continues collecting data. The kids notice that Mike and Marci are both sixty-one inches and want to check it out. Marci and Mike stand back-to-back. Marci is about two inches shorter.*]

JENNISE: I'm sixty-four inches and I think Mike's shorter than me.

CATHY: Let's compare you two. (*There does seem to be about a three-inch difference when Marci and Mike stand back-to-back.*) What do we know now?

JONATHAN: Maybe we should remeasure Marci's group.

[*The class is now enthusiastic. Kids want to do more back-to-back checks. Either checking data against reality is intriguing or they are just having fun with the back-to-back comparisons. Cathy decides to move on because of the time.*]

CATHY: The purpose of this discussion is to point out how important accuracy in your measurement is. There are some flaws in our data. We'll have to use this information tomorrow. As early as we can tomorrow morning we'll invite the first graders to come up here, and your group of three will measure two or three first graders. Watch for the kinds of things we did today so you can get as accurate a measurement as possible. What I want you to do now in your group is to take this data and organize it so that we can collect some information from it.

RUTH: Do you want them to find out how tall a typical fifth grader is?

CATHY: What we can learn about the height of fifth graders. We better have them write something on there too. You need to display your data, maybe in a couple of ways, and describe what you can learn from that data.

Most everyone used their time productively during the twenty minutes they were given. The following morning Cathy talked with the class about how the first graders might feel about coming upstairs and what the class might do to make them feel more comfortable. Jonathan and Bo went to get them, and others taped their papers on the wall in preparation. Both groups of kids seemed to enjoy the measurement task. Many of the same imprecisions in measurement were repeated, but some groups did try to be more precise. The measuring took about fifteen minutes, after which Cathy pulled the class together:

CATHY: What were some of the things you had happen today?

BRYAN: (*Although Cathy and I had earlier commented on how small the first graders looked.*) It seemed like they were giants. One of them was fifty-three inches, and we asked Zachary and Joseph how tall they were and Joseph was fifty-three and a half and Zachary was fifty-four, so that first grader is probably going to be like six feet when he goes into fifth grade.

CATHY: What other observations or problems or comments from your measuring experience?

ALLIE: We had to raise our paper because they were so tall.

CATHY: I saw some of you putting your paper too high and moving it down. Everybody should have written down the heights of the first graders that they measured. You'll need to work in your groups to organize and analyze your data. One thing we're going to ask you to do is make sure you have a title on your paper. Be sure we can look at your work and know you are finding out how tall a typical first grader is.

RUTH: When I was looking at your papers from yesterday, I noticed that a lot of you were making statements about the numbers that were on your graph. But nobody made comments about how tall a typical fifth grader is. So when you're analyzing the data you collected today, try to keep in mind that what you're trying to do is see what does the data tell you about how tall a first grader is. What are you learning about first graders' heights?

CATHY: In your group of four now, you're going to take these data and organize the data like you did yesterday in two ways and then write what you have learned about heights of first graders. How tall do you think a typical first grader is?

Children were given about thirty minutes to complete the task. They worked without much apparent enthusiasm. When most everyone had finished displaying their data, Cathy asked for comments about what they had learned:

J.R.: Lots of first graders are between forty-eight and fifty. There's a big cluster there.

JENNISE: I rounded up the shortest first grader and subtracted it from my height and got eighteen inches.

CATHY: Okay, but that's comparing our class with first graders, so save that thought.

MICHAEL: More than half the first graders were more than forty-five inches tall. There's two clumps from forty-four to forty-six and then forty-eight to fifty.

JOSEPH: They aren't usually very, very tall or very, very short. There's only one on each end.

MICHAEL: Fifty-three is an outlier.

JENNISE: I'm surprised how tall some of the first graders were.

CATHY: Now you're going to try to come up with a display that lets you compare how tall fifth graders are with first graders. You'll be inventing new ways to display the data, so first you'll come up with an idea that will let you compare the two sets of data, then you'll try out the display, see if the result is reasonable, and try another display if necessary. There will be two parts to this, but this is the first part, so I'll have you do that first, then I'll explain the other.

RUTH: You have to invent something you haven't done before so try to get yourselves into a creative mode, and play with the data and see if you come up with an idea. Try it out and if it doesn't work try to invent another way.

Groups went right to work. Cathy didn't have any idea how they would compare their data. I didn't either, but I was sure they would invent ways. Cathy wanted to take notes on how groups were working so she could talk about that during processing. We both took notes, and Cathy shared what she had seen when she pulled the class back together at the end of the period:

CATHY: It was interesting to watch you work today. I saw some nice things happen in the groups. I heard someone in group 5 say, "Don't worry, this is not our final copy." I also heard, "Let someone who hasn't had a chance write next." I think that was group 5 again. I saw Michael and Paul pull Zachary and Timmy back into the group with a question when they were tuned out. I even heard John say, "I need something to do." That's great. He went to his group and said, "I need something to do." How do you feel about how you worked in groups?

MARI: We were trying to work together but sometimes we told one person (*Referring to Ray*) something and they didn't listen.

CATHY: I see. I saw that happen in other groups and I saw ways that they brought the people into the group. So you guys have a problem you have to solve here. How you say something is very important. There's probably something for you to look at about what you're doing. There are ways to get that person involved that you need to be aware of.

Cathy then had several groups share the displays they were working on. The following day, groups were given forty-five minutes to finish their displays and data analysis. Most of them had finished and posted their results by 9:50 a.m. Cathy decided to stick with the deadline and let the two groups that had not completed the task complete it on their own time.

Cathy asked for volunteers and three groups shared the findings from their data. Groups had invented a number of ways to display data. For samples of their displays see Figures 5–14, 5–15, and 5–16.

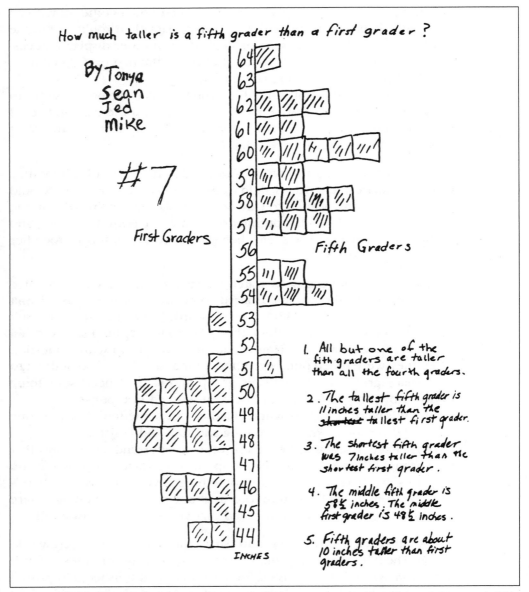

Figure 5.14. Group 7's data display comparing heights of first and fifth graders.

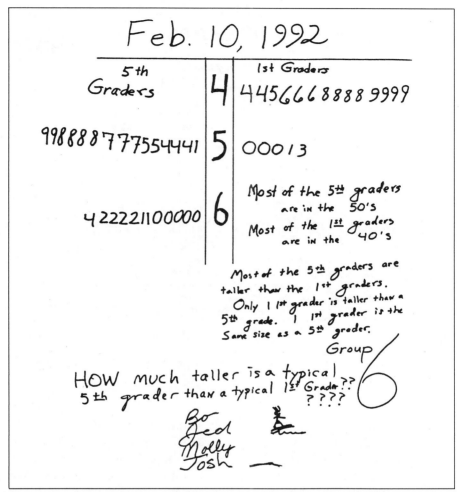

Figure 5.15. Group 6's data display comparing heights of first and fifth graders.

Some groups made comments about the numbers on their graph rather than talking about heights of first and fifth graders. Only one group answered the question, "How much taller is a typical fifth grader than a typical first grader?" This might indicate they were approaching this as a task to be completed rather than a question they were curious about. It might also be that "typical" is a hard concept, with one (typical) thing standing for many. On displays, children gave specific, concrete examples. "Typical" may be a difficult abstraction for them.

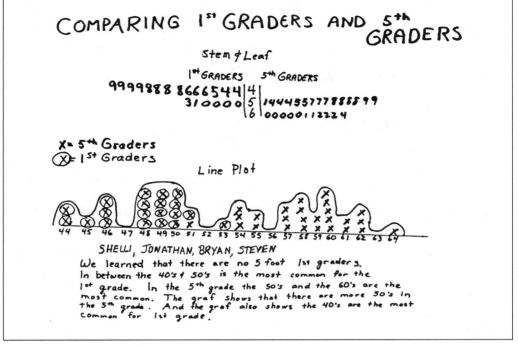

Figure 5.16. Group 4's data display comparing heights of first and fifth graders.

Children's interest level varied during this entire data collection and analysis unit. The same was true for Cathy and me. There seemed to be a spark missing that had been part of math until this unit, and the reasons weren't obvious. Although children were inventing ways to display data, lessons felt a bit too predictable. We didn't find as many opportunities to build on children's ideas. It's difficult to determine if four weeks had been too long a stretch and we were all just ready for a break or if the problems we had posed hadn't captured children's curiosity or challenged their thinking.

Cathy had commented several times that it was nice to have the lessons outlined clearly so that she knew what to do. I think, for me, that had been a deterrent. There is a dynamic missing when I'm not inventing lessons based on children's interests. If I hadn't been doing discrete research on the data collection and analysis unit, we might have spent two weeks on the unit initially, then dispersed the remaining lessons throughout the year. In retrospect, I now know this would not have been a good decision.

As it was, Cathy and I met after school on the last day of the height-measuring exercise. We decided to take a break from data collection and analysis and come back to it in two weeks, when the children would conduct a statistical investigation of a question of interest to them. We would see what ideas the children used after being away from the unit for two weeks.

The Role of Processing:
A Measurement Unit

Wanting a change of pace after our four weeks with data collection and analysis, Cathy and I decided to do a one- to two-week project in which the children would build scale models of the classroom. That would give us a context for helping children develop their measurement skills. Cathy agreed a change of pace was needed but expressed some fear about working with scale models since she has never understood how to draw things to scale. She said she didn't know what to watch for. I suggested she join a group and work with them for a while so she could experience the mathematics involved.

In preparing for the unit we once again consulted the NCTM *Standards* (1989) and the California State Department of Education's *Mathematics Model Curriculum Guide* (1987). We wanted to be aware of the important ideas within the measurement strand as we planned and carried out the unit. Standard 13: Measurement of the *Standards* states:

> In grades 5–8, the mathematics curriculum should include extensive concrete experiences using measurement so that students can—

- extend their understanding of the process of measurement;
- estimate, make, and use measurements to describe and compare phenomena;
- select appropriate units and tools to measure to the degree of accuracy required in a particular situation;
- understand the structure and use of systems of measurement;
- extend their understanding of the concepts of perimeter, area, volume, angle measure, capacity, and weight and mass;
- develop the concepts of rates and other derived and indirect measurements;
- develop formulas and procedures for determining measures to solve problems.

The Essential Understandings for measurement as identified by the *Mathematics Model Curriculum Guide* are:

1. When we measure, we attach a number to a quantity using a unit which is chosen according to the properties of the quantity to be measured.
2. Choosing an appropriate measuring tool requires considering the size of what is to be measured and the use of the measure.
3. Measurement is approximate because of the limitations of the ability to read a measuring instrument and the precision of the measuring instrument. The more accuracy you need, the smaller the unit you need.
4. For an accurate drawing or model to be made, a constant ratio between the lengths of the model and the lengths of the real object must be maintained.

Getting Started

Cathy introduced the measurement investigation to the class by telling the children they would be making a scale model of the classroom that included the floor and walls, with doors and windows cut out. There were a variety of measurement tools from which the children could choose, including metersticks, yardsticks, rulers, a trundle wheel, and string. There were three different sizes of graph paper available. Children were to choose a measuring instrument, then record their estimates for the length, width, and height of the room, decide on their scale, and then begin work on their model. The floor plan of the room is quite complex (see Figure 6–1). Although Cathy asked groups to

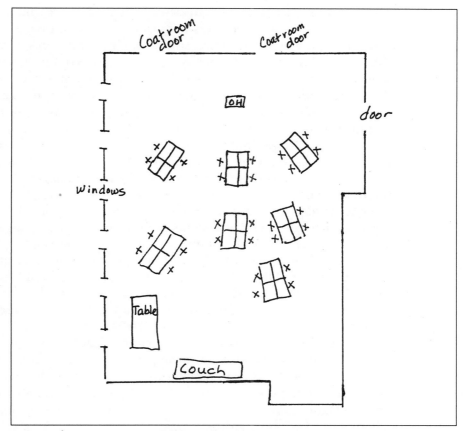

Figure 6.1. Floor plan of Cathy's classroom.

spend some time planning what they were going to do, most groups spent less than thirty seconds doing so, then got their measurement tools and began measuring.

All the children were out of their seats measuring and talking about what they were doing. Cathy said to me, "This lesson would drive some teachers right out of teaching." I asked if she was bothered and she said, "No. They're all busy." The lesson on scale modeling came from *SPACES* (Fraser 1982) but we adapted the problem considerably. The *SPACES* version says to give every group a meterstick and two-centimeter grid paper and have them use a scale of two centimeters equal to one meter. It also suggests taking students through the directions for how to tape the grid paper together and make the floor plans. It suggests that if the room is not rectangular, students should be told to pretend it is. There would probably have been less confusion had we followed the lesson plans, but we would have been structuring the children's thinking and they would not have had as many problems to solve on their own. We would not have gotten as much information about what they could do. Using different tools and grid paper would allow us to examine the mathematical ideas of similarity, congruence, ratio, and proportion. We would also be able to see whether the children could determine and use a scale. Some teachers might view the process we had decided on as too messy. We found the messiness desirable. We wanted children's processes to model those used by professional mathematicians. We wanted them to confront the messiness and to search for order.

As children worked there were wonderful opportunities to observe their thinking and ask challenging questions. It was surprising to see that most groups took just two measures, the length and width of the room, then began building their models. Cathy wondered how they were going to find the height of the ceiling. This was an old school and the ceilings were over ten feet high. I told her I didn't have a clue but that it would be interesting to see what they did. Rachael's group tried to stand on the couch and roll the trundle wheel up the wall, but they gave up and estimated when they couldn't reach to the top. Steven figured out that they could tape string to the end of a meterstick, stand on the desk, touch the meterstick to the ceiling, drop the string to the floor, and cut and then measure the string. This was probably the most clever solution any group came up with. Steven, once again, seemed fully involved with his group.

Two minutes into the lesson Sean came over to me and asked, "Can I go see if the janitor has a tape measure? That's what real builders would do." I said sure, and he went in search of a tape measure. Twenty minutes into the lesson, I walked by Jennise's group, who were already assembling the walls and floor. They had taped four sheets of graph paper together and cut out grids measuring eleven squares by eleven squares from the four corners. They then folded the walls up and began to tape. I asked a question:

RUTH: Have you folks already measured your floor plan?
JENNISE: We don't have to.
RUTH: What do you mean you don't have to?
JENNISE: Well, we found out the walls were eleven feet high, and our scale is one foot per [graph-paper] square, so we cut out the corners so they were the height of the walls and we just have to fold them up.

RUTH: Are you sure that will give you the dimensions of the room?

JENNISE: Yes. Four walls determine what the room is. That's all we need to know.

RUTH: I can see that you have the height of the walls figured out, but how do you know how long they need to be?

JENNISE: We don't need to know that 'cause there's just one way to . . . Oh wait . . . (*Walking off, yardstick in hand*) Oh, come on you guys, we need to do some more measuring.

Jennise's argument about walls determining the space had sounded reasonable. The group just hadn't considered all the information they needed to.

There were also wonderful opportunities to observe children's lack of precision in measuring. Bo measured the long wall using a yardstick, but each time he moved the stick there was a two- to four-inch overlap in what he measured. Joseph's group used string to measure the distance of the room but didn't seem to notice or mind a large bow in the string. Michael and Shelli's group used a trundle wheel and measured around objects instead of finding a way to remove the objects. Sean's group, who had gotten their tape measure, taped one end of it about three inches from the corner without noticing.

Cathy and I talked about what we were observing:

CATHY: It was so great to see Steven come up with that solution for measuring the ceiling. And his group gave him credit when I asked them how they figured that out.

RUTH: What other things are you noticing? You said you weren't sure what to look for.

CATHY: Well, everybody's really involved. They seem to be doing the task. What are you seeing?

RUTH: (*After telling her my experience with Jennise's group*) I'm somewhat surprised by their gross imprecision in measurement. It looks like this is their first experience with measuring. That is something we'll want to watch over time.

CATHY: What do you mean?

RUTH: Well, watch how Shelli is measuring the wall. She doesn't know what to do when she runs into the wall protrusion and the yardstick doesn't fit. She's just estimating now. I think I might interact with Shelli, maybe even offer a suggestion, since I know she won't use the suggestion unless it makes sense to her. Jonathan and Sean didn't seem to notice their tape measure was taped three inches from the corner. Look at Michael rolling the trundle wheel around objects while he tries to measure the length of the room. I just heard Bo say the walls are three meters and eight inches high. He doesn't see any problem mixing measurement systems. I wonder what he'll do when it comes to translating that to scale. Bryan is wrapping string around a ruler, content to ignore the quarter inch on each end of the ruler. He'll probably be off by six or eight inches. Most kids only measured one length for the room and one width even though both dimensions have wall protrusions.

CATHY: I wonder if I'll ever know what to look for. You're seeing so much and I'm saying, "They're all working."

RUTH: I think that comes from understanding the big ideas or "essential understandings" in measurement. I wanted to know if kids would choose appropriate measuring tools and if they would use units appropriate to the properties they're measuring. I want to observe what level of precision they're using, and where errors are happening, so we can process that with them.

CATHY: What will we do with this information?

RUTH: I think during processing time we can list their measurements for the length and width of the room. That'll give them an opportunity to see if their measures agree and to explore why they might not. I'm aware of the rich opportunity for assessment here as we watch kids work.

CATHY: Yes, this is where I should be writing notes if I knew what I was looking for. Maybe I should try that. Would you do the processing today so I can watch? I don't feel ready for this.

A Look at Processing

Groups worked on their scale models for an hour before Cathy called the class together. Groups reported on progress they had made. I then asked groups to tell me their measures for the length of the room and I recorded them on the board. They were: 9 meters; 8 meters, 30 centimeters; 11 yards; 32 feet; 11 yards; and 8.75 meters.

RUTH: What's the difference between group 1's and group 2's measures?

JONATHAN: Seventy centimeters.

RUTH: Do you think that's a lot or pretty close for measuring the length of this room?

JOHN: I think it's a lot. It's almost a meter off.

RUTH: How do you think that happened?

SHELLI: We couldn't get our trundle wheel into the corners so we estimated.

RUTH: Could that be the difference?

SHELLI: Some of the difference.

TONYA: Maybe somebody used the wrong end of the measuring stick and read the wrong numbers.

PAUL: They could have measured on a crooked line.

MARCI: Maybe they weren't careful when they moved the meterstick.

RUTH: There are a lot of things that might have happened. We want to have the scale models be as precise as you can make them, so some of you might want to double-check your measures tomorrow.

Here the bell rang, and although kids seemed engaged in figuring out the reason for the discrepancies in their measures, we dismissed the class for recess.

Observers in the Classroom

The following day visitors came to observe our classroom. Cathy told them she didn't know what to expect from the lesson but they were welcome. She introduced the lesson by telling kids they would continue working on their scale models, but first we wanted to share what we'd noticed from yesterday.

CATHY: Yesterday some of you got to a place where you thought there wasn't much left to do. In some groups one or two people were working on building the scale model and the others were just watching. I was surprised that most groups only took two different measures and thought they were done. I want you to help me generate a list of what measures you'll need to do, because there is a lot to do, and you won't finish on time unless you come up with a plan and divide up the work so everyone is working.

She asked the class what measures they would need and listed their responses on an overhead transparency. The list was long and included things like distance of door from corner, height and width of door, distance to wall protrusions, length and width of protrusions, height and width of windows, distance between windows, placement and size of coat-closet doors. After encouraging groups to make a plan so that they could use their time wisely, she told them to go to work. I interrupted and asked if I could share something.

I told the class I wanted to show them what I had observed yesterday and see if they could tell me what the problems were. Without naming names, I modeled how Bo (and others) had overlapped yardstick measurements. Jonathan told us what the problem was. When I asked if it would make a small or large difference in their results, they thought it might make a big difference. Next I fastened the tape measure to the wall about three inches from the corner and measured to the other side of the room leaving some sway in the tape measure and measuring higher at one end than the other. Kids were able to identify all the problems. When I asked if they thought the sway would make a big difference or a small difference, opinions varied. I decided to measure both ways. We weren't sure of the answer, and it would give us another opportunity to do mental computation in context when we tried to determine the difference. After reminding the class that they might want to double-check their measurements, we let the kids go to work.

The room was very busy and everyone was involved. Most groups decided to redo their measurements. About fifteen minutes into the lesson I looked around the room and wondered what our visitors were seeing. Would they notice Michael and Jonathan laughing at the front of the room and think they were off task? How could they know the brilliant work Michael has done all year and the intellectual challenges he continually gives himself, the rest of the class, and us? How could they know that it's wonderful to see serious Michael laughing? Would they notice children's errors in measurement and wonder why we didn't try to explain how to measure correctly? Would they notice Steven, who has struggled with school, measuring precisely? Would they notice noise? Would they notice productivity? I know how difficult it is to observe a classroom for a short period of time and interpret what you are seeing. Before they left, the visitors thanked us and said they had enjoyed the day, but Cathy and I didn't have time to talk with them about what they'd seen. The following week we received a note thanking us and mentioning how impressed they were by the relaxed yet challenging environment.

Finishing Up

The class worked for five days on their scale models. I arrived at school early on the last day of the project. Cathy had playground duty so we talked outside.

RUTH: I was thinking about these kids on the way here this morning. I realized that there has only been one other classroom I've taught in lately where I could play with kids, joke intellectually, and when I need them back seriously looking at an idea, or listening, all I have to do is ask once. In a lot of classrooms I've been in there is a feeling that you have to keep the lid on or things are going to get out of control real easily.

CATHY: Yes. But I believe this can happen with any class. I think we're seeing the payoff for trying to turn responsibility back to them. I think they're now kids who know they're respected, and they know how to act responsibly. In those other situations where you fear loss of control I think it's because the teacher is the one who's taking responsibility for the control, rather than giving it back to the kids. In those situations there's no opportunity for kids to develop self-control.

RUTH: So you credit our efforts, early in the year, to help them become the ones who solved the problems that came up?

CATHY: Yes. Absolutely. Trust and responsibility, challenging their minds, and not being the resource with all the answers. The substitute wrote another wonderful note. They always mention how motivated these kids are. Now for today. Should I be giving them more time or holding to the deadline?

RUTH: I think that decision depends on how productively they're using their time. If kids work productively and don't finish, the deadline was probably unrealistic. If they waste lots of time and don't finish, then you want them to face the consequences of having chosen to waste time.

CATHY: Since we were both gone yesterday I think I'll give them thirty minutes to finish up and then we'll begin processing.

After the bell rang Cathy addressed the class:

CATHY: The note from the substitute yesterday was good as usual. You guys are great. It's really nice to hear that you act responsibly.

BRYAN: We had trouble yesterday working on our model because Joseph was gone and he was the one with all the information.

CATHY: What did you do yesterday?

BRYAN: We tried to do some measuring but we kind of fell apart.

CATHY: Where were you keeping your notes and your work?

BRYAN: We kind of had some stuff, but Joseph had our measures.

CATHY: (*To the class*) Where were the rest of you keeping your notes?

SEAN: In our group folders.

CATHY: That's one of the reasons why we keep them in this file. If you have all your working materials here, and you have your measurements or whatever data you've collected in here, then if someone's absent you can go and get them.

JENNISE: (*To Bryan's group*) Well, why didn't you take the measurements all over?

BRYAN: (*To Jennise*) Well, that's sorta what we did, but then we kinda quit.

CATHY: What did you get accomplished yesterday?

JENNISE: We got our walls and windows and doors done. Then we worked on making the desks.

CATHY: So you're finished with the required part of the task. Do you still have things to do today if I give you more time?

JENNISE: Yes. We want to put all the desks in the classroom.

TIMMY: We got all the windows and bumps [wall protrusions] done.

JONATHAN: We were getting the final measurements and drawing the plan onto the graph paper.

SHELLI: We have the room done, but we have to make the bumps and put in our desks.

TONYA: We were really finished.

CATHY: Did you understand what your choices were when you were finished? Or what your challenges were?

TONYA: Uh-huh.

CATHY: What about group 5? You're all very quiet back there.

NATHAN: (*After silence and then some chuckling from that group*) We got one wall and the floor done.

CATHY: Okay, thirty minutes? Does that sound about right?

SEVERAL KIDS: Forty-five minutes.

CATHY: How many of you could be finished if you had forty-five minutes? (All but group 5 raise their hands) Okay. Go to work.

All the groups went to work right away and I wandered over to Jennise, Molly, Zachary, and Ray, who were mass-producing desks. They had cut out all twenty-eight desks, small two-by-two-centimeter grids. I asked if they had made the desks to scale and Jennise replied, "Yeah, sort of." I pushed farther:

RUTH: I notice you have two-by-two squares for the desks. Are your desks square?

JENNISE: Pretty close.

RUTH: Can you show me how you measured them? (*Jennise takes out a ruler and measures, showing me what she did to be precise, and the desk measures two feet across*) What about the other dimension? Is it two feet also? (*She finds that it's one and a half feet*) So do you think the two-by-two squares are precise enough?

JENNISE: It would be a lot easier to make them this way.

ZACHARY: Let's just cut these so they're two-by-one-and-a-half. That's easy.

RUTH: (*To Molly, who has cut sixty quarter-inch straws to use for desk legs*) I have a question for you too, Molly. Did you cut those to scale?

MOLLY: No. Do we have to do that?

RUTH: So you didn't measure how tall the desk is?

MOLLY: No.

RUTH: Well, your challenge was to add furniture and things to your model, but everything that goes in should be made to scale.

MOLLY: Jed, why don't you measure and see how long we should cut these?

Meanwhile Cathy noticed that Ray and Steven were not working with their respective groups. She decided to talk to Ray first, but came up to me a couple of minutes later:

CATHY: I just talked to Ray and told him he needed to work with his group or I'd give him another task to do. He perks up and says, "What?" He wanted another task! I don't want to just give him an out. I have a feeling if I give him that fractions thing to do he'll enjoy it. So I don't want to give it to him. He's one who likes to work alone. He doesn't want to work in his group and would rather do something on his own, and I don't want to reward that.

RUTH: Is he aware that he has the choice of working with his group or not but since this is a group task the consequence of choosing not to work with the group is that the best grade he can get on his rubric is two 1's: one for dropping out of the task, and one for not working with the group?

[*For an explanation of the scoring rubric we used, see Chapter 9.*]

CATHY: So he still gets the score for the task they're doing.

RUTH: You might tell him you'll give him another task because he needs to be working during math time, but he needs to know his grade will be 1, 1 for the task he's quitting.

CATHY: (*After Ray decides to work with his group*) What I'm finally realizing is these kids need to understand that they can't sit and wait for someone in their group to tell them what to do. They have to be proactive and take responsibility for looking at the job and seeing what needs to be done.

Cathy then went over to talk to Steven, the other dropout, and he too soon rejoined his group. I wondered what she'd said to him:

RUTH: Can you tell me anything about your meeting with Steven?
CATHY: I brought Josh out to see if he had said anything unkind and if that was why Steven was upset. I don't think that was it. I think it was that they all knew what to do and were all going to work, and Steven didn't know what to do, so he was just left sitting. So I talked to him about not waiting for everybody in the group but instead thinking ahead about what needs to be done and then jumping in and saying, "I can do this." When I came back I sat with the group and made them have a planning meeting and talk about what still has to be done. Timmy was going to do all the walls and the rest of them were just sitting there with nothing to do.

Another Look at Processing

The class continued to work on the task for about forty-five minutes. Then Cathy brought them together for processing. I have included the complete transcript of this processing session because it is a good illustration of opportunities to examine both mathematics and social issues:

CATHY: Would you use your next two minutes to clean up your area? (*Then*) Who has a finished project you'd like to share? (*Michael, Shelli, and Sean come up*) Can you tell us about what you did to complete your model?
MICHAEL: We had two squares to a meter. Our windows are off, because we rounded off a little bit. But there are so many windows, we didn't realize that would throw the whole wall off.
CATHY: Any other problems you ran into?
MICHAEL: Yeah, we made the bump [wall protrusion] and we made it the same size as the door so we had to make a new one.
CATHY: In other words, you made the bump, put it up and looked at it and said, "Oops, it's the same size as the door" and made another one?
SHELLI: That's not really what happened.

CATHY: How did it happen?

SHELLI: Well, they did it when I was in orchestra, and when I came back, I said, "It doesn't look right, it's the same as the door."

CATHY: Did you figure out what had gone wrong? Had you measured wrong?

MICHAEL: Yeah.

CATHY: So you had to go back and remeasure.

RUTH: How'd you feel about having to do that? Did you feel okay having Shelli say it was the same as the door, or did you resist, or what'd you do?

MICHAEL: We thought we measured it right, but we must have, like, put down the wrong measurement.

RUTH: So when Shelli raised a question about the size of it, I'm kind of curious about what you did then. What was your response to her? Did you say, "Good observation, Shelli, we'll go measure again?" Or what did you do?

MICHAEL: Well, we kinda thought she was wrong and our measure was right, and it wasn't the same. Then Shelli showed us by measuring it.

SEAN: We didn't listen to her and we sorta denied the fact that it was wrong.

CATHY: So you had a little disagreement. But you worked through the problem. Any questions from any of you about their project?

PAUL: The sides of your walls don't look like they're the same and they should be the same.

MICHAEL: Yeah, well, we rounded off a little on the windows, but there were a whole bunch of them so the wall's not quite right.

RUTH: So you discovered that if you are off by a little, but multiply that by six windows, you can end up off by quite a bit.

MICHAEL: Yeah.

BRYAN: How did you make the bump? We're kind of confused about how to do that on ours.

MICHAEL: Well, we made the room first then added the bumps. It was kind of confusing.

CATHY: Would you do anything differently if you were to do it again? What would you do differently if you were given the same project?

MICHAEL: We'd measure more carefully. Especially when we did the windows so it would be easier to make the walls.

RUTH: Did anyone else use two squares to a meter for your scale?

BO: We did.

RUTH: Are you using the same-size graph paper?

BO: It's smaller.

J.R.: Our grid is—one square is fifty centimeters.

RUTH: So what should we be able to say about your two models?

CATHY: Would you ask that question again? I don't think everybody heard you.

RUTH: J.R. says their scale is one square is one-half meter. Michael said their scale is one meter for two squares. So what should be true about their models?

J.R.: They're the same.

RUTH: What do you mean by the same?

CATHY: Bring yours over and let's see.

RUTH: If we put these two on top of each other everything should line up. The bumps and the doors and everything should line up. (*When we try, one nestles inside the other. The windows don't match and one closet door doesn't match*) Oh, look at this, they nestle in. The bumps nestle into each other. Oops, look at these closet doors, guys. Can you see these doors?

MICHAEL: One of the doors lines right up.

RUTH: One of the doors looks pretty precise. So do the wall protrusions. You knew your windows wouldn't line up precisely.

SEAN: I wonder which closet door is in the right place?

RUTH: You might want to check that. We'll leave the models out on the table in the back of the room for awhile and you can investigate and see what you can figure out.

CATHY: Group 2, do you want to share yours with us? (*They bring their model up*) You finished yours last week, right? To what do you attribute the fact that you finished last week?

J.R.: We measured most of it the first day. While we were measuring, the other person was drawing it on our plans. We had fun.

JONATHAN: I think one of the reasons why they got it done faster is most of the groups measured two or three times. They started over.

CATHY: Why do you think that happened?

JONATHAN: We didn't get it right the first time.

CATHY: So you think they were more accurate the first time?

J.R.: Well, we always had two people measuring and one person drawing. We'd have one person mark the spot then move the meterstick, so it wasn't like one person trying to do it on their own.

CATHY: So having two people helped a lot with measuring.

J.R.: (*Holding up a scale model of Bryan*) And I made Bryan, and he's exact.

RUTH: So how tall is Bryan?

J.R.: Well, I didn't do it to exact scale. He's a little over one meter, no, not one meter. He's almost one and a half meters.

BRYAN. I'm five feet, one-and-one-half inches.

RUTH: Oh, he measured you in feet and inches? Their scale is meters. How did you figure out the scale then, J.R.?

J.R.: No, I measured him in meters.

CATHY: Did your group have any problems? (*Tonya and Marci giggle*)

J.R.: Yes, but I won't say.

CATHY: Can you tell us what problems you had?

J.R.: One person complained a lot, but they didn't measure, and they didn't help draw. They cut, but that was all they did. They complained a lot about what we did, but they didn't offer suggestions for making it better.

CATHY: So if they had a complaint, you would have appreciated having them offer a solution to the problem?

J.R.: Yeah.

CATHY: Group 3, is your group finished? Would you bring yours up? (*Turning to me*) This isn't what you were thinking about for processing, is it.

RUTH: You're doing fine.

ZACHARY: Our scale is one square is one foot.

J.R.: We didn't get to put the desks in because we ran out of time.

CATHY: What about the original assignment part?

ZACHARY: We started out not using the bumps. But when we heard the challenge, we decided we should put the bumps in. We added the bumps in. One on the inside and one on the outside.

JENNISE: Our windows are kind of off, because we used two feet, then when we tried three feet they were off.

RUTH: Can I introduce a mathematical idea?

CATHY: Yes.

RUTH: Would you leave your model here? J.R., you said yours were alike. There's actually a mathematical term for shapes that fit right on top of each other. Does anyone know what it is?

A NUMBER OF KIDS: Congruent.

J.R.: You wrote it on the board.

RUTH: I wrote two words up there. How do you know congruent is the right one?

J.R.: We learned about that earlier in the year and I remembered it.

OTHER KIDS: Yeah.

RUTH: We did? I don't even remember it. You're right. These two are congruent. Or they should be if the measurement was precise. There's something we can say about table 1's model and table 3's model also. Anyone know what we can say about them?

MICHAEL: They're similar.

RUTH: What does it mean for shapes to be similar?

MICHAEL: It means even if they aren't the same size or something, if one, like, somehow you shrunk it to the same size it would be congruent. All the bumps and doors and stuff would be the same place if you shrunk it.

CATHY: Could I interrupt for just a minute? I'm very aware that there are about five or six of you who seem to think that because you don't have anything to contribute to the conversation, it's not important for you to listen. And I want you to know that this is probably one of the most important parts of the whole lesson. A lot of the learning that you've been doing is getting summarized and processed now, so that you'll understand what the learning was the last three or four days. And if you're checking out to do other things, you're missing some of the meat of what we've just accomplished. Please check back in again.

RUTH: Actually that description is about the nicest description of similar I've ever heard. Could you try it again?

MICHAEL: It would be, like, if there were two models and they were just the same with the same scale they would be congruent. That means when they're compared to each other, everything is in the same place. The doors and stuff. And for similar they're the same shape but one is bigger, so if you shrunk one to the right size then they would be congruent.

RUTH: A nice way to test for similarity, if I can move this building without destroying it, is to stand over them, and close one eye and move this smaller one on top up or down and see if I can get it to line up exactly with the bottom one. Like right here, I'm seeing the front doors line up precisely, the bumps line up precisely. Oops, I can't even see the closet door, so the models aren't similar in terms of where the doors are placed. You don't have agreement about distances for where the left closet door is placed. The windows aren't aligned, but you knew they were not precise. So you might want to play with these that way and see where things are aligned.

SHELLI: Maybe if you used ours the closet doors would match, because ours didn't match theirs.

[*Shelli understands that we can use logic to get more information about which measures might be precise. If models 1 and 2 don't line up at the left closet door, and models 2 and 3 don't line up there either, we should compare models 1 and 3 to see if they line up. This will give us useful information.*]

RUTH: That might be an interesting way to try to find out which is placed more precisely, or to see if these two match up.

CATHY: So we have three completed projects. Can any of you tell us why others didn't get completed?

BRYAN: We didn't get finished 'cause Joseph was in charge and he hasn't been here for two days. Then we had this big sheet of paper on the floor and we don't know what he's doing.

CATHY: So you were all relying on the person who isn't here.

NATHAN: We had a lot of disagreements on measurements. We'd measure and someone else would go measure and say they disagree and we'd go do it again.

HEIDI: We forgot to put the door in.

CATHY: So planning maybe will be important to you? I want to tell you what I observed. I observed that in the groups that didn't finish, almost every time I observed the group or came to the group, there was somebody who wasn't actively involved in the process of getting the task done. And that wasn't just once around. It was several times. And it wasn't necessarily the same person but there were always one or two people who were sitting or fiddling or off somewhere talking, or doing something else. So that tells me there's still some work that needs to be done in terms of learning to plan and to divide up the responsibility for how to get the job done. It also occurred to me in coming around to the groups that there's a reliance on the part of some of you to wait for somebody else in the group to tell you what to do. It's as if, "Now here's our group. Now let's find out who the leader is and let's let them tell us what to do." And you sit and wait to get told what to do. And there's a couple of things that happen with that. One, if the person is absent then you're out to lunch in terms of what you do next; and number two, if you're relying on other people to do the thinking for you, then you don't know what to jump in and get ready to do because you haven't thought through this project yourself. It doesn't mean that when we have a group we've got one or two people who are the thinkers and the rest of us are the workers. You should all take responsibility for the thinking process and the planning process so that you can be an integral part of getting the project done. (*The room is quiet and children seem to be paying attention*) I saw this group over here. One of the reasons they got done is because every one of them was involved in understanding what this project was and what had to get done. I don't think I even once saw them just goofing around. I think they really worked on task.

NATHAN: It could be 'cause they only had three of them here for two days, so they all worked.

CATHY: So you think four was too many people?

SEVERAL KIDS: Yeah.

CATHY: But what does that mean you have to do as a group?

RUTH: It's interesting that three can get the job done and four can't.

CATHY: I find that kind of amazing. Think of what you're saying. You're saying that if we had a job to do, the job is going to get done faster and better with fewer people?

JONATHAN: If a few people better understand the problem and more people don't understand it, it will get done faster.

[*The children may have a valid point. With some jobs, three could work more efficiently than four. This wasn't the case with the scale model task, however.*]

CATHY: (*Thinking the children are looking for an excuse and not giving them an out*) Does that mean when there's a group of four or five, there are some people who think I'm the best and the rest of them aren't any good, so I'm going to do the job? That bugs the heck out of me. That really bugs the heck out of me. And I see that happening sometimes in here. You just sort of make the assumption that the other person or the other two aren't capable to dig in and do this. And you aren't learning to work together when you do that. What I observed in some groups was that you had somebody sitting and waiting till others went to get the measure and came back and told you. And I'm going, "Now wait a minute. If there are four walls in the room and things to put in there, it seems to me that there's more than enough to do to keep everybody involved." Four groups didn't get the job done. I don't think you were using your time very well. How many of you had a planning session today? (*Nobody raises hands*) I didn't say anything about it but have we talked about having planning sessions before? (*Shelli mumbles something about three working better and Cathy laughs*) Yeah, I know you. But I'm going to be real stubborn. 'Cause I think when you move to threes you move away from one of the purposes of groups of four, which is to learn to cooperate, plan, and problem-solve together. And as uncomfortable and as difficult as that process is, it's a reality for your future.

RUTH: Should I tell them about the Boeing interview?

CATHY: Yes, please do.

RUTH: Picture yourself in this situation. Think about how you've been working the last three days and then ask yourself, Would Boeing hire me? One of the teachers in my class this summer had a son who just graduated from the University of Washington as an engineer. He applied at Boeing for a job. At his job interview, when he walked in the door the person hiring greeted him and sat him down at a table with three other people who were also applying for the same job. The Boeing person gave them a real engineering problem that the company had to solve, and watched the four people as they worked together all morning trying to solve the problem and preparing and presenting a report at the end of four hours. Boeing was only going to hire one of the four. They wanted to hire someone who was a good problem solver and who knew how to work effectively with others. And businesses are starting to do that now. They're saying, We want workers who can use their time productively. And the way we're going to find them is to give them a real problem to solve and watch them and see how they work.

CATHY: The priority is really to work collaboratively in teams. Even as a member of a staff of teachers, I have to learn to work together with other people, even though we each have our own classroom. We have to make decisions now at our building level about how the money is spent, what supplies you need, what we want to focus on next year. If we can't get along and plan together, things get wasted. Money gets wasted. Time gets wasted. Progress doesn't get made.

BRYAN: We wasted time and didn't make progress because we relied on that one person. (*Meaning Joseph*)

CATHY: Good point.

JOHN: I know somebody that makes the manuals for flying planes at Boeing.

CATHY: Does he have to work with others to do that?

JOHN: Yeah.

CATHY: Okay. Those of you who have not finished the task need to finish it by using your recess time. But you need to decide as a group how you're going to get that done. How many of you can get it done with the recesses you have today. (*All but group 5 raise their hands*) Okay, if you've finished your model, you're excused for recess.

While the others were going to recess, Bryan came to me and said, "We relied way too much on Joseph. We shouldn't have, because now that he's absent we have to do all the work over again." I agreed and suggested that would be a good thing to remember next time. All but one of the groups finished their models during the fifteen-minute recess break. Bryan's group didn't finish but made more progress than they seemed to have made during the two previous days. In this case, working on their own time appeared to motivate them to complete the task. It would be nice to believe that the class discussion also acted as a motivator.

After recess Cathy showed the class how we could nestle the models and, using a string attached to the center of the models, test for proportionality. (The string will cross common points on all of the models if they are built to precision.) As part of an upcoming measurement menu, we planned to label the scale models and have the children use the string to see what they could discover about the precision used in making them.

Although we were finished with the scale-model investigation, it was clear that children would need many more opportunities to work with measurement and to develop their understandings within the strand. We planned to provide ongoing opportunities.

After the scale-model investigation, Cathy spent a week on the *Seeing Fractions* (CDE 1991) unit and a week on a number menu before we returned to data collection and analysis. We were very eager to see what the children would do after three weeks away from the unit.

## Chapter Seven

Developing Mathematical Understanding over Time: *Revisiting Data Collection and Analysis*

When we took our break from the unit on data collection and analysis earlier in the year, both Cathy and I were somewhat disappointed with it. We had hoped children would have an opportunity to experience statistics, or data collection and analysis, and recognize its importance as a tool for making sense of their world. There was not much evidence that they were experiencing either the power or importance of the mathematical ideas. If I hadn't been focusing my doctoral dissertation on this unit, Cathy and I might have decided not to return to the unit at all. And indeed, when we did return, it was without much enthusiasm. It is only through hindsight, of course, that we realize what we would have missed had we not done so.

In returning to the unit, we decided to have our students do a second statistical investigation of an issue in which they were interested. But before asking them to do these investigations, we wanted them to have explored the issues of random sampling and sample size. That first day we had them do two sampling tasks. For the first task, Cathy had placed ten color tiles in a bag. She told the class there were only ten tiles in the bag and that individual tiles could be either red or green. She asked if anyone was confident he or she knew how many red and how many green tiles there were. Bo said he was so confident there were five of each that he would bet his recess on it. Others said what they thought it might be, but no one else was sure.

Cathy asked for a volunteer to tally results as they conducted the experiment. Children took turns drawing a tile out of the bag, marking its color on a tally sheet, and then putting the tile back in the bag. Cathy shook the bag after each tile was replaced. When she asked why children thought she was doing that, Zachary said, "So the same one doesn't stay on top. Cathy replied, "Yes. I want to be sure we're getting a random sample." After every ten draws, Cathy asked for predictions. After thirty draws, the class thought they would be confident after ten more draws. When those were inconsistent with the other draws, they thought it might take a hundred draws in order to have confidence in the data. They did ten more draws, for a total of fifty, then made their predictions and emptied the contents of the bag. Most of the class had predicted there were six green and four red tiles. They discovered that there were seven green and three red tiles in the bag.

For the second sampling experiment, groups of children selected one of several bags labeled A, B, or C. They were told the contents of all the bags, but not which bag had which contents. One bag had fifteen blue cubes and five yellow cubes; a second bag had ten blue and ten yellow cubes; and the third had five blue and fifteen yellow cubes. Groups selected a bag and then sampled one cube at a time, recording the color, replacing the cube, and shaking the bag after each draw. They continued this process until they felt they could confidently predict the contents of their bag. One group thought they knew the contents after just twenty draws. One group did a hundred draws.

Cathy processed their findings and talked about the relationship between sample size and confidence in the data. She mentioned that some children might be sampling a population of people outside the classroom for their statistical investigations, and that they would need to make decisions about the size of the sample needed and ways to be sure they were taking random samples when appropriate. We knew the children would need many more opportunities to experience and investigate sampling issues. But because time was of the essence (my defense was just a month away), we decided to begin the statistical investigations the following day. Cathy asked groups to spend the last fifteen minutes before recess brainstorming a list of questions they might want to investigate. Groups shared their lists with the whole class, and Cathy suggested that for homework they should share their lists with their parents and ask them for additional suggestions of ideas to investigate.

They had two days to gather additional ideas before beginning their data collection and analysis survey.

At the next math class, Cathy asked for volunteers to share their lists of ideas. Molly was first. Her list included: How many people recycle at home? Should we save the whales? Do you think we should save trees for birds and other small animals? (This is a hot political issue in the Northwest.) Why do people shop at K-Mart? Rachael was next: Do you think the rat should have babies? Should we lower the sales tax? Should we put more money up to find a cure for AIDS? Should we start school at 8:30 and get out at 3:00? Should we eliminate daylight savings time? (It was easy to see that the lists had been influenced by additional ideas generated at home.) Tonya and Heidi shared their list: If you had a choice, what country would you live in? How many people recycle? What is your favorite season? What's your favorite kind of book? What region would you like to live in? What's your favorite kind of music? Should skateboards be allowed downtown? What is your favorite kind of weather?

After several more children had shared their lists, Cathy asked partners to decide on a question together and make plans for gathering data. They were to determine their population and other data-gathering issues before beginning to collect data. She told the class they would have three ninety-minute math periods to work on their projects, that they would also need to work on them outside of class, and that they should be prepared to present their findings in two weeks. As the kids went to work, the level of discussion was intense. Most pairs had several good ideas to choose from, so making a final choice was often difficult. J.R. and Bryan quickly decided on, "Do you litter?" and began asking everyone in the room. When they asked Cathy she responded, "Gosh, I don't know if I'd tell you if I did. Do you suppose you're getting honest data?" J.R. was sure they were, so they kept on. In about fifteen minutes several twosomes were gathering data. Only a few were still planning. Zachary and Paul were trying to find out if people recycle plastic. When they asked me, I answered, "Yes. But do you think some people might say yes because they know they should?" Zachary was convinced this was not a problem because two people had answered that they use plastic and throw it away. The children seemed convinced that because some people answered honestly, everyone would.

When we revisited the notion of sensitive data during processing, the kids felt that questions about recycling, littering, or wearing helmets weren't sensitive data. They were convinced that because some people had acknowledged they didn't do those things, everyone was telling the truth. I suggested some of them might want to investigate this idea by collecting the data both anonymously and face-to-face. I didn't know if anyone would follow up on that idea.

During the three class sessions provided for this data collection and analysis project, partners worked industriously. They reflected on their progress each day in their math learning logs (see Shelli's portfolio entries in Chapter 9). When children were ready to display their data, many tried to use line plots or stem-and-leaf graphs and found those methods didn't work with their data. Cathy and I were a little surprised that the data display methods we had taught during the *Used Numbers* lessons did not fit the kinds of questions kids were asking. Some children used bar graphs instead, others invented their own methods of recording. Graphs were posted before spring break, and processed after vacation. The initial processing session was lively. Cathy asked for volunteers willing to share their data, and Zachary and Paul offered to be first. (Their data display is included as Figure 7–1.)

ZACHARY: We wanted to know what people do with their plastic. It's an important question 'cause they don't recycle plastic in curbside recycling, so it takes even more energy for people to take their plastic down to the recycling center. We found out that not very many people throw plastic away without recycling it. Most people reuse it. Our population was twenty-seven.

JENNISE: Twenty-seven what?

ZACHARY: Us. We asked people in here.

JOHN: What do those rectangles mean?

ZACHARY: Oh. Each rectangle is one person.

CATHY: John, are you suggesting it would be easier for the reader if that was more clearly labeled?

JOHN: Yeah, it was hard to tell.

CATHY: What would make it easier to read?

JOSEPH: If they wrote, "Number of people" on the side.

RUTH: Did you ask people directly?

PAUL: Yes.

RUTH: Did any of them say how they reuse plastic?

ZACHARY: Well no, but there are a lot of ways. We refill ours with water in the refrigerator, and we cut plastic bottles and use them in the garden to keep the birds away. (*Several kids have their hands up*)

J.R.: We use a lot of those margarine tubs. Then we wash them and use them for leftovers.

MOLLY: We keep water in ours.

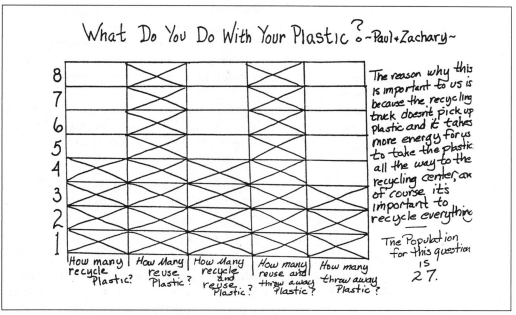

Figure 7.1. Zachary and Paul's graph from their statistical survey, "What do you do with your plastic?"

JONATHAN: We cut off the tops of the big plastic milk cartons and make little greenhouses for our plants in the garden.

CATHY: Something we're hearing more of lately is precycling. Does anyone know what that is?

ZACHARY: It means you think about what you buy before you buy it. So if something is in plastic and you have a choice you don't buy the plastic.

CATHY: I'm thinking it might be fun to write a newsletter on what you found out in your surveys. Maybe you and Paul could write an article to go with your data display that gives people ideas how to reuse plastic, or makes them aware of precycling.

RUTH: Some people may not think about having a choice when they buy ketchup, for example. You can get either glass or plastic.

J.R.: Well, you can't squeeze the glass.

RUTH: Oh. So you think people will only recycle or use environmentally sound products when it's convenient? Does that mean it's not really a very important issue?

ZACHARY: No, it's real important. Plastic stays forever and doesn't ever break down. It never goes away and our landfills are filling up. We're running out of places to put our garbage. And it takes oil to make plastic so it uses our oil supply. And that's another big problem.

RUTH: It sounds like you know enough to write an interesting article for a newsletter. You might even ask people to consider if they would be willing to go to the inconvenience of shaking a ketchup bottle. You could probably get us to think.

CATHY: This sounds like a newsletter that we would want to get out into the community. (*To the class*) Would all of you be interested in doing a newsletter on your findings? (*Almost everyone is*)

Several children notice the graph of a smoking survey (see Figure 7–2) on the wall and want to talk about that. Cathy asks Ray and Josh if they're willing to share:

JOSH: You read it, Ray.

RAY: Okay. (*Reading their findings*) Nobody said they will smoke. Fifty-one people said they won't smoke. Only seven people said they have tried to smoke. Forty-four people said they haven't. No one said they do smoke. Fifty-one people said they don't smoke. This project was fun because it kept us busy and working. It was an interesting project, how you see who's smoked or not.

CATHY: Does anyone have any questions for Ray and Josh?

MOLLY: How did you get fifty-one people?

JENNISE: Yeah, who was your population?

JOSH: We asked everybody in here, and everybody in Mrs. Bailey's room [the combined fourth/fifth grade across the hall].

MICHAEL: What does it mean if people said yes they have smoked? I mean, does it mean, like, they used to smoke a lot or, like, they tried it just once?

RAY: We think it means they just tried it.

CATHY: Can you tell that from the way you collected your data?

JOSH: Well, most kids just try smoking once to see what it's like, like I tried smoking when my mom was there 'cause she wanted me to see how bad it was.

[*Josh is not responding to Cathy's question about data collection. He's more interested in his experiences and related theories. Other children are also eager to share what they think.*]

CATHY: (*Trying to bring the discussion back to statistics*) Is there a way you might have asked your question differently so that you could find

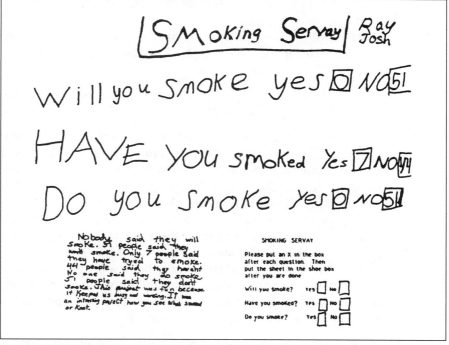

Figure 7.2. Ray and Josh's graph from their statistical survey on smoking.

out the answer to what Michael is curious about? How could you ask your question so that you would know if kids have just tried cigarettes once?

RAY: Maybe we could ask, "How many times have you smoked?"

JENNISE: When you read your findings, you just told us the things we could already see. Maybe you should tell us the things we can't see. (*Ray shrugs his shoulders*)

CATHY: So Jennise, you're suggesting that there is some information that would help you more. Can you give them some suggestions? All of you should be thinking about these things so that you'll know what you should do if we're going to publish a newsletter on your findings.

JENNISE: Well, we need to know who the population was. It should maybe say fifty-one fifth graders at our school.

CATHY: Okay. So knowing the population surveyed is important information. Anything else?

MOLLY: How do people know now they won't smoke? We don't know. We may think we won't smoke, but there'll be peer pressure and we don't really know.

JOSH: We just said people said they won't smoke. That means they think they won't smoke now.

RUTH: Molly raised the issue of peer pressure. What do you two think would happen if you gave the survey at the middle school? Do you think you would get the same results?

[*A lot of hands go up. Several children explain why they think more kids smoke at the middle school.*]

RUTH: It might be interesting for you two to conduct a survey at the middle school, maybe at sixth, seventh, and eighth grades. You might find out some interesting information about when kids start smoking. Think about whether you want to do that before we publish.

TONYA: How do you know people told you the truth?

JOSH: We don't know they told the truth. But we had them answer by putting *X*'s on a piece of paper, then put their paper in a shoebox. So nobody saw what they said.

CATHY: So you collected the data as if it's sensitive data. That probably increases the likelihood that people will give accurate information.

RUTH: Molly and Allie had an interesting experience with that idea. Would you two mind sharing your results?

[*When I first saw the display Molly and Allie posted (see Figure 7–3), I was disappointed. I didn't have a clue what they had done, and the information was very sloppily presented. It was only when I read their math learning logs that I could interpret their findings. Molly had written, "We learned that twenty-five people say yes they do recycle at home on one graph and only seventeen people said they do on the other graph. There's a difference when you ask the people right up to their face than if you ask them to check off a piece of paper and put it in a can or something like that. We asked the same people each time, but they answered different on paper. We learned if the question is sensitive, you better ask on paper."*]

CATHY: Were you surprised by your results?

ALLIE: Yeah, we thought everybody would say the same thing. We didn't think it was sensitive data. But Ruth said we might want to check and see, so we did.

CATHY: Is there anything you'd do differently if you did this again?

MOLLY: Well, our line for twenty-five looks shorter than our line for seventeen. That makes it hard to tell. We'd do our scale the same next time.

CATHY: Anyone have any questions?

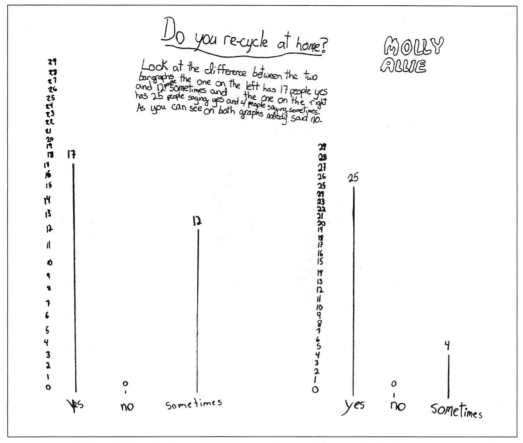

Figure 7.3. **Molly and Allie's graph from their statistical survey on recycling.**

RUTH: You found out some very interesting information, but when I read your graph, I didn't have any idea what you were reporting. What information would help your audience know what you have done?

ALLIE: We would need to label the two graphs so people know who we asked and how we collected the information. Also, our bar graph should be neater, but Molly did it when I was sick and she had her arm in a sling.

CATHY: Okay, you might want to think about what else you want to know and what you want your reader to know when you publish. Your findings are interesting.

MICHAEL: If they got different information on recycling when they asked people and when they had them record on paper, I wonder if Zachary and Paul would get different information if they did a survey on paper.

Figure 7.4. Nathan and Mike's graph from their statistical survey on music-listening habits.

CATHY: Zachary and Paul, you might want to find that out before we publish the newsletter.

Next Nathan and Mike shared their graph on their music survey (see Figure 7–4). Children had questions for them as well:

J.R.: What does it mean that seven people said they never listen to music their parents don't want them to? Are we talking about radios or tapes?

MOLLY: Well, I put never, because my parents don't care what music I listen to.

RUTH: Oh, I thought those were the seven good kids who never listen to music their parents don't want them to.

JED: I put never, and my parents don't care what I listen to.

CATHY: You two might want to figure out how to ask the question differently so that we know what never means if you're going to publish. Okay. We have lots to think about if we're going to be ready to publish a newsletter. It's recess time already. I can't believe it. You contributed a lot of good ideas today that will help people know what they need to do.

BRYAN: Are we going to have more time this time? We barely got our survey done and we rushed.

CATHY: Yes, I think we'll have about three weeks this time.

BRYAN: How about a month?

CATHY: It might take us a month. How many of you want to collect more information as a result of our discussions? (*Most groups raise their hands*) Some of you might want to survey at the middle school. We can arrange for that. Well, be thinking about what you need to do before we publish a newsletter. These are all issues that are important to the community. I think it will be very important for you to share your findings with them. Okay, you're excused for recess.

Talking with parents about issues that might be important seemed to have influenced the kinds of surveys children did. Discussions throughout the next two days were lively as children shared their findings. These were issues kids seemed to care about, and they were quite articulate about their issues.

To summarize: Our first response when we saw the children's data displays was disappointment. They looked quite primitive. The line plots and stem-and-leaf plots that we had introduced during the data collection and analysis unit didn't fit the questions they were asking. Kids needed to invent new ways to display the data. Some used bar graphs (there were a few hanging bar graphs), others just gave the information in boxes. Much information that would have been helpful to the reader was not included on the displays. But children had opportunities through the processing to talk about these issues. We looked forward to what they would produce when they published their newsletter, which would provide an audience for their writing. Children also had opportunities to encounter the messy issues surrounding data collection and analysis. They were talking about sensitive data, the population surveyed, random sampling, clarifying their questions, and ways to present findings. They were also experiencing data collection and analysis as a way to find out information that can be used to influence people's thinking and actions. They will need additional opportunities over time to continue to develop their understanding. But by trying to discover information they care about, these children were developing the understandings outlined in the NCTM *Standards*. They are having opportunities to explore statistics in real-world situations so that they can:

- systematically collect, organize, and describe data;
- construct, read, and interpret tables, charts, and graphs;
- make inferences and convincing arguments that are based on data analysis;
- evaluate arguments that are based on data analysis;
- develop an appreciation for statistical methods as powerful means for decision making. (NCTM 1991, p. 105)

Their understanding was by no means mastered. In fact, the very notion of mastery seems meaningless because many of the ideas the children encountered during this unit were recent inventions within the mathematics community. As statisticians search for more meaningful ways to analyze and display data, they will continue to invent new ideas and tools. In statistics, as in other domains, mathematics is an expanding, dynamic field. These children, also, will continue to invent new and more sophisticated understandings as they work to make sense of their world.

We hoped they would have opportunities over time to do so. Eight months of doing mathematics was a start. Yet if children are to become mathematically powerful, as that term is defined in *Professional Standards for Teaching Mathematics* (NCTM 1991), then the educational community must find ways to ensure that these children, and others, have ongoing opportunities to do mathematics: to conjecture, invent, ponder, describe, represent, communicate, solve, create, and search for the patterns and relationships that surround them. They must have ongoing opportunities to learn that mathematics is a powerful tool for making sense of and for impacting their world. The unfortunate reality, however, is that in all likelihood these twenty-eight fifth graders will instead face roughly 240 pages of routine, outdated textbook mathematics next year.

Number Concepts:
An Alternative

Paper-and-pencil algorithms taught and practiced in isolation are still the mainstay of most mathematics textbooks and thus of most mathematics classrooms. The value of such practice has been challenged by mathematics educators (Burns 1992; Sowder 1990) who question the usefulness of these algorithms to the changing needs of society in the technological world of the 1990s. If, as the NCTM recommends, students are allowed free use of calculators, then the ability to do estimation and mental calculation, the development of "number sense," and an understanding of number relationships become much more important and proficiency with paper-and-pencil algorithms becomes much less useful. Sowder (1990) suggests that the teaching of standard algorithms does little to help children understand number relationships or perform mental computation. Findings within Cathy's classroom suggest that proficiency with paper-and-pencil computation may, in fact, interfere with children's ability to use number relationships to do mental computation.

In planning for the year, Cathy and I decided not to teach standard paper-and-pencil algorithms. We would, instead, provide opportunities for children to (1) use numbers, number relationships, and invented algorithms to solve problems; (2) develop an understanding of number concepts in the context of mathematical investigations; and (3) invent arithmetic concepts before being formally instructed in those concepts. Our focus throughout would be to consider and encourage diverse algorithms. This decision involved a major change in teaching priorities for Cathy and demonstrates how willing she was to take risks. In previous years, standard algorithms, rules, and procedures were the very skills she felt most accountable for. This decision not to teach standard algorithms would be considered by many to be a radical and perhaps unreasonable departure from the norm.

Children Invent Arithmetic Concepts

Throughout the year children were frequently asked to make sense of mathematical ideas they had not yet been formally taught. The discussion in Chapter 4 of the "How did you get to school today?" graph, for example, illustrates the thinking these fifth graders displayed with regard to fractions.

The following discussion occurred when the children were given their scores from their first menu. As described in Chapter 4, many children wasted time during their first menu experience and few were successful in completing the menu. Grades ranged from a low of 7 points to a high of 20.5. Interpreting these scores became a vehicle for examining what children understood about percent prior to instruction:

CATHY: Do you have a sense of what your grade would be based on your score?

CLASS: No, not really.

CATHY: Well, unfortunately, next year, in middle school, you are going to receive grades of A, B, C, D, and F. Most of your teachers will probably grade you based on 90% to 100% is an A, 80% to 89% is a B, and so forth. Do you have a sense of what your grade would be from that?

CLASS: No.

RUTH: I'm curious what you do know about percent. What if you scored twenty points on your menu. Do you know what percent that would be?

CLASS: (*Lots of hands go up*) A hundred percent.

RUTH: What if you got zero points, what percent would that be?

CLASS: (*Again, lots of hands*) That would be zero percent.

RUTH: Well, what if you got ten points, what percent would that be?

CLASS: (*Hands up quickly again*) Fifty percent.

RUTH: So you do know about percent. What percent would it be if you got two points?

[*This time I had to give them time to think about the problem. They hadn't yet been taught percent, but I was curious about what they would do to make sense of this information prior to any formal instruction. After about half the class had their hands up, I called on several students to explain their thinking.*]

MICHAEL: I thought there are twenty points to make 100% and five twenties make one hundred, so each point would be 5%. Two points would be 5% and 5% and that's 10%.

RUTH: Did anyone think about it differently?

J.R.: I thought twenty points makes 100% and ten points make 50%, so five points would be 25%. Then I had to think in fives. Five fives makes twenty-five so each point is 5% and two points is 10%.

RUTH: Did anyone else think about it differently?

SEAN: Well, I thought that twenty points was 100% and I divided them both by ten so two points was 10%.

RUTH: Why did you divide them both by ten?

SEAN: Because there was twenty points and I wanted to find out two points. There are ten twos in twenty so I just took off the zero. Then I took off a zero from 100%.

RUTH: Why did you take off a zero?

SEAN: Because we already discovered that to multiply times ten you just have to add a zero, and division is exactly the opposite.

[*I wasn't trying to pester Sean here, but rather, I was curious to understand how he thought about the problem. Probing is often necessary if our goal is to uncover children's thinking.*]

RUTH: Okay, does anyone else want to share how they thought about the problem?

JOSEPH: Well it's really not about the problem, but I got 20.5 points and I think I know my percent.

RUTH: Okay, do you want to tell us what you got and how?

JOSEPH: Yeah. I knew twenty points was 100% so my score had to be more than 100%. First I thought it was 105%, but then I thought each point equals 5% and I only have .5 extra and that's a half a point, so it's half of five and that's two and a half, so my score would be 102.5%.

[*These ten-year-olds are making sense of percent without ever having been taught percent formally. We were to discover over and over again throughout the course of the study that kids are powerful sense makers when they are given situations to make sense of.*]

CATHY: Do the rest of you want some time to figure out your score as a percent?

CLASS: Yeah!

We watched as everyone went to work figuring out their percents with no further instruction from us. They were motivated to know, and had given each other ways to think about the information. That seemed to be all they needed. The children worked to invent procedures and make sense of their information. On a recent California Assessment Program (CAP) test, only 50% of eighth graders tested were able to successfully answer the question, "How much is 100% of 32?" Could this poor showing be the end result of mathematics instruction that focuses on the memorization of rules and procedures? Is it possible that many students believe that if they can't remember the rule (e.g., for finding percent), then they can't solve the problem? Several studies do suggest that children's mathematical errors are often rulebound, but might it also be that teaching rules and procedures can interfere with children's sense-making processes?

Developing Number Concepts
Through Mathematical Investigations

Although we never taught number concepts directly during the year, the children often explored number theory or number concepts in the context of their investigations. During the four-day unit on multiplication in September, children found all the possible rectangles that could be made from the numbers one to twenty-five. They used these rectangles to explore patterns of primes, composites, square numbers, multiples, and factors. They examined patterns from multiples on a multiplication table and made and tested predictions about what patterns would occur if the table was extended.

When the class read an article about the national debt, some children decided to find out how long a million, a billion, and a trillion seconds were. They used calculators, as they often did. I expected an answer of 11.57 days, since that's the answer I hear from most adults. Some children gave this answer, but others claimed that a million seconds was eleven days, thirteen hours, forty-six minutes, and forty seconds.

Seeing Fractions (CDE 1991) provided opportunities for children to develop an understanding of fractions through work in geometry, probability, proportional reasoning, and measurement. Building a scale model of the room involved measurement, computation, decimals, and proportional reasoning. When placing six windows on the outside walls of their models, children had an opportunity to examine what happens when errors are compounded. When trying to determine how much taller a typical fifth grader is than a typical first grader, children again had opportunities to use numbers and to consider issues related to precision in measurement. When two children were measured as equally tall yet revealed an apparent two-inch difference in height when they stood back-to-back, children examined what might have happened with the numbers and with the measurement.

These are just a few of the ongoing opportunities children had to use and investigate number concepts in context: in the process of doing mathematics.

Mental Computation

Starting early in the year, we asked the students to practice mental computation once or twice a week. Typically, Cathy put a problem on the overhead, gave students time to come up with answers, collected all the different answers students volunteered, then had children explain what they did to get their answers. Her emphasis throughout was on encouraging children to come up with diverse approaches to the problems and to take risks with their thinking. The following session took place in November:

CATHY: One request I have before we start today. Ruth made an observation yesterday that those of you participating the most are all male, and that there were very few hands from the female contingent of this classroom. Now, we only have nine girls; however, are we powerful or what?

SOME BOYS: No!

CATHY: We can't let this happen here. The challenge is that you should all be involved. Yesterday I had the feeling that some of you don't feel real confident in being able to raise your hands 'cause you're afraid you might not have the right answer. Or maybe you feel like your brain doesn't work very well unless you can write things down, which is pretty much the way I feel. I'm not good at this, but I can tell I'm getting better. I want you to go through the process of trying to figure these out. So how many girls are here today? (*Counting*) Six. There are three absent. Well, the six of you really have to carry the weight today. (*Writing 65 × 10 on the board*) Let's start out with an easy one for warm-up.

MARCI: I just added zero 'cause of Joseph's theory.

[*Joseph had discovered earlier that when you multiply by ten, one hundred, one thousand, etc., you can just annex the zeros. Marci had labeled this idea "Joseph's theory" after the inventor of the idea in this classroom.*]

MICHAEL: I just put one times sixty-five is sixty-five and then added a zero.

CATHY: Okay, let's go on to another one. (*Writing 75 × 3 on the board and waiting until lots of hands are raised*)

JED: I added seventy-five and seventy-five and got one hundred and fifty—

CATHY: How did you add seventy-five and seventy-five?

JED: I knew seventy-five cents and seventy-five cents was a dollar fifty. Then I added another seventy-five to that.

J.R.: I added seventy three times and got two hundred and ten, then I added the fifteen and got two hundred and twenty-five.

CATHY: What did you do mentally to add seventy three times?

J.R.: I guess I knew three times seven was twenty-one and I added the zero 'cause it was really three times seventy, not three times seven.

MICHAEL: I did three times fifty is one hundred and fifty, then there'd be seventy-five left, so it was just two hundred and twenty-five.

CATHY: How come you added seventy-five?

MICHAEL: Because I took off twenty-five three times. It was like three quarters.

CATHY: So in your brain you said, "I don't like multiplying three times seventy-five so I'll make that something easier to multiply by, like fifty?"

MICHAEL: Yeah.

CATHY: That is what we were talking about yesterday—some of you who are reluctant to see if you can make the problem easier.

SHELLI: (*Who consistently used the standard algorithm for solving the problems*) I did three times five is fifteen so I put down the five and carried the one. Then I said three times seven is twenty-one plus the one I carried makes twenty-two, so that's two hundred and twenty-five.

SEAN: I thought of seventy-five as three quarters so that would be nine quarters. Eight quarters is two dollars, so nine would be two dollars and twenty-five cents, or two hundred and twenty-five.

BRYAN: (*Turning to me*) Is money easier to go by?

RUTH: Well, sometimes it's easier for me because I've used money so much that I already understand those relationships. It probably depends on whether or not you've used it a lot. What do you think, Sean?

SEAN: It's easy for me to think about quarters and dollars.

CATHY: Let's do another one. (*Writing 130 ÷ 5 on the board*) This is not a race. Just think about what to do. (*Waiting about twenty seconds*) It sure is easy to tell who's working on this and who isn't. See if you can make yourself try. These only get easier if you keep trying to figure them out, then listen to everyone's ideas. (*Waiting about twenty more seconds*) Okay, let's record some answers here.

[*The children volunteer several different answers, including fifteen, sixteen, twenty with a remainder of three, and twenty-six. Cathy records them on the overhead.*]

CATHY: Who's willing to share your thinking? Oh, good.

SHELLI: I said five into thirteen was two and five into thirty was six.

RUTH: Shelli, why did you do five into thirty?

SHELLI: Well, I . . . no . . . I . . . no . . . I didn't do that.

CATHY: You can think about what you did for a minute while I hear from some others.

[*Shelli had done the problem correctly, but when I questioned her she became flustered and couldn't explain her thinking. I was surprised, because asking kids to explain their thinking was a common practice in the classroom. I had not seen Shelli respond like this before. Perhaps it was because she was following a procedure she had memorized without understanding.*]

RACHAEL: (*Who's been in the gifted program for three years and also always uses the standard algorithm during mental computation*) I did it sort of like Shelli did. I put five goes into thirteen two times, and two times five is ten. So there was three left over, and I brought down the zero, and said five into thirty goes six.

RUTH: Is that what you did, Shelli?

SHELLI: Yes.

PAUL: I did five goes into thirty six times and it goes into one hundred twenty times, so that's twenty-six.

JOSEPH: I did one hundred and thirty divided by ten and got thirteen, because you have to take off a zero and then I multiplied it by two because five is half of ten, and I got twenty-six.

CATHY: Joseph, would you explain that one more time? I'm not sure I followed your thinking.

JOSEPH: If you were to multiply thirteen times ten you'd get one hundred and thirty because of my theory. So if you divide it you take off the zero because it's the opposite from multiplying, so that's thirteen. Then I had to multiply it because you're not dividing it by so much. You're dividing it by half as much, so you multiply it by two and get twenty-six.

BRYAN: Five goes into thirty six times and five goes into one hundred twenty times, I did it by fives, then I added six and twenty.

CATHY: You said that when you divided it into one hundred you did it by fives. What did you mean by that?

BRYAN: Well, I knew ten would go into one hundred ten times, and five was five down so it would be twenty times.

CATHY: Okay, let's see.

SEVERAL KIDS: Give us a hard one.

CATHY: Do you want multiplication or division? (*The response is split. She writes 26 × 13 on the board and waits until most hands are up.*) Ooh, that's hard. Make it simpler for yourself. Let's get some of your answers up here.

BO: Two hundred and seventy-five.

MIKE: Two hundred and seventy-six.

HEIDI: Three hundred and thirty-one.

TONYA: Two hundred and ninety.

J.R.: Two hundred and seventy-eight.

RACHAEL: I'm not very confident in my answer but I got two hundred and eighteen.

[*Cathy has been working all year at getting Rachael to take more risks. She is aware that this is the first time she has volunteered an answer she is not sure of during mental computation.*]

CATHY: Thanks for risking, Rachael. Jed, are you going to gamble with an answer?

JED: (*Who also usually only volunteers when he's sure of his result*) I'll try it, three hundred and fifteen.

CATHY: Let's hear how some of you thought about it.

BRYAN: I think it's two hundred and eighty-six. I did twenty-six times five (*By adding five on his fingers twenty-six times*) and I came up with one hundred and thirty, and then I multiplied that times two and got two hundred and sixty. Then I did three more was fifty-two plus twenty-six . . . was . . . wait, I got this wrong. It would be fifty-two and twenty-six is seventy-eight, so I have two hundred and sixty and seventy-eight so that's . . . Oh, I don't know.

[Bryan is making sense of the problem, but reaches a point where he can't keep track of all the information.]

MIKE: I did six times three is eighteen, so I put down one on top of the two. Then I did three times two and put the seven down. Then I did two times one is two. So I got two hundred and seventy-six.

[Mike appears to be following a recipe he has learned but part of the recipe is missing for him. There is no indication that he is using relationships. But he is taking a risk and sharing his thinking.]

J.R.: (*Using relationships but not dealing with three times twenty*) Twenty-six times ten is two hundred and sixty and six times three is eighteen, so it's two hundred and seventy-eight.

JOSEPH: Twenty-six times ten is two hundred and sixty. Then I added two twenty-fives and that was three hundred and ten, then I added twenty-five and that was three hundred and thirty-five, then I added three more 'cause I took one off three times. So that's three hundred and thirty-eight. Twenty-five was easier to work with than twenty-six.

[Cathy is not questioning children's thinking as much on this problem, probably because of her own discomfort with the problem.]

TONYA: Two hundred and ninety. Instead of multiplying by thirteen, I multiplied by three so twenty-six times ten was two hundred and sixty, then ten times three was thirty, so that is two hundred and ninety.

[I wondered what Tonya would do with this problem on paper or in an interview. It's not easy to determine where her thinking is in error.]

MICHAEL: I did ten times twenty-six was two hundred and sixty. Then I put three times twenty is sixty and three times six is eighteen and that comes out to seventy-eight. Then I just added it and it was three hundred and thirty-eight.

SEAN: I used quarters again. First I did thirteen times twenty-five and that was three hundred and twenty-five. Then I did thirteen more and that was three hundred and thirty-eight.

J.R.: I know what I did wrong now. I forgot to do three times twenty, so I agree with three hundred and thirty-eight.

CATHY: Well, we'd better move on. It's so amazing that it's so easy to tell who's working on these. I think if we keep doing mental computation on a regular basis you're going to see yourself getting better and better at it, with more and more confidence. That's the goal.

We did get more responses from girls than we had previously. Cathy continued to provide time for practice with mental computation and/or estimation once or twice a week. She also used opportunities that came up in the context of other work. For example, when Michael reported that kids in this class had one hundred and twenty-eight pets all to-gether, Cathy asked the class how many pets that would be on average.

Over time, as the problems for mental computation became more difficult, Shelli, Nathan, Rachael, and Heidi rarely contributed ideas. They seemed unable to let go of the standard algorithms even though they became cumbersome and were no longer useful. Their facility with traditional algorithms actually appeared to interfere with their ability to use relationships to solve mental computation problems. If this is true, it has serious implications for instruction.

Are We Ready for Unrestricted Use of Calculators?

By February, Cathy was a little nervous that she had not focused on paper-and-pencil algorithms at all and that she had not assessed who could perform which algorithms. She wanted an assessment that could be done in context rather than as computation problems in isolation, so she asked students to work alone, and without a calculator, to answer the following questions using the information on Tonya, Sean, Jed, and Mike's data display (shown in Figure 5–14, p. 106).

1. How much taller than the tallest first grader is the tallest fifth grader?
2. How much shorter than the shortest fifth grader is the shortest first grader?
3. If you lined all the fifth graders up on the playground, head-to-toe, how long would the line be?
4. How much taller is a typical fifth grader than a typical first grader? Explain your thinking.
5. If you combined the heights of the tallest and the shortest fifth grader, how would that compare with the combined height of the tallest and shortest first grader?
6. What is the average height of a fifth grader? Explain your thinking.

Children's responses revealed a range of understanding, from Allie, who consistently took the smaller number from the larger number whenever she subtracted, to Michael, who invented an algorithm for the division problems, to Rachael, who added large columns of numbers precisely and divided using the standard algorithm to find the average.

Cathy and I had mixed feelings about not allowing the students to use calculators during the assignment, a proscription we'd never imposed before. The children didn't seem to mind, but why was it important to get information about what the children would do using paper-and-pencil algorithms if they were able to do mental computations and able to solve problems accurately using calculators? Were we tied to an antiquated mathematics paradigm, or was it still necessary to be able to do algorithms without using a calculator? Cathy's students would likely be placed in mathematics classes at the middle school next year based on their performance on tests composed primarily of isolated computations. Was it her responsibility to prepare students for these placement tests? Because of these pressures, Cathy decided to schedule more menu time during the remainder of the year, so that she would have time to meet individual student needs regarding computation.

What does the NCTM mean when it suggests that children have unlimited use of calculators in class, on homework, and on tests? Perhaps the more important question is, How important is the ability to perform paper-and-pencil algorithms in the technological world of the 1990s? It *is* important that students understand number relationships so that they can use numbers to make sense of information and situations. It *is* important that they be able to determine what operations are needed to solve a problem. But is it important that they be able to do these computations using paper and pencil? Clearly, it is *not* important that they be able to do this using any one standard algorithm. This is an issue worthy of further investigation and discussion within the mathematics community.

Results from the National Assessment of Educational Progress (NAEP) and international assessments of mathematics suggest that while children in this country are able to add, subtract, multiply, and divide, they are unable to use those skills to solve even simple problems (Dossey et al. 1988). This very likely is a result of a mathematics curriculum that emphasizes the memorization of algorithms that are taught in isolation. And very likely, too, children who experience number in context, who are asked to invent diverse algorithms based on number relationships, and who encounter frequent opportunities to use numbers to make sense of complex mathematical situations will be better prepared not only for mathematical competency assessments but also for life in the 1990s.

The professional mathematics community has not clearly established whether or not paper-and-pencil proficiency is still considered an important goal for mathematics instruction. Until this issue is more fully addressed, teachers and textbooks will continue to place a major emphasis on assuring computational proficiency with paper and pencil and students will continue to have very little classroom time in which to do real mathematics.

Assessing Mathematical Understanding

_____

This chapter describes the various assessment practices we used to evaluate the children's understanding of mathematics:

1. Observations
2. Learning logs
3. Rubrics
4. Portfolios

Cathy and I wanted to align assessment with current efforts in mathematics reform. This meant that paper-and-pencil tests of isolated skills would not be sufficient. We wanted more authentic measures of students' performance in mathematics.

Observations of Children at Work

Our most frequently used assessment technique was to observe the students while they were working. Children were always encouraged to talk with one another about their thinking as they worked to solve problems. Thus we had an ongoing opportunity to hear the children explain their thought processes and to observe their understanding as they worked together. This process is described throughout the book and therefore is not detailed here.

Math Learning Logs

Writing in the mathematics classroom has received increasing attention in the past several years. Writing about their thinking can help children gain clarity and can reveal their level of understanding.

> Communication in mathematics has become important as we move into an era of a "thinking" curriculum. Students are urged to discuss ideas with each other, to ask questions, to diagram and graph problem situations for clarity. Writing in mathematics classes, once rare, will now be vital. (Stenmark 1989, p. 11)

When students were not working in menu books, they recorded their work in their math learning logs. Thus, they had a record of their work in mathematics and we were able to assess their development of mathematical understandings over time.

Writing about mathematics did not come easily for the students. Early entries in their learning logs focused for the most part on how they felt about a problem. They had not been asked to write about their thinking before now, and they were both unsure of what was wanted and inexperienced in examining their thought processes.

During the first weeks of school, Cathy collected the math learning logs frequently. We spent a lot of time writing comments that we hoped would help children learn to write about the mathematics involved in a problem and about their own thought processes. This was not easy for Cathy. She was used to writing comments like "Good work" or "Excellent" on student papers. She had not had opportunities to write about her own mathematical thinking and was unsure of what kinds of ideas we wanted the children to write about and what kinds of comments would help elicit those responses. Early on she frequently asked whether I would make comments on children's papers so she could get a sense of what to write. After a few weeks she began writing her own comments but often asked me to read behind her and add comments of my own. The children's writing about mathematical ideas got better over time, as did Cathy's confidence in her responses to the students' work.

Rubrics

Since children were no longer getting papers back with the number of wrong or right items marked and a letter grade at the top, we wanted to find a way to assess their work that would convey both how the students had done and what they might do better. We were changing the game, and we wanted to convey what performing the new game well entailed. Although our initial attempts to develop such an instrument were primitive, their impact on the children's work was dramatic, as we saw when we used a scoring guide for the patterns and functions menu (see Chapter 3). That menu evaluation sheet and one we used for collaborative group work are shown in Figures 9–1 and 9–2.

We knew these initial forms did not really convey what good performance was. The generic rubric we developed in January (the left side for the task assigned, the right for the group process—see Figure 9–3) came closer, but it was still dissatisfying.

Introducing this rubric was an interesting process. Cathy put the form on the overhead projector and covered all but the top two categories on the group process side. She asked the students to read those two descriptions and tell her the difference between them.

MENU EVALUATION FOR _____ Topic _____ date _____				
	Identify your problem (1 pt)	Show evidence of problem solving (2 pts)	Tell what you learned (2 pts)	TOTAL POINTS
SQUARES FROM SQUARES				
MORE SQUARES FROM SQUARES				
POINTS DIVIDING A LINE				
THE DIAGONAL PROBLEM				

Comments:

POINTS EARNED _____
POINTS POSSIBLE   20
GRADE _____

Figure 9.1. Our first menu evaluation sheet.

```
┌─────────────────────────────────────────────────────────────────┐
│              Group Evaluation          for _____       │
│   Date _____    Task _____   _____       │
│                                             _____       │
│                                             _____       │
│   1. Worked together cooperatively as                             │
│      a group.                               _____       │
│      Comments: _____                         │
│      _____                      │
│      _____                      │
│                                                                   │
│   2. Stayed with the task.                                        │
│      Showed persistence and worked                                │
│      industriously.                         _____       │
│      Comments: _____                         │
│      _____                      │
│      _____                      │
│                                                                   │
│   3. Explained your thinking and findings.  _____       │
│      Comments: _____                         │
│      _____                      │
│      _____                      │
│                                                                   │
│   4. Listened attentively, asked questions                        │
│      and/or offered suggestions or comments                       │
│      when other groups shared their findings. _____     │
│      Comments: _____                         │
│      _____                      │
│      _____                      │
└─────────────────────────────────────────────────────────────────┘
```

Figure 9.2.   Our first evaluation sheet for collaborative group work.

JONATHAN: Three says you work well together most of the time and 4 says you use all of your time productively.

TONYA: For a 3 it says you are pretty good at listening to each other and for a 4 you build on each other's ideas.

SHELLI: Three says everyone in the group is treated with respect. Does that mean that's important for 4 also?

CATHY: Yes. It means you can't get a 3 unless group members treat each other respectfully, but that would be true for a 4 also. (*Covering up the 4 and revealing 2 and 3*) Now would you read 2 and 3 and tell me what the difference is between those two?

PAUL: For 2 you just work together some of the time and for a 3 you work together most of the time.

Name(s) _____ _____ _____ Date_____

TASK _____

	Group Process	

4
I, (we) fully achieved the purpose of the task, including thoughtful, insightful interpretations and making conjectures.
I, (we) raised interesting or provocative questions.
I, (we) communicated our ideas and findings well.
I, (we) went beyond what was expected.

We used all of our time productively. Everyone was involved and contributed to the group process and product. Problems didn't deter us. We listened to each other's ideas and other groups' ideas and built on those ideas. **4**

3
I, (we) accomplished the task and communicated our findings effectively. I, (we) understood the task and learned from it. I, (we) worked persistently to overcome problems I, (we) encountered.

We worked well together most of the time. We were pretty good at listening to and using each other's and other groups' ideas. We worked together to overcome problems we encountered. **3**

2
I, (we) completed most of the assignment and communicated our ideas and findings.

We worked together some of the time. Not everyone contributed equal effort to the task. We might have worked more productively as a group. **2**

1
I, (we) did not accomplish our task.
I, (we) didn't finish the investigation and/or weren't able to communicate our ideas very well.

We really didn't pull together or work very productively as a group. Not everybody contributed to the group effort. Some people did more work than others or else nobody worked very well as a group. **1**

Figure 9.3.   Generic rubric for individual and group tasks.

JOHN: Some people do more work than others for a 2. Everybody's not helping.

JENNISE: For a 3 you worked together pretty well and for 2 you didn't. It says, "We could have worked more productively."

CATHY: Okay, how about the difference between a 2 and a 1?

TIMMY: For a 1, nobody really worked together.

JOSH: And some people didn't do anything to help the group, or else nobody works very well.

CATHY: Does that help you understand what we're looking for when we give you a group grade?

Because I wanted to give some real examples of what we were looking for, I interrupted her at this point and told the students I was going to describe how some groups were working and I wanted them to read the rubric and silently decide on a score. Then, after everyone had a chance to decide individually I would say, "One, two, three, show" and they would all hold up their score on their fingers at the same time. I described scenes I had observed in the classroom during the previous few days (without, of course, naming names). Children used the rubric to determine a score and revealed their score on the count of three. We then looked around at the fingers raised. When there was disagreement, children told why they had selected the score they did. If the explanations were not based on information on the rubric, I explained they needed to justify the scores based on the rubric. After the third scenario, the children consistently agreed on their scores, and they seemed to be enjoying the process.

Cathy then took them through the same process on the task side of the rubric. When they weren't sure about the vocabulary used, she asked them to predict what the word meant. Several children got dictionaries, but they didn't tell the dictionary definitions until the invented meanings had been shared.

Two days later we used the rubric during a group task in which the children built free-standing straw structures. The day after they did the task, Cathy passed back their rubrics and gave the groups time to talk about them. Sean, Tonya, Jed, and Mike were angry. They told Cathy they thought they should have gotten a better score because they had all worked. Mike said he worked hard and built a structure right there on his desk. Sean also said he was working even though he dropped out for a while. Cathy asked Mike what his structure had to do with the group's structure. Mike said, "Nothing." She asked them what they had produced as a group, and they replied, "Nothing, but we did the work ourselves." Cathy then explained that the score in question was a score for how well they had worked as a group. She asked them to read the rubric and to tell her which category best described how they had worked as a group. After doing so, they agreed with the score Cathy had assigned. That same day groups were assigned the task of inventing a way to display data to compare the heights of first graders and fifth graders. There was a dramatic change in how Mike, Tonya, Jed, and Sean worked. They hunched over their desks fully engaged the entire time. They also invented a creative way to display the data.

When Sean got up during processing time to share his group's display, he said only one sentence before Mike stood up and took over. This was very different behavior for Mike, who usually sat uninvolved during group tasks. He obviously felt included in the ownership of this display.

After the discussion, the kids in this group were talking as they left for recess:

SEAN: You know what I think about why we worked better today? I think it's because we tried.

RUTH: That makes a big difference. You guys are all capable. When you try, you've got powerful stuff going on.

TONYA: We're kind of afraid people are going to copy our ideas now.

RUTH: That's an honest response. But you know what, if they do, maybe you can say, What a compliment. They loved our idea.

CATHY: (*After the children have gone*) The rubric in a way feels false because they're working for a grade. But it really isn't because it lets them know what they can do and what good performance is.

RUTH: Yes. We've changed the game on them, and I think the rubric is an attempt to help them understand what's expected. It may also work as coercion for some students.

CATHY: Next year will sure be easier. We can use rubrics from the beginning of the year. We won't have to invent all of this in January. Portfolios will be easier too. We can just get so many more routines going from the beginning of the year.

The rubric in Figure 9–3 is generic. For some investigations we needed to develop a rubric that more specifically fits the mathematics involved in the task. The development of specific rubrics will no doubt get easier over time as well.

Cathy has also asked her students to develop their own rubrics. She erases or whites out the names on the papers and has pairs of students read and sort them into three piles: high, middle, and low. The high pile is then subdivided into two: exceptional and very good. The children then write about why they gave the papers the ratings they did. Cathy feels that this process has been very useful in getting children to recognize quality work.

Portfolios

Deciding whether and how to implement portfolios evolved during numerous conversations. Cathy was somewhat hesitant to use them because she was unsure of their value. I wanted to try them for two main reasons: first, the idea of portfolios is being embraced by the professional mathematics community as one alternative to current standardized tests, and I wanted to find out whether they were helpful in revealing children's understanding of mathematics or in assessing our mathematics program as a whole; second, I understood from teachers who had piloted mathematics portfolios in California that the process of selecting work for a portfolio that would represent them as mathematicians is an important process for students.

Cathy and I expected our initial attempts at developing portfolios would be primitive and that new questions and adaptations would occur throughout the year. Portfolios would be collections of a student's work over time. We hoped they would provide these benefits:

1. Students would take responsibility for their accomplishments. They would make decisions about what items to put in the portfolios and would be responsible for communicating to readers of their portfolios (parents, teachers, and others) what they would see in the portfolios and why particular selections were made.

2. Moving a selection from the working folder to the portfolio would require students to undertake an important time of reflection. They would review their work from the past month and decide what tasks represented their most challenging work or showed how their understanding of mathematics had grown. If there were no finished tasks or tasks they wanted to include in the portfolios, that too would provide the student (and the teacher) with important information.

3. They would provide a basis for student/teacher conferences and for student/teacher/parent conferences.

Cathy and I talked frequently about using portfolios, but we didn't initiate them until the October parent/teacher conferences were nearly at hand. A week before we asked the students to go through their working folders and their math learning logs and select three or four items for their portfolios. They were to pick items that:

1. Demonstrated the most challenging work they had done so far.
2. Showed how their understanding of a mathematical concept had grown.
3. Exemplified a group task they had been part of.
4. Revealed their reflective thoughts about mathematics, such as what it means to be good at mathematics or how they felt about themselves as mathematicians.

They were also asked to (1) write about why each item had been selected and (2) write a cover letter telling Cathy and their parents what they were going to see in the portfolio. We found that giving these two writing assignments concurrently caused the children to approach them simply as something to be finished. We decided that if we wanted them to give thoughtful consideration both to their reasons for their selections and to what they wanted to convey to readers of their portfolios, we would need to treat the tasks as separate processes and assign them on separate days.

Cathy knew she would not be able to review the portfolios thoughtfully with the parents in the brief time allotted for each conference, so she sent the portfolios home and asked parents to review them prior to coming in for their conference. That way they would have a better opportunity to raise relevant questions.

Although we talked often about needing to establish a monthly routine by which students would review their working folders and make selections for their portfolios, we hadn't yet done so by March, when the children made their third group of selections (a second group of items had been selected in January). By March, Cathy was convinced of the value of portfolios. Before this they had just been one more thing needing attention when she was already overwhelmed by all the new things she was trying to do. She now knew them to be an important representation of a student's work over time. She also felt that their main benefit to the student was as an ongoing opportunity to reflect on his or her growth as a mathematician.

When children wanted to extend their portfolio pieces because they recognized that they could take the task further, we encouraged them to do so. The new work was simply stapled to the old as evidence of their growth. Students who had not accomplished much or had not completed assignments were clearly reminded of earlier lack of effort.

Although their greatest value is to the child, portfolios are revealing in other ways. We found that we could observe the children's growth and also the growth in our correspondence with them. We could see the changes we had made in rubrics. The children revealed nonmathematical characteristics as well. For example, before I read their portfolios I was unaware of Shelli's artistic talents and unaware that Timmy was such an excellent writer.

Entries from Shelli's portfolio are grouped at the end of this chapter, arranged chronologically to show her progress over time. Although her vividly colored originals have of necessity been rendered in black-and-white, you will still see changes in Shelli's attitude and understanding and her growth in confidence. These portfolio entries also serve as an overview of the various aspects of our mathematics program.

Some of our richer and more complex tasks (e.g., the scale models of the classroom) were not represented in the portfolios, since we did not provide a way to include large projects or products. To remedy this in the future, we will take photographs of works in progress and of the final products. Students will be able to attach these photos to learning log entries made while the projects were being worked on and submit them as portfolio entries.

Oct. 28

Dear Mrs Young and Mom,

This letter is about math.

The future from right now looks
like we're going to have lots
of math. As a mathematician
I like the challenge. I think
I'm good at working out problems
and not just leaving them behind.

I do have some faults like
explaining what I think. Because
I usually have everything my
head but I forget that people
can't see <u>inside</u> my head.

Being good at math means
understanding and using and
enjoing it. I enjoy it because
it's actually never ending. I also
think it's challenging. When I
say challenging I mean exitingly
challenging.
                Signed,   SHELLI
                                 SEALY

Figure 9.4. **Shelli's October cover letter. It reflects her enthusiasm for mathematics but also her real struggle in learning how to communicate her thoughts in writing, which she regards as a "fault."**

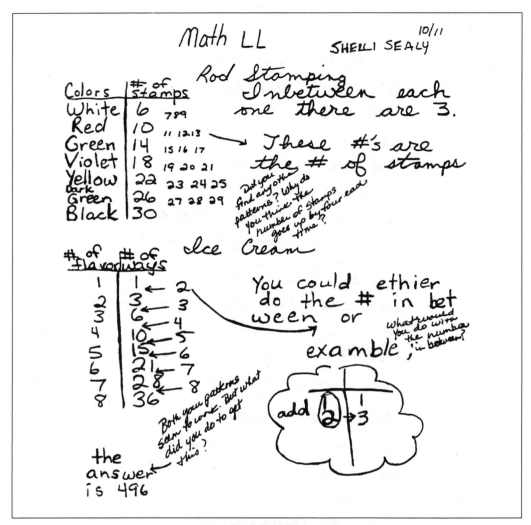

Math LL   SHELLI SEALY   10/11

Rod Stamping
Inbetween each one there are 3.

Colors	# of stamps	
White	6	789
Red	10	11 12 13
Green	14	15 16 17
Violet	18	19 20 21
Yellow	22	23 24 25
Dark Green	26	27 28 29
Black	30	

These #'s are the # of stamps

Did you find any other patterns? Why do you think the number of stamps goes up by four each time?

Ice Cream

# of flavors	# of ways	
1	1	2
2	3	3
3	6	4
4	10	5
5	15	6
6	21	7
7	28	8
8	36	

You could ethier do the # in between or example;

what would you do with the number in between?

Both your patterns seem to work. But what did you do to get this?

add 2→3

the answer is 496

Figure 9.5. One of Shelli's math learning log entries. Early in the year Cathy and I spent quite a bit of time corresponding with children in these learning logs, asking questions that would help them examine and communicate their thinking. (We found that we had to set aside time for the children to answer our questions or they remained largely unanswered.)

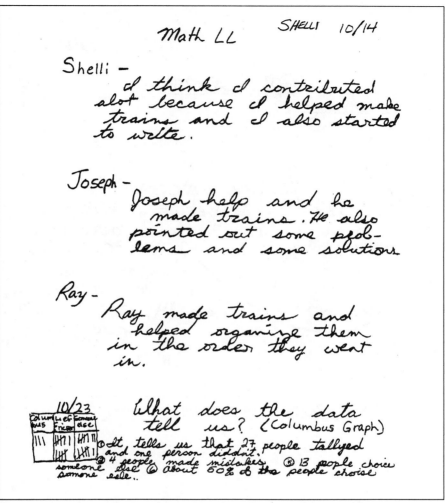

Math LL   SHELLI 10/14

Shelli -
 I think I contributed alot because I helped make trains and I also started to write.

Joseph -
 Joseph help and he made trains. He also pointed out some problems and some solutions.

Ray -
 Ray made trains and helped organize them in the order they went in.

10/23   What does the data tell us? (Columbus Graph)

① It tells us that 27 people tallyed and one person diddn't. ② 4 people made mistakes ③ 13 people choice someone else ④ about 60% of the people choise someone esle..

Figure 9.6. Another of Shelli's learning log entries. Children were sometimes asked to reflect on how their group worked together and on individual contributions to the group task. (They knew ahead of time they would be asked to share these reflections with their group members.)

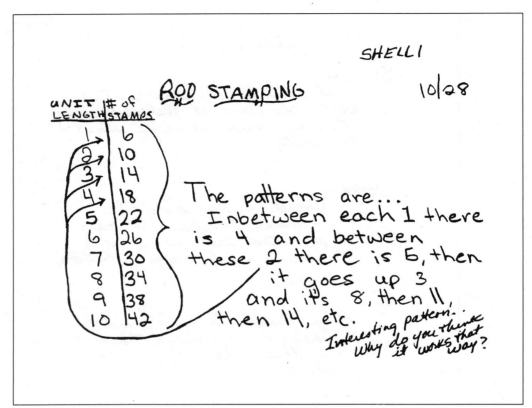

Figure 9.7. Shelli's third learning log entry.

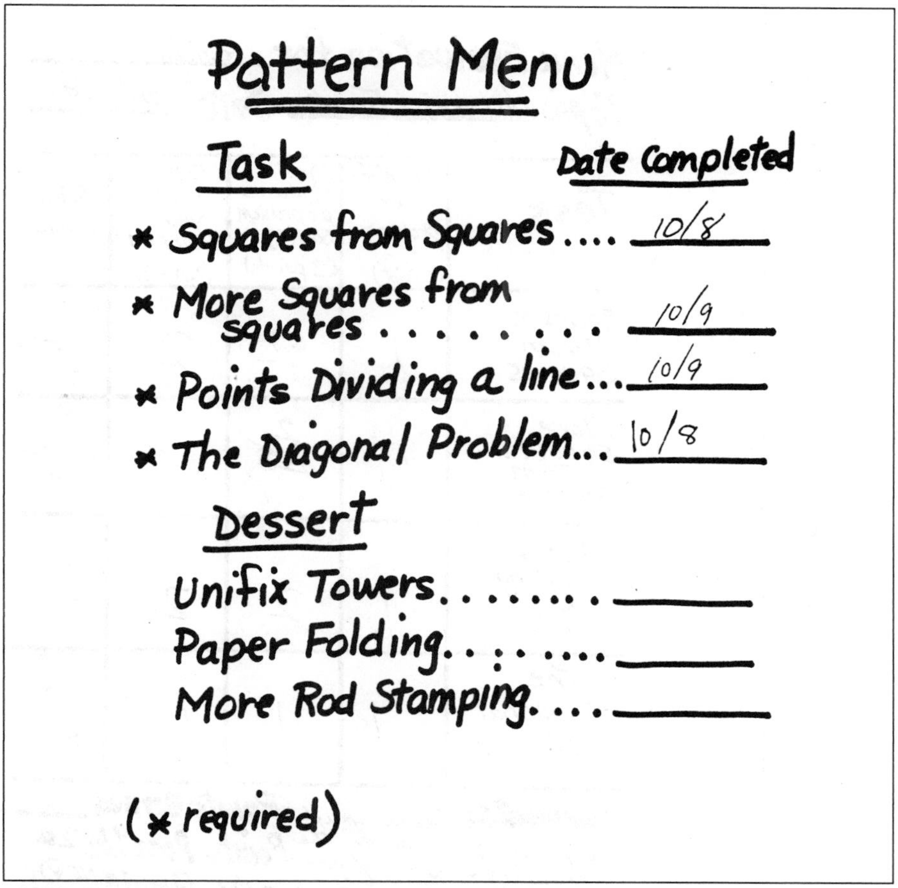

Pattern Menu

Task   Date Completed

* Squares from Squares .... _10/8_

* More Squares from
   squares . . . . _10/9_

* Points Dividing a line... _10/9_

* The Diagonal Problem... _10/8_

Dessert

Unifix Towers. . . . . _____

Paper Folding. . . . . _____

More Rod Stamping. . . . _____

(* required)

Figure 9.8. Shelli's pattern menu cover sheet (a sheet the children glued inside their menu cover so they could keep track of their progress).

Menu Evaluation for Shelli
Topic Patterns & Functions Date 10/14/91

Task	Identify your problem (1 Point)	Show evidence of problem solving (2 points)	Tell what you learned (2 points)	Total Points
Squares From Squares	1	2	2	5
More Squares From Squares	1	2	15	45
Points Dividing a Line	1	2	2	5
The Diagonal Problem	1	1	1	3

Comments: Sarah, you did a pretty good job on the required tasks. If you have time, trying some of the dessert problems can help a lot.

Points Earned 17.5
Points Possible 20
Grade NI ⊘ +

Figure 9.9. Shelli's menu evaluation sheet. This was one of the first forms we used to assess students' work. Required tasks were each worth five points. Optional tasks, which could be done only after the required tasks were completed, were worth one point. (The required tasks were weighted more heavily so students would approach them thoughtfully rather than rush to get more tasks done.)

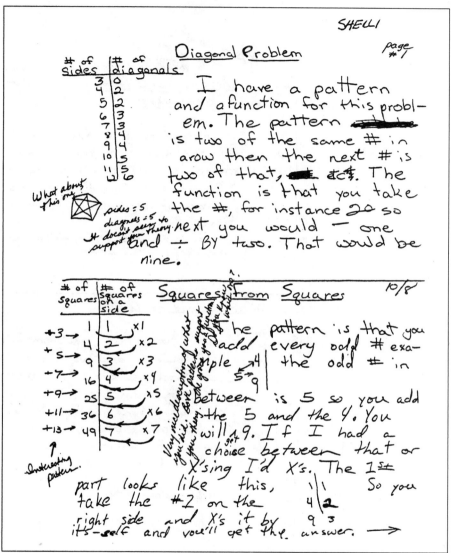

Figure 9.10. Shelli's pattern menu entries.

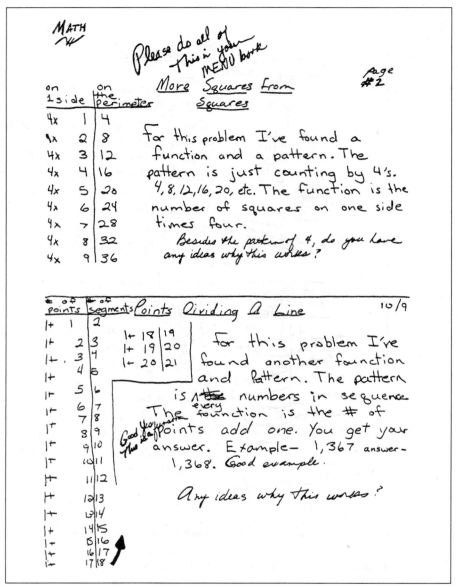

MATH

Please do all of
This in your
MENU book

Page #2

More Squares From Squares

on 1 side	on the perimeter	
4x	1	4
4x	2	8
4x	3	12
4x	4	16
4x	5	20
4x	6	24
4x	7	28
4x	8	32
4x	9	36

For this problem I've found a function and a pattern. The pattern is just counting by 4's. 4, 8, 12, 16, 20, etc. The function is the number of squares on one side times four.

Besides the pattern of 4, do you have any ideas why this works?

Points Dividing A Line

10/9

# of points	# of segments		
1+	1	2	
1+	2	3	
1+	3	4	
1+	4	5	
1+	5	6	
1+	6	7	
1+	7	8	
1+	8	9	
1+	9	10	
1+	10	11	
1+	11	12	
1+	12	13	
1+	13	14	
1+	14	15	
1+	15	16	
1+	16	17	
1+	17	18	

1+ 18	19
1+ 19	20
1+ 20	21

For this problem I've found another function and Pattern. The pattern is numbers in sequence every The function is the # of points add one. You get your answer. Example— 1,367 answer— 1,368. Good example.

Good you this.

Any ideas why this works?

Figure 9.11. Shelli's pattern menu entries (continued).

Math Cover Letter   1-7-92

Both of these math assignments were fun & they were two of my best pieces of work. I'm very glad with the way I took my time and by doing that they turned out well.

I spend time on all of my math work and for some reason only a few turn out to be my best I had (for example) always spent the same amount of time on my fractions pages but this fractions work is my favorite of all of them.

Shelli

Figure 9.12.   Shelli's January cover letter.

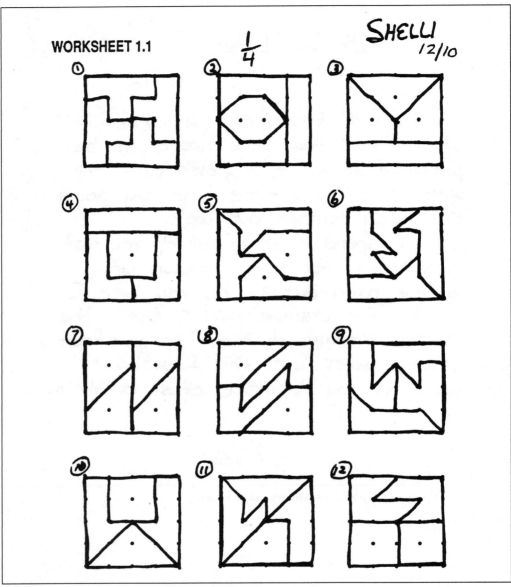

Figure 9.13. Shelli's fractions entry. Children were asked to divide a geoboard into fourths in as many ways as they could and then reproduce their favorite solutions on dot paper. Shelli's designs were done in deep purples and blues with silver lines, and had a wonderful sense of balance. (This was the first time we really noticed Shelli's artistic talents.)

```
GEOMETRY MENU           NAME Shelli
DUE DATE  12/9          Date 11/25/91
```

REQUIRED TASKS   DATE COMPLETED

TANGRAM SHAPE................................... 12/8

HOLD & FOLD..................................... 12/4

GEOBLOCKS: Build a Structure............... 12/6

SQUARE PARTITIONING........................ 12/8

MAKE A CUBE................................... 12/6

SPAGHETTI MATH............................... 12/7

CAN YOU MAKE THIS?....................... 12/7

FRACTION KIT [small group instruction]..... _____

DESSERTS

GEOBLOCKS #1... _____
NAME CREATURES................................... 12/7
HOLD & FOLD #2.................................... 12/8
~~PERSPECTIVE ART~~.............................. _____
Magic mirror

Figure 9.14.   Shelli's geometry menu cover sheet.

	Evidence of your work & thinking (4 pts)	What you learned & problems (4 pts)	Neatness & clarity (2 pts)	TOTAL POINTS
TANGRAM SHAPE	3	3	2	8
HOLD & FOLD #1	4	4	2	10
GEOBLOCKS	4	4	2	10
SQ. PARTITIONING	4	4	2	10
MAKE A CUBE	3	3	2	8
SPAGHETTI MATH	4	4	2	10
CAN YOU MAKE THIS?	4	4	2	10

EVALUATION FOR *SHELLI* date 11/25

Comments: Lots of good work! +2 desserts

TOTAL PTS. +68

% _____

Figure 9.15. Shelli's geometry menu evaluation form. Cathy developed this form in November. I was uncomfortable with "Neatness" and lobbied for "Clarity of communication" instead, since the important issue is the ability to communicate effectively. (Since assessment tools clearly reflect what is valued, we need to carefully examine what we are conveying as important.)

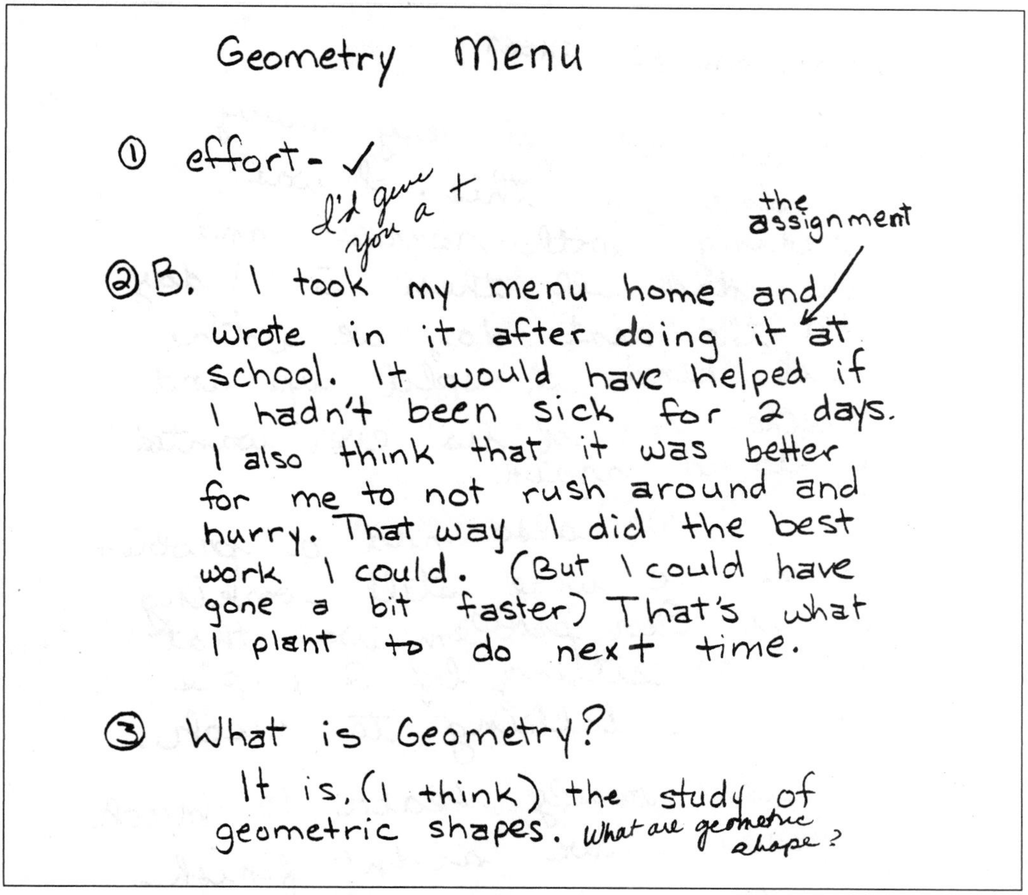

Geometry Menu

① effort - ✓

I'd give you a +

② B. I took my menu home and / *the assignment*
wrote in it after doing it at
school. It would have helped if
I hadn't been sick for 2 days.
I also think that it was better
for me to not rush around and
hurry. That way I did the best
work I could. (But I could have
gone a bit faster) That's what
I plant to do next time.

③ What is Geometry?
It is, (I think) the study of
geometric shapes. *What are geometric shape?*

**Figure 9.16.   Shelli's self-evaluation of the geometry menu. (The children
were often asked to assess their own effort and learning.)**

TANGRAM SHAPES SHEET

I did not get very many done on this. I was working with Rachael and we did all these in 1 day but the next day we both just kind of split up and niether one of us ever wanted to do it again.

We also had a problem while we were still working on it. Our problem was that we were sitting by 2 people who were talking to much.

I didn't really learn to much because we didn't finish.

I kind of dought anybody finished though.

What problems did you have using the tangram pieces to build the various shapes?

SHELLI
12/8

Figure 9.17.   A geometry menu entry.

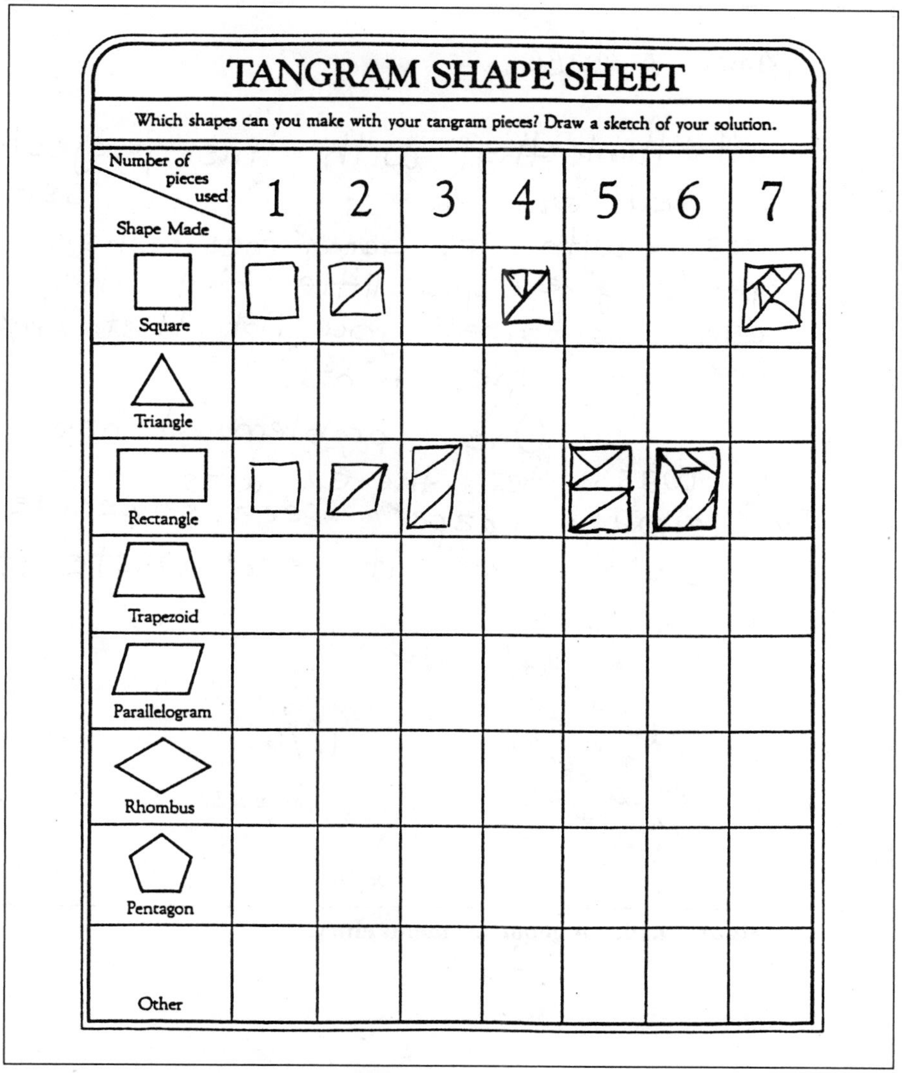

Figure 9.18. A geometry menu entry.

179

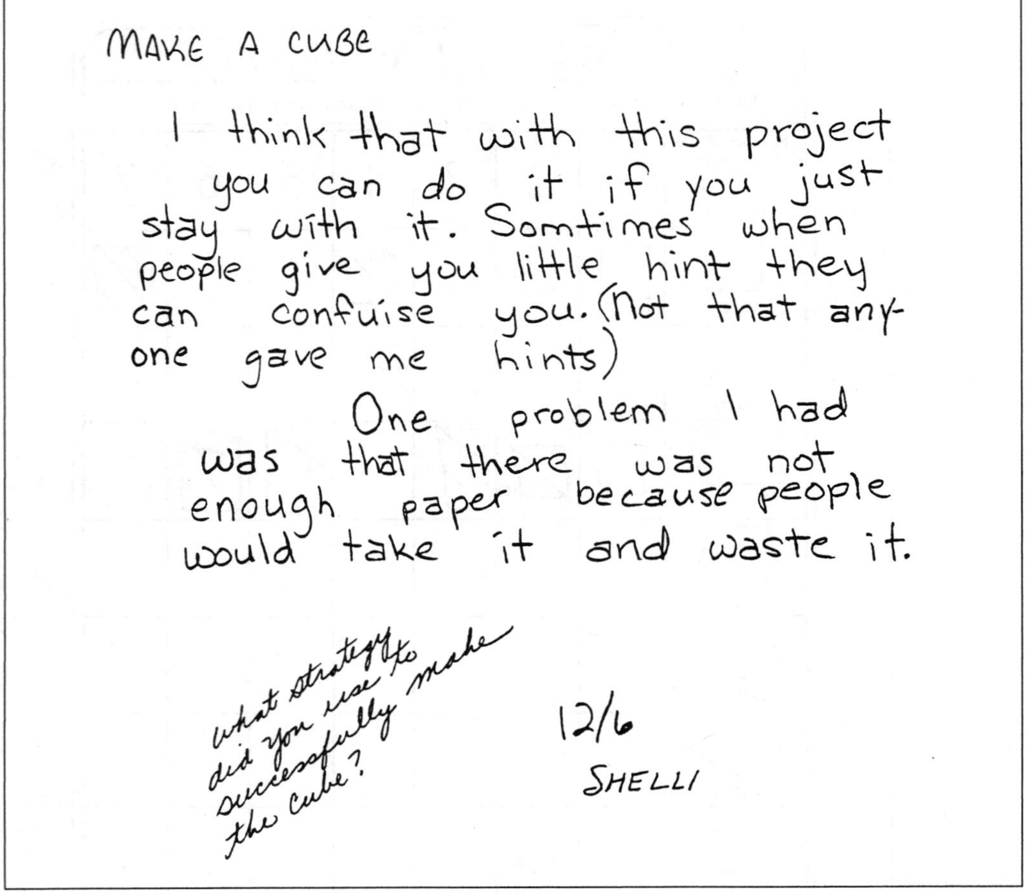

MAKE A CUBE

I think that with this project you can do it if you just stay with it. Somtimes when people give you little hint they can confuise you. (Not that any-one gave me hints)

One problem I had was that there was not enough paper because people would take it and waste it.

what strategy did you use to successfully make the cube?

12/6
SHELLI

Figure 9.19.   A geometry menu entry.

GEOBLOCKS- BIULO A STRUCTURE

12/5

The first person I did this with was Mari. I thought that you could easily make it hard for yourself or you could make it easy. I made It kind of easy. I'm not sure what Mari thought about hers, but I'd give hers an inbetween easy and hard.

In my oppinon the hardest part was explaining and the furiest part was guessing. It was fun guessing because it was odd somtimes at the end to look over at your parteners and see that you were todaly off track.

12/6
SHELLI

Figure 9.20.   A geometry menu entry.

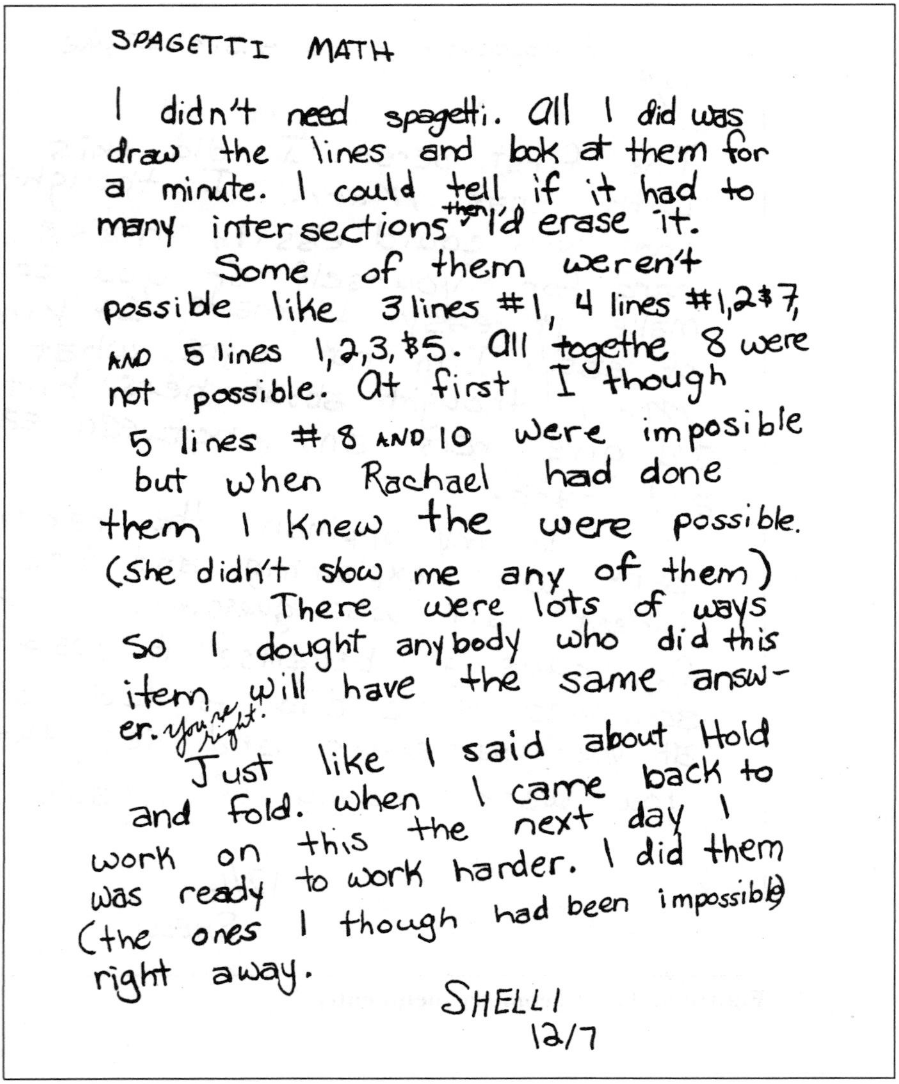

SPAGETTI MATH

I didn't need spagetti. All I did was draw the lines and look at them for a minute. I could tell if it had to many intersections then I'd erase it.

Some of them weren't possible like 3 lines #1, 4 lines #1,2 & 7, AND 5 lines 1,2,3, & 5. All togethe 8 were not possible. At first I though

5 lines #8 AND 10 were imposible but when Rachael had done them I knew the were possible. (She didn't show me any of them)

There were lots of ways So I dought anybody who did this item will have the same answer. you're right!

Just like I said about Hold and Fold. when I came back to work on this the next day I was ready to work harder. I did them (the ones I though had been impossible) right away.

SHELLI
12/7

Figure 9.21.   A geometry menu entry.

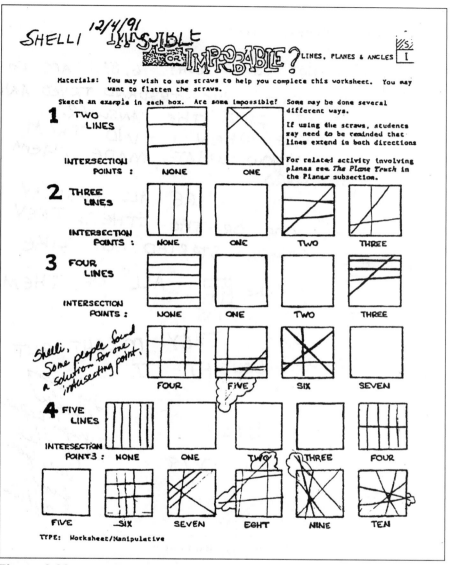

Figure 9.22.   A geometry menu entry.

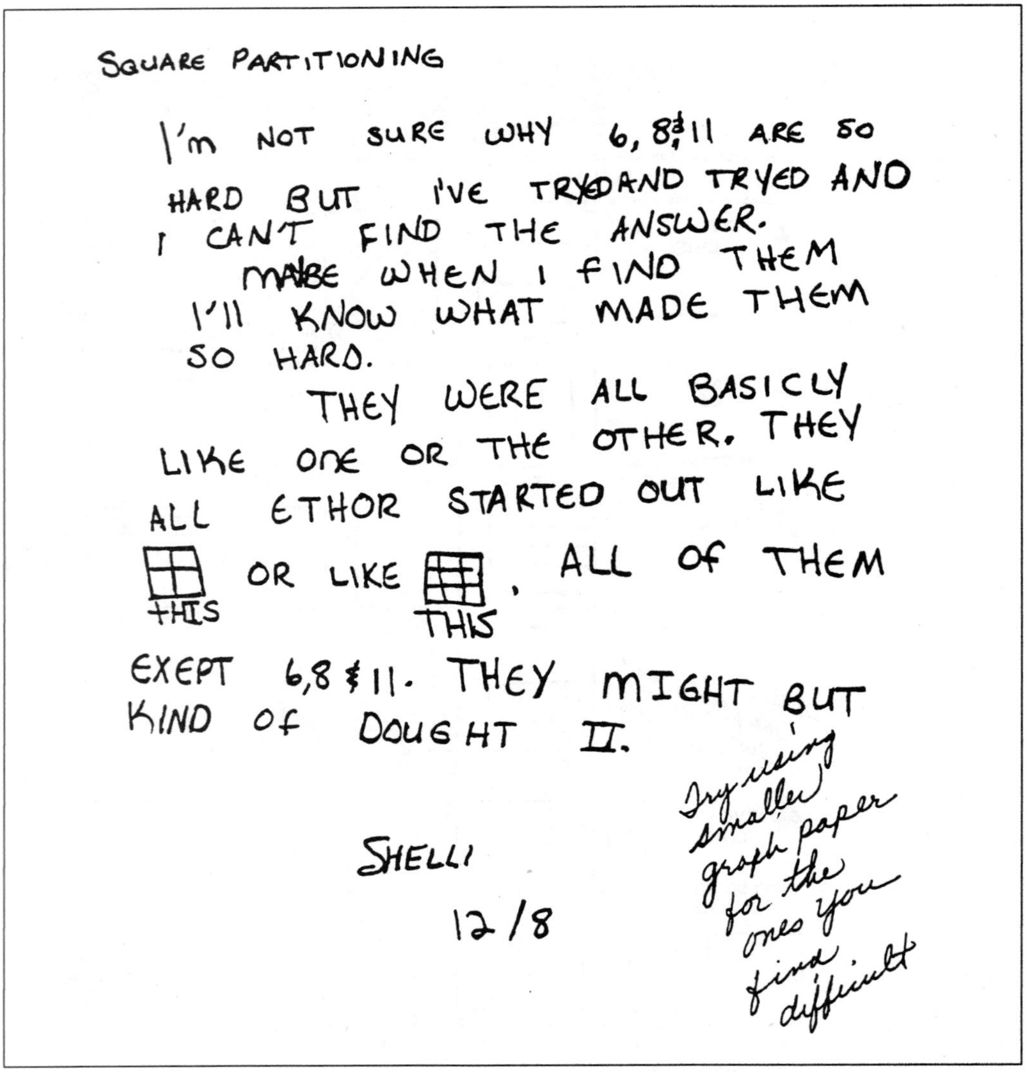

SQUARE PARTITIONING

I'm NOT SURE WHY 6, 8 & 11 ARE SO HARD BUT I'VE TRYED AND TRYED AND I CAN'T FIND THE ANSWER.

MAYBE WHEN I FIND THEM I'll KNOW WHAT MADE THEM SO HARD.

THEY WERE ALL BASICLY LIKE ONE OR THE OTHER. THEY ALL ETHOR STARTED OUT LIKE ⊞ OR LIKE ⊞ THIS, ALL OF THEM EXEPT 6,8 & 11. THEY MIGHT BUT KIND OF DOUGHT II.

SHELLI

12/8

Try using smaller graph paper for the ones you find difficult

Figure 9.23. A geometry menu entry.

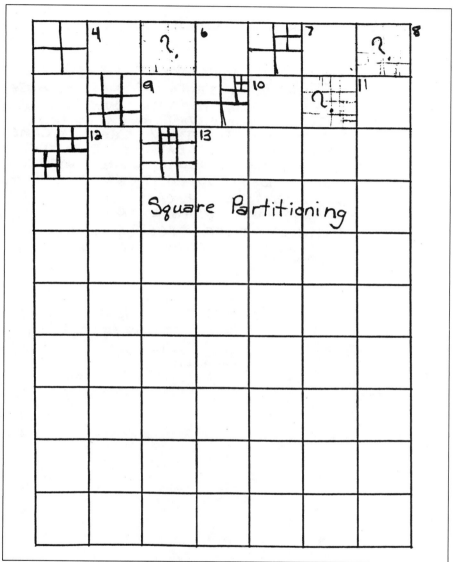

Figure 9.24. A geometry menu entry.

HOLD AND FOLD #1

DURING THIS ASSIGHNMENT I FELT
(DISCURIGEO) I THINK IT WAS BECAUSE
WHEN I CAME TO THE ONES I THOUGHT
WERE IMPOSSIBLE, (JUST FOR A WHILE.) I cow-
dn't do them. SO THEN WHEN I CAME
BACK TO IT TODAY I DID THE 2
THAT I HAD THOUGHT WERE IMPOSSIBLE
RIGHT AWAY. SO I THINK I WAS JUST
TO BORED THEN I CAME BACK AND THEY
WERE EASY. ANOTHER REASON MIGHT BE
BECAUSE OTHER PEOPLE HAD SOLVGD
IT AND I KNEW IT WASN'T
IMPOSSIBLE.

SHELLI
12/4

Figure 9.25. A geometry menu entry.

Hold & Fold (Dessert)

I liked this Hold and Fold better. I'm not sure why but it might be because I had time to practice on the Hold and Fold #1.

I'm not sure if its me or if this one seem alot easyer. But if the ones on the bottem part of the page are supposed to be hard, they aren't.

I didn't have any problems. I just cut out the fold piece of paper and d row by row.

Shelli
12/8

Figure 9.26. **A geometry menu entry.**

NAME CREATURES (DESSERT)

This was fun to do because you ussualy think of Math Menus as hard and challenging. But this was differant because we got to draw and color. You had to your imagineations and it was fun to see what other people did with their names.

Usualy 1 letter gives you the whole idea for your creature.

I really had to thing with my name and I definatly used my imagineation.

I think most of all I liked looking at other peoples ideas and how they explained theres.

I think it sould have been a partener activity because we all helped each other out and shared opinouns.

SHELLI
12/8

Figure 9.27.   A geometry menu entry.

188

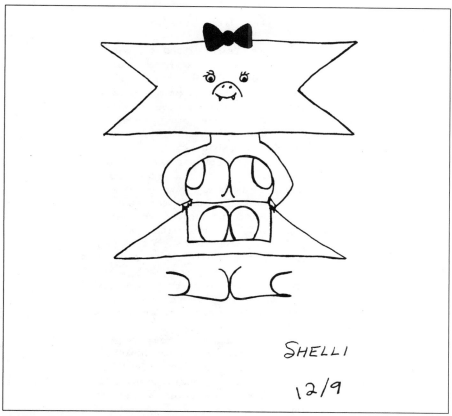

SHELLI

12/9

Figure 9.28. **A geometry menu entry.**

Math Cover Letter

3/12
Shelli

1. To me being good at math means you understand how it works and all the thing it can help you do. Being good at math also means you willing to learn more about math and you willing to try new ways of using it.

2. I have really grown as a mathematician. I have been going the extra mile on my work and I have learned to understand it. Unlike in the beginning of the year when I did all the work the same. for intants when we first started fractions the fractions I was doing were all the same. Now I'm spending more time on whatever fractions assignment we have.

3. I defenately have to get better at division. I know how to divide last year but over the summer I forgot. Other than that I'm doing fine on all my math subjects.

4 I chose this math assignment because it shows how I've used fractions. This piece was kind of challenging because

I wanted to make it harder than all my other math assignments. This piece of math was diffecult to start because my grid was different than I usually did.

Figure 9.29. Shelli's March cover letter. It indicates that she values mathematics and has grown as a mathematician. Several other students also indicated they needed to do more long division, even though they had been using mental computation, estimation, and invented algorithms to solve division problems in context. They had not discarded their traditional views of what is important in fifth-grade math.

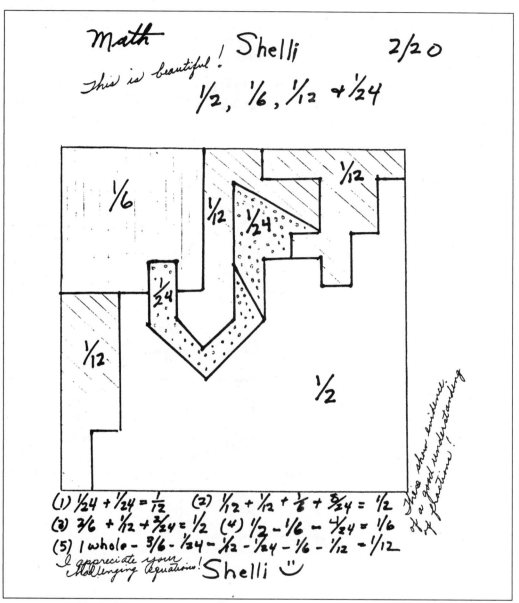

Math

This is beautiful!   Shelli   2/20

1/2, 1/6, 1/12 + 1/24

(1) 1/24 + 1/24 = 1/12   (2) 1/12 + 1/12 + 1/6 + 3/24 = 1/2
(3) 3/6 + 1/12 + 2/24 = 1/2   (4) 1/2 − 1/6 − 4/24 = 1/6
(5) 1 whole − 3/6 − 1/24 − 1/2 − 1/24 − 1/6 − 1/12 − 1/12

I appreciate your challenging equations! Shelli ☺

These show evidence
of a good understanding
of fractions!

Figure 9.30. One of Shelli's fractions entries. Children were given an un-marked square and asked to divide the square using three different fractions. Shelli invented a challenging solution demonstrating her understanding of fractional parts of a whole. (Her number sentences contain an error that Cathy didn't catch.)

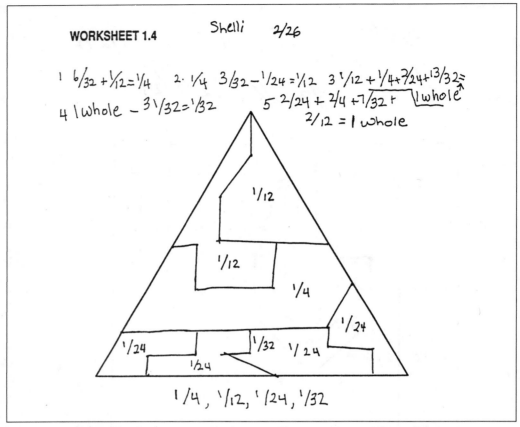

WORKSHEET 1.4   Shelli   2/26

1 $6/32 + 1/12 = 1/4$ 2. $1/4$ $3/32 - 1/24 = 1/12$ 3 $1/12 + 1/4 + 7/24 + 13/32 =$

4 1 whole $- 31/32 = 1/32$ 5 $2/24 + 2/4 + 7/32 + $ 1 whole

                                    $2/12 = 1$ whole

$1/12$

$1/12$

$1/4$

$1/24$

$1/24$ $1/32$ $1/24$

        $1/24$

$1/4, 1/12, 1/24, 1/32$

Figures 9.31.   One of Shelli's fractions entries. Children were given an unmarked triangle and asked to divide it using at least three different fractions. Shelli's solution is inaccurate and it is difficult to determine the cause of her errors.

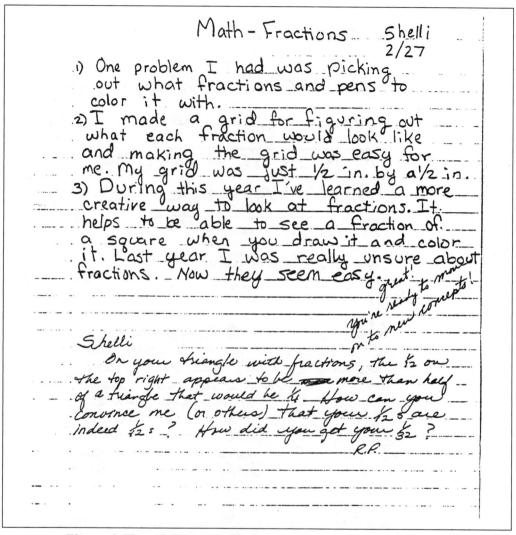

Math - Fractions   Shelli
2/27

1) One problem I had was picking out what fractions and pens to color it with.

2) I made a grid for figuring out what each fraction would look like and making the grid was easy for me. My grid was just ½ in. by a ½ in.

3) During this year I've learned a more creative way to look at fractions. It helps to be able to see a fraction of a square when you draw it and color it. Last year I was really unsure about fractions. Now they seem easy.

great! you're ready to move on to new concepts!

Shelli
    On your triangle with fractions, the ½ on the top right appears to be ~~was~~ more than half of a triangle that would be ¼. How can you convince me (or others) that your ½ s are indeed ½ s? How did you get your ½₃₂?
                    R.P.

Figure 9.32. Shelli's self-evaluation of the fraction tasks. Cathy did not notice that some of Shelli's solutions were inaccurate. Children sometimes give very sophisticated or complex solutions, and teachers need to have ongoing opportunities to increase their own mathematical understanding.

Math L.L.

Jan. 8 –

$$1/8 - 1/4 - 1/8 - 1/16 - 1/8 - 1/16 - 1/16 - 1/8 - 1/16$$

$$4/8 + 1/4 + 4/16 = 1 \text{ whole}$$

$$1/8 - 1/8 - 1/16 - 1/8 - 1/16 - 1/8 - 1/16 - 1/16 - 1/4$$

$$4/8 + 4/16 + 1/4 = 1 \text{ whole}$$

$$1/8 - 1/8 - 1/2 - 1/16 - 1/16 - 1/16 - 1/16$$

$$2/8 + 1/2 + 4/16 = 1 \text{ whole}$$

Jan. 13 –

When we do mental computation
all the problems are differant
and since their all differant
some are easy and some are
diffecult The ones that are
hard for me I don't always
do them. I just wait until
I see other peopl do it then
I relize how easy they really
are.

Jan 17 – I don't really think I've made
any progress I've just stayed
the same. I like it but I can't
find a better way to do the →

Figure 9.33. A series of Shelli's learning log entries. Her descriptions of mental computation corroborate my observation that proficiency with paper-and-pencil algorithms seems to inhibit children's ability to use relationships to solve problems using mental computation.

Math L.L.   *Shelli*

problems. I just do them the way I was tought. Like this:

The more you try, listen and watch, the more you will learn. Maybe, challenge yourself to use a new method once and awhile — And jump in & work on the tough ones! "a partly solved problem is better than no solution at all."

25
× 13
‾‾‾‾
75
+ 350
‾‾‾‾‾
answer = 425

This is a good way!

Shelli, This works for you when you're using paper + pencil, but it's a hard way to do mental computation.

1/24

1. $3/4 + 6/16 + 1/8 = 1$ (T) or F
2. $4/16 + 1/4 + 1/2 = 1$ (T) or F
3. $1/4 + 1/8 + 1/16 = 1/2$ T or (F)
4. $3/8 + 2/16 + 8/32 + 1/4 = 3/4$ T or (F)
5. $1/8 + 1/8 + 1/2 + 1/2 + 1/2 = 1 3/4$ T or (F)
6. $6/32 + 4/32 =$ T or F

3/2

The Length of our room might be 10 meters and the width might be 7 meters. and the hight 4 1/2 meters

Figure 9.33   (continued).

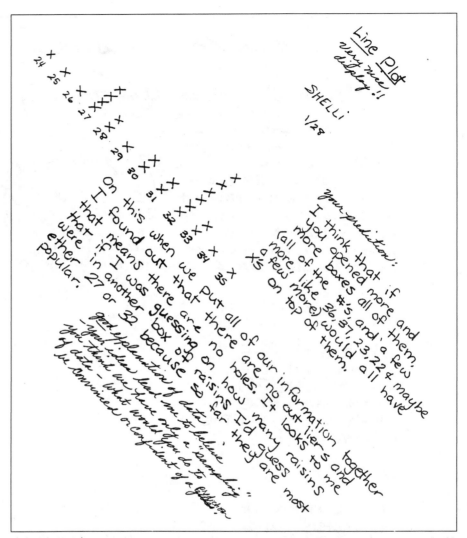

Figure 9.34. Shelli's statistics entry on the number of raisins in one-half-ounce boxes.

196

Math L.L.   SHELLI

3/23-

1   Do you think the rat should have babies?
2   Should we lower Sales Tax prices?
3   Should we try harder to get rid of Sadom Husain?
4   Should we put more money up for finding a cure for aids?
5   Should they serve better food in the cafiteria?
6   Should we start school at 8:30 and get out at 3:00?
7   Should we elemenate daylight savings time?

                    Should We Elemenate DayLight?
                                    SAVINGS OF TIME
3/26-   Our group didn't make a plan so we
just started asking questions. But when we
came to Mrs. Young she made us think
about our question and now we might
even change our question. Everybody
didn't think about our question exept
Mrs. Youngy and she asked some questions
like ~~~~~ "does this question have any
importance?" and, "do you know ~~~~ why
we have Day Light Savings Time?"
We didn't know.
        I thougt this was a good idea
but now that Mrs. Young made me
think about it.   SHELLI

Figure 9.35. Another series of Shelli's learning log entries, offering her reflections on her progress during a multiday statistical investigation.

197

Should We start School at 8:30 and get
out at 3:00?

3/27 – Today we started a new question as a
trial. Our question was Should We Start
School At 8:30 and Get out At 3:00?
I called it a trial question because our
group agreed to use this question if
we got results that were mixed. I didn't
get to mixed answers exept 1. That was
a didn't care. I think that person
said he didn't care because he
was busy talking about something else.
The next time we get together ⌃ I ~~can't~~
~~it~~ we should ~~z~~ anilize our data. Right now
I'm not sure if Id want A keep
this question.

3/30 We didn't do much today exept
we answered other peoples
questions. we agreed that we
needed a new question but we
didn't think of one.
The next time we meet
we'll think of a new question.

3/51 – ① What time do you go to bed?
② Should you get allowence for
chores or just being part of the
family?
③ ~~How~~ much allowence do you
get?
Today we didn't have a question
so we asked Mrs. Young for some
help. She made us think of some
quistions we could ask and we liked 2

Figure 9.35 (continued).

198

(Statistics cont.) MATH L.L.   SHELLI

of them. What time do you go to bed and do you think you should get allowence just for being in a family or for doing chores. I didn't want one of them but my ~~person~~ wanted the one I didn't. We decided to partoners one (the one they wanted) and if half the class has the same answer we'll try the other one.

4/3—

1. Yesterday I started asking people my question and today I finished asking. Now I'm putting my data on a chart.

2. I had 1 problem. Some people didn't fill-out my paper the way I wanted but that might have been my fault for not explaining it very well.

3. Now I would tell people more about how to fill out my papers for sensetive data.

4. It vary from school days to weekends. I had to tell people to do it on the time of a school day.

5. I had 2 parteners and we had to seperate because we all had to do differant things at differant times.

Grades: Task   I   Process   ✓

Figure 9.35 (continued).

TASK "How Much Taller..."	Group Process

4	I, (we) fully achieved the purpose of the task, including thoughtful, insightful interpretations and making conjectures. I, (we) raised interesting or provocative questions. I, (we) communicated our ideas and findings well. I, (we) went beyond what was expected.	We used all of our time productively. Everyone was involved and contributed to the group process and product. Problems didn't deter us. We listened to each other's ideas and other groups' ideas and built on those ideas.	4
3	I, (we) accomplished the task and communicated our findings effectively. I, (we) understood the task and learned from it. I, (we) worked persistently to overcome problems I, (we) encountered. *Effective display; easy to read. More specific comments on the height of 1st and 5th graders would have improved your product. Contrasting colors would have made comparisons easier to see on the line plot.*	We worked well together most of the time. We were pretty good at listening to and using each other's and other groups' ideas. We worked together to overcome problems we encountered.	3
2	I, (we) completed most of the assignment and communicated our ideas and findings.	We worked together some of the time. Not everyone contributed equal effort to the task. We might have worked more productively as a group.	2
1	I, (we) did not accomplish our task. I, (we) didn't finish the investigation and/or weren't able to communicate our ideas very well.	We really didn't pull together or work very productively as a group. Not everybody contributed to the group effort. Some people did more work than others or else nobody worked very well as a group.	1

Figure 9.36. A rubric evaluating a group task in which Shelli participated as a group member.

Math Cover Letter

Shelli
June 5, 92

I chose my number bracelets tasks because I improved them inbetween menus. With Rachael help, I did all 100 bracelets. (Rachael did 50 & I did 50.)

This piece shows that if take the time I can do a better job on a project. I took more time to improve on my summary statement and the way I did my paper like how I aranged it and kept track of how many bracelets I had done and how many I had to do.

I think I took to much time on it because I didn't get anything else done in my menu. But I think I needed to do it with that much time because Its an involving task.

Shelli

Figure 9.37. Shelli's June cover letter indicates that she has learned to value her own persistence in investigating complex problems. She justifies this and seems less concerned that she was unable to complete other tasks on the menu.

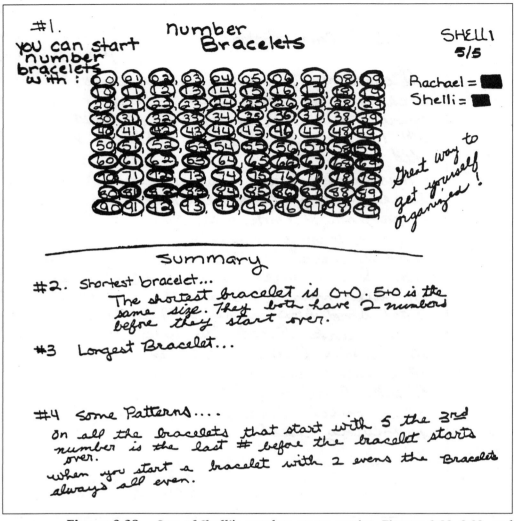

#1.
you can start number bracelets with:

number Bracelets

SHELLI
5/5

Rachael = ■
Shelli = ■

Great way to get yourself organized!

Summary

#2. Shortest bracelet...
The shortest bracelet is 0+0. 5+0 is the same size. They both have 2 numbers before they start over.

#3 Longest Bracelet...

#4 Some Patterns....
On all the bracelets that start with 5 the 3rd number is the last # before the bracelet starts over.
when you start a bracelet with 2 evens the Bracelet always's all even.

Figure 9.38. One of Shelli's number menu entries. Figures 9.38, 9.39, and 9.40 show Shelli's work on number bracelets. It is clear that she was challenged by and engaged in the task.

Number Bracelets   Shelli
                                           5/5

1) 01123583145943707741561785381909987529 10/
2) 03369549325729101123583145943707741561785 38
   19099875279651673 0/
3) 0550/
4) 07741561785381909987527965167303369549325 72
   910112358344594370/
5) 0886404482022460662 80/
6) 12358314594370774156178538190998752796516 7
   30336954932572910110/
7) 145943707741561785381909987527965167303369
   549325729101123583 1/
8) 21347189763 92/
9) 2358314594370774156178538190998752796516
   7303369549325729101 12/
10) 25729101123583145943707741561785381909987 5
    279549 32/
11) 26842/
12) 279651673033695493257291011235831459 43
    7077415617 853819099875 2/
13) 280886404482022460662/
14) 291011235831459437077415617853819099875 27
    96516730336954932572/
15) 32572910112358314594370774156178538190998
    75279651672033695493/
16) 347189763 9213/
17) 35831459437077415617 853819099875279651 67
    3033695493257291011 23/
18) 3819099875279651673033695493257291011 23
    583145943707741561785 3/
19) 41561785381909987529101123583145943707 7
    4/
20) 4370774156178538190998752910112358314
    594/
21) 448202246066280886 4044/
22) 471897639 2134/
23) 493257291011235831459437077415617853819
    099875279651673 03369 54/
24) 505/
25) 527965167303369549325729101123583145 943
    70774156178538190998 75/
26) 549325729101123583145943707741561785381 90
    998752796516730 33695/

Figure 9.39. Shelli's number bracelets. These exercises are an example of
opportunities for children to practice arithmetic drill in the context of solving
problems that also ask them to think and reason and search for patterns and
relationships.

203

27) 561178538190998752796516730336954932257
29101123583145943707741S/
28) 57291011235831459437077415617853819099875
27965167303369549325/
29) 640448202246066280886/
30) 65167303369549325729101123583145943707741
56178538190998752796/
31) 718976392137/
32) 730336954932572910112358314594370774156178
53819099875279565167/
33) 763921347897/
34) 796516730336954932572910112358314594370774I
561785381909987527/
35) 808864044820224606628/
36) 85381909987527965167303369549325729101/23
583145943707741156178/
37) 886404482808/
38) 910112358314594370774156178538190998752796
5167303369549325729/
39) 932572910112358314594370774156178538190999
8752796516730336954/
40) 954932572910112358314594370774156178538I9
09987527965167303369/
41) 97639213471897189/
42) 5943707741561178538190998752796516730336954
93257291011235834S/
43) 774156178538190998752796516730336954932257
910112358314594370/
44) 819099875279651673033695493257291010123583145
943707741561178538/
45) 820224606628086404448/
46) 83145943707741561785381909987527965167303369
549325729101I2358/
47) 864044820224606628088/
48) 909987527965167303369549325572910112-3583145
9437077415617853819/
49) 92134718976397
50) 94370774156117853831459/

Number Bracelets   3/17/92

1 93257291011235831459437077415617 8
5381909987 5/2910112358314594370741 7
85381909987 5/291011

2 12358314594370774156178538190998752 0
22460662808864044 8/2 02246066280886 4
044 8/2 02246

Longest   60   ← these numbers mix themselves up.

3 5617 (853) 81909987527965167303369549
32572910112 (358) 3145943707741/5617853
81909987527965167303369549325729101123
5831459437077741/561785

4 741561785381909987527965167303369280886
4044820224606 4/28088640448202246066/28
0886

Shortest   12
5 897639213471/897639213471/897639

Longest   60
6 4156178538190998752796516730336954932 5
7291042358314594370777/41561785381909987 52
7965167303369549325729101123583145943 70
77/415617

I LIKED THIS PROJECT BECAUSE I LIKE TO
FIND PATTERNS AND I LIKE ADDING.
    I NOTICED THAT THE NUMBERS SEEMED
TO MIX THEMSELVES UP. LIKE THIS: ONCE THE
NUMBERS 60 853 THEN THEY CHANGE TO 358.
    I'M NOT SURE WHY SOME ARE LONGER THAN OTHERS BUT
AT FIRST I THOUGHT IT MIGHT HAVE HAD SOME-
THING TO DO WITH THE NUMBERS YOU CHOOSE IN
THE BIGINNING.   IT DIDN'T.

This shows Evidence of lots of work & thought!

(4)₃

Figure 9.40.   More number bracelets.

To start a number braclet here are all
the possible ways: 0-0 0-1 0-$\overset{2}{2}$ 0-$\overset{3}{3}$ 0$\overset{4}{4}$ 0$\overset{5}{4}$
0$\overset{6}{5}$ 0$\overset{7}{6}$ 0$\overset{8}{7}$ 0-8 0$\overset{10}{9}$ 1-$\overset{11}{1}$ 1-$\overset{12}{2}$ 1-$\overset{13}{3}$ 1-$\overset{14}{4}$ 1-$\overset{15}{5}$ 1-$\overset{16}{6}$
1$\overset{17}{7}$ 1$\overset{18}{8}$ 1$\overset{19}{9}$ 2$\overset{2}{2}$ 2$\overset{21}{3}$ 2$\overset{22}{4}$ 2-5 2$\overset{24}{6}$ 2$\overset{25}{7}$ 2$\overset{26}{8}$
2$\overset{27}{9}$ 3$\overset{28}{3}$ 3-4 3$\overset{30}{5}$ 3$\overset{31}{6}$ 3$\overset{32}{7}$ 3$\overset{33}{8}$ 3$\overset{34}{9}$ 4$\overset{35}{4}$ 4$\overset{36}{5}$
4$\overset{37}{6}$ 4$\overset{38}{7}$ 4-8 4$\overset{40}{9}$ 5$\overset{41}{5}$ 5-6 5$\overset{43}{7}$ 5$\overset{44}{8}$ 5$\overset{45}{9}$
6-6 6$\overset{47}{7}$ 6$\overset{48}{8}$ 6$\overset{49}{9}$ 7$\overset{50}{7}$ 7$\overset{51}{8}$ 7$\overset{52}{9}$ 8-8 8$\overset{54}{9}$ 9$\overset{55}{9}$
      55 ways to start a bracelet.

The shortest number bracelet I found
was the one that started with
8 and 7. That one had 12 numbers
befor I found the pattern.

The longest number bracelet I found
was the one that started with 5 and 6.
I found another bracelet that had
the same amount of numbers. It
started with 7 and 2. They both had
60

I found a pattern that whenever
you start a number bracelet with
an odd and an even the pattern
goes, odd, odd, even, odd, odd, even,
odd, odd, even, etc. It's also like
that when you start with 2 odds.

4606628086404482022/46066
When you start a bracelet with 2 evens
all the numbers a even.

Figure 9.40 (continued).

206

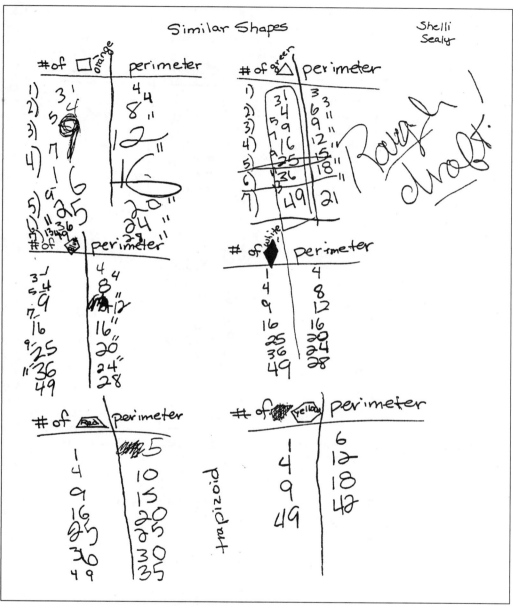

Figure 9.41. Shelli's rough draft of her similar shapes entry. Children used pattern blocks to build similar shapes and kept track of any patterns or relationships they discovered.

Similar Shapes

SHELLI SEALY

# of ▢	perimeter
3 — 1	4 — 4
5 — 4	8 — 4
7 — 9	12 — 4
9 — 16	16 — 4
11 — 25	20 — 4
13 — 36	24 — 4
49	28

# of △	perimeter
3 — 1	3 — 3
5 — 4	6 — 3
7 — 9	9 — 3
9 — 16	12 — 3
11 — 25	15 — 3
13 — 36	18 — 3
49	21

# of ◇	perimeter
3 — 1	4 — 4
5 — 4	8 — 4
7 — 9	12 — 4
9 — 16	16 — 4
11 — 25	20 — 4
13 — 36	24 — 4
49	28

# of ◊	perimeter
3 — 1	4 — 4
5 — 4	8 — 4
7 — 9	12 — 4
9 — 16	16 — 4
11 — 25	20 — 4
13 — 36	24 — 4
49	28

# of ▱	perimeter	
3 — 1	5	
5 — 4	10	
7 — 9	15	
9 — 16	20	counting
11 — 25	25	By
13 — 36	30	5's
49	35	

# of ⬡	perimeter
1	6
4	12
9	18
(messed up) ↓	(messed up) ↓

Figure 9.42. Shelli's refined similar shapes entry. She did not feel she had adequate time to complete this investigation.

> I wish I had had more time!
> I really would have liked to
> finish and if I had had a lot
> more time I would have gone
> back and do all the harder
> math blocks over again.
> I didn't get finish the
> yellow one. (the hexagon)

Figure 9.42 (continued).

Reflections

Going into Cathy's classroom after twelve years spent working to re-define mathematics education at the university, state, and national lev-els, I had a myriad of questions about children, mathematics, and teacher decision making in a mathematics classroom. This chapter deals with (1) how content decisions were made, (2) how the children's understanding of number was developed, (3) what it means to teach mathematics in ways responsive to children, (4) meeting the needs of *all* children in a self-contained classroom, and (5) traditional beliefs and practices that Cathy had to reexamine in working to align her teaching with the NCTM *Standards*. The chapter concludes with a discussion of the kinds of support Cathy and other teachers will need as they work to make their mathematics programs more meaningful.

Decisions About What Mathematics to Teach and How to Teach It

Data collection and analysis, geometry, patterns and functional relation-ships, measurement, logic, number theory, and number sense were not integrated into an existing curriculum in Cathy's classroom. Rather, they became the core of the curriculum. The strands of mathematics and the connections linking mathematical ideas within and among the strands were the basis for all our decisions regarding mathematics instruction. The NCTM *Standards* (1989) and California's *Mathematics Model Curriculum Guide* (1987) also provided guidance as we planned instruction around the important mathematical ideas identified within those documents.

Teaching mathematics in this new way meant giving up the textbook. There is no way to develop mathematical power through the primary use of textbooks that continue to focus on skills taught in isolation. We did find the curriculum replacement units *Seeing Fractions* (CDE 1991) and *Used Numbers: The Shape of the Data* (Russell and Corwin 1989) consistent with reform goals. Cathy felt that both resources were very accessible, helping educate her about mathematics while providing children with relevant mathematical experiences. Additional resources are currently being developed in many parts of the country with the support of the National Science Foundation and other educational organizations. As these become available, classroom teachers will have more materials to choose from that can support their efforts at mathematics reform.

Our lessons were geared toward involving children in meaningful mathematical investigations. Wanting children's work in mathematics to mirror the work of real mathematicians, we purposefully provided problems and situations that were "messy" and "ill defined." (For example, we opened up the lesson on building a scale model of the room to include messy raw data and asked the children to solve complex problems.) Children had ongoing opportunities to "do" mathematics: to conjecture, invent, play, discover, represent, apply, prove, experiment, and communicate.

Children Inventing Algorithms

Throughout the course of the study we gave students problems to solve and watched to see how they solved them. Children repeatedly invented procedures for dealing with mathematical ideas such as percent, fractions, division, and multiplication without formal instruction. They invented diverse algorithms that were based on relationships within and among numbers, and they were able to articulate these algorithms to others.

One interesting finding was that some of the children most proficient with paper-and-pencil algorithms were not successful at the more difficult mental computation problems. Several of these students continued to rely on the standard algorithms although they were unable to keep track of the isolated symbols and unable to solve the problems that other children solved easily with their invented procedures. If it is true that proficiency with paper-and-pencil algorithms can interfere with children's ability to compute mentally and if mental arithmetic is becoming increasingly important while paper-and-pencil skills are becoming less useful, the implications for future mathematics instruction are serious indeed. This is an area requiring further research.

What Does It Mean to Teach in Ways Responsive to Children?

Cathy and I wanted to teach mathematics in ways that were responsive to the understanding and interests the children revealed. This meant that although we were purposeful in planning for instruction, we needed to be flexible. Our ongoing instructional decisions were responsive to children's emergent interests and understanding. We assigned complex tasks, watched to see what children were able to do, and adjusted our plans accordingly. For example, in the process of determining how much taller a typical fifth grader is than a typical first grader, our students demonstrated that they did not fully understand measurement or the precision it required; we therefore decided to introduce a unit on scale modeling as a context for measuring and for developing their understandings about measurement. When children were unable to provide mathematical arguments to support their ideas about fractions of geometric shapes, we interrupted the *Seeing Fractions* unit to explore area on the geoboard. When in the middle of a planned six-week unit on data collection and analysis it became evident that the students needed a change of pace, we shifted directions, then returned to the unit at a later date. We provided menu experiences in which children made choices, thus allowing us to observe individual interests and understandings. Teaching in ways that were responsive to children meant that we often had to be less concerned about meeting our preestablished agenda and more concerned about meeting the ever-emergent needs and interests of the children.

Meeting the Needs of All Children

We continually asked ourselves whether we were meeting the needs of all the children. High achievers were using our open-ended problems to take the mathematics involved to levels we could not have predicted ahead of time. Michael's work with dividing square and triangular regions into fractional parts, for example, provided a real challenge to us and to other students. These "high-end" children clearly benefited from our attempts to teach mathematics, not just arithmetic. Several children who had not previously been identified as "gifted" displayed surprising talent in mathematics, consistently outperforming the two children who *had* been identified for the district's gifted program. Cathy often remarked about how current practices for identifying children for the gifted program often fail to identify children who are truly and diversely gifted.

Determining whether the needs of low achievers were being met was more difficult. We will adapt our future efforts so that they will better meet these children's individual needs. But many things about the program supported them. We provided open-ended tasks that could be experienced at a variety of levels. For example, all the children were engaged in measuring and constructing the scale models of the classroom. All had opportunities to refine their measurement skills even though only some were able to use proportional reasoning in determining the similarity and/or congruence of the models or report findings in fractions of an inch or use decimals in dealing with meters. Our job as teachers was to provide lessons that had the potential for all children to learn. It was not to expect that all children would learn the same thing from the same experience.

Through work in collaborative groups, children were able to hear the thinking going on around them. They were not left to work in isolation. As individuals and groups invented and communicated diverse approaches and solutions to problems, children benefited from hearing more than one way to approach and solve problems.

Because children were actively involved in "doing" mathematics, we were able to observe their misunderstandings and respond accordingly. When children failed to grasp an important idea, we were able to provide experiences over time that would help them develop their understanding. Important ideas were not addressed for two days and then abandoned, as they are in many textbooks. Rather, children were immersed in multiday and multiweek units of study designed around important mathematical ideas.

By teaching mathematics rather than the traditional arithmetic curriculum, many "low achievers" were able to find areas of mathematical strength. Steven, who had spent years in special education classes, continued to struggle with computation but found he had real talent when it came to spatial relationships and measurement. Ray, who came to us convinced that he was "no good at math," learned that he loved to do statistical investigations and to explore fractions in the context of geometry. Cathy's comment when discussing report cards in February is illustrative:

> Let's see. Who else? Ray. I think Ray has made terrific progress this year. It's remarkable. That last thing he did with the triangle I think was a triumph for him. And I think that was really important because he finally did something that was even better than a lot of other people in the class. And usually he's the one who can't do things. At least that has been his experience in previous years and it's his image of himself. I remember how angry he was at the beginning of the year and how he isolated himself from everyone. He's really changed. He has much more self-control now, and he gets along with lots of kids.

By experiencing mathematics, not just arithmetic, children were able to recognize their different areas of strength and interest. The same children were not always the "low kids." Children learned that they all brought unique strengths and weaknesses to varied situations.

The menu technique we used also provided support for all children. They not only were able to make choices and pursue their own thinking on their own timeline while working on a menu, but they also learned to work independently of the teacher, providing time for Cathy to meet the needs of individuals or small groups. Cathy will provide more menu experiences in the future for just this reason.

And there are other things we can suggest strengthening so that the needs of all children will be better met: Implement portfolios from the beginning of the year so that children have opportunities to reflect on their past work and their own progress. Make better use of math learning logs. Continue to develop rubrics that better communicate what good performance in mathematics is. But, on the whole, we felt our mathematics program supported all children's development of mathematical power to a much greater extent than a traditional curriculum has.

We found that practices that align with the NCTM *Standards* and other reform efforts are the very practices that help the individual child succeed: surrounding children with models for doing and thinking about mathematics; providing open-ended problems in context; probing for and valuing diversity; writing and talking about learning; designing units that will develop understanding over time; offering experiences across the breadth of mathematics; using mathematical reasoning and logic to validate ideas; and being part of a collaborative community of learners are all essential practices that support the development of mathematical power.

Beliefs and Practices
That Inhibit Restructuring Efforts

As Cathy worked to restructure her mathematics program, she frequently had to reexamine her beliefs. At times they acted as barriers to change. Some of the barriers Cathy faced are:

1. *Old beliefs about what is important in mathematics.* In order to teach in ways aligned with the *Standards,* Cathy had to let go of her previously held belief that her main responsibility was to ensure that children were proficient at paper-and-pencil computation skills, particularly in the areas of fractions and long division, the mainstays of her previous curriculum. She had to overcome her fear of how her students would perform on standardized tests and whether they would be expected and able to do long division.

2. *Structuring children's thinking.* Like Cathy, many teachers feel their job in mathematics is to help children learn correct procedures for specific kinds of problems. They learn that the way to do this is to teach procedures and then observe as children practice them. Even popular new mathematics materials often structure potentially rich and engaging tasks so that children are doing little more than filling in creative forms and charts. The real thinking is done ahead of time by some adult(s). Cathy had to learn the value to children of confronting messy situations. She had to view her role as helping children develop persistence and mathematical thinking in order to make sense of such situations. Her job was to learn to value and encourage diversity in children's thinking and approaches. She had to ask herself, "Who's doing the thinking here?" Cathy was often uncomfortable when I asked children to make sense of mathematical situations that she herself didn't know how to make sense of. She understood the value of doing this and was continually impressed by the children's mathematical reasoning, but her lack of confidence in mathematics often inhibited her ability to challenge children mathematically.

3. *The fear that some children won't "get it."* Numerous times throughout the year Cathy was aware that some of the children didn't understand the ideas we were studying. Her tendency was to say, "This doesn't make sense," and to want to go back to something more familiar. She needed frequent reminders that important mathematical ideas develop over time and that all children shouldn't be expected to get the same thing from the same experience. It is important to mathematics reform efforts for teachers to learn that confusion, rather than something to be avoided, can be a valuable and necessary part of the process of learning. Our desire to intervene and "fix" children's erroneous thinking is well ingrained. We need to reexamine this practice and learn instead to provide ongoing opportunities for children to confront their incomplete understandings and actively construct new understandings. Our "fix-it" efforts all too often close down the process so that children no longer have opportunities to invent wonderful ideas.

4. *Confusing children's ability to do procedures with understanding.* In mathematics, memorizing rote procedures and understanding the concepts behind the procedures have little in common. Children's proficiency with algorithms and procedures often masks fundamental misunderstanding. National and international assessments continue to suggest that students in the United States are proficient at computation yet unable to use those skills to solve problems (Dossey 1988). As mentioned previously, some of the children in this study who seemed most proficient with algorithmic procedures showed little understanding of number relationships and were unable to solve new problems. Cathy knew that in teaching for understanding she also needed to move beyond current assessment methods that focus on proficiency with isolated computation skills.

5. *Current assessment practices.* The traditional practice of teaching a skill and testing for mastery is inconsistent with the notion of providing ongoing opportunities for children to construct their understanding of important mathematical ideas over time. Cathy sometimes worried when children didn't immediately demonstrate an understanding of mathematical ideas. She came to realize that children need many and diverse opportunities to encounter important mathematical ideas.

District standardized tests also were barriers to Cathy's restructuring efforts. She worried about how students would perform on district tests and middle school placement tests that focused primarily on paper-and-pencil computation. She knew that assessment practices should align with instructional goals and that these current practices did not support her goals for children as mathematicians.

Cathy and I worked to implement performance-based assessment in mathematics using (1) observations, (2) learning logs, (3) rubrics, and (4) student-selected portfolios. Over time Cathy was able to integrate assessment with instruction. Children as well as teacher took responsibility for assessing growth in understanding.

By April, Cathy had not given any tests. This was a major change for her. At times she worried that she didn't know enough about her students and what they could do. At other times she said she knew these students better than any of her previous classes. Her knowledge of and experience with the "essential understandings" throughout the strands were tentative. In previous years, when her program consisted primarily of arithmetic, Cathy knew all the skills she was responsible for assessing. In teaching this expanded version of mathematics, she struggled to identify what it was she should be assessing. This is not surprising, and it is an issue currently being addressed within the professional mathematics community. National leaders in mathematics education are struggling to define the very assessment issues Cathy grappled with in her classroom.

Assessment direction needs to be forthcoming from the mathematics community if teachers like Cathy are to align their curriculum and instruction with mathematics reform goals. It is unfair to expect Cathy to teach mathematics if she continues to be held accountable primarily for children's proficiency with arithmetic skills.

6. *Viewing the teacher as the locus of control.* If our goal is to promote knowledgeable, thoughtful, and responsible decision making, then children must have opportunities to take responsibility for their actions and their learning. When decisions are not made responsibly, children need to be able to reflect on those decisions and to consider alternatives. Much effort, early in the year, was devoted to giving the students responsibility for decisions and solutions. Cathy played an important role in helping children learn to be reflective, to consider various viewpoints in coming to decisions, and to take responsibility for their behavior. She provided an environment in which children made choices and were asked to reflect on their learning and their actions and interactions with others. And it was not only we who observed growth in the students' interactions with each other and the environment; substitute teachers consistently commented on the work ethic in the classroom and on how responsible and helpful the class was.

7. *The teacher as validator of ideas and answers.* In order to create a classroom environment in which children act as a community of learners, they must be encouraged to challenge and extend one another's thinking and to use mathematical evidence, logic, and mathematical reasoning to validate ideas rather than look to the authority of the teacher or answer book. Children quickly accepted that Cathy and I were not going to give answers to problems. They learned to question, challenge, and extend one another's ideas. Learning to ask appropriate questions proved challenging as Cathy worked to change her role in the mathematics classroom. The processing-type questions identified in the introduction to *Professional Standards for Teaching Mathematics* (NCTM 1990) provided guidance as she worked to help children learn to listen to and challenge one another's thinking.

  8. *External manipulation through praise and rewards.* If our goal is to control children's behavior, such external rewards may work in the short run. But if our goal is to have children learn to control their own behavior and take responsibility for their learning, then practices that have the potential to interfere with those goals must be reexamined. Several educational researchers suggest that praise and rewards can have a debilitating effect on learning, creativity, and behavior (Curwin and Mendler 1988; Dreikurs 1953; Kohn 1986). Cathy had to reexamine her practices of providing praise both orally and in written responses. Her former practice of dispensing points and related rewards for groups and individuals no longer seemed appropriate. These practices convey that the teacher will take responsibility for children's behavior and learning. As such, they did not support Cathy's goals for children. Cathy decided to stop using external rewards. She worked to replace comments that indicated praise with words of encouragement and questions that challenged the children's thinking. The reward of being intellectually challenged by the mathematics and by one another proved far more productive, as children stretched themselves mathematically in ways we would never have imagined possible. Extrinsic rewards were neither provided nor needed.

Support for Teachers

Numerous times throughout the year, Cathy commented that she didn't really understand the math the children were doing. Thus she was often unable to respond to or build on the children's mathematical ideas. She sometimes found herself frustrated and wanting to return to something more comfortable. Her confidence in my understanding of the mathematics, the ongoing support I provided, her recognition of her own fear and dislike of the mathematics she had been taught, and her realization that this way of teaching mathematics aligned with her own philosophical goals for children combined to give her courage to continue to discard old practices in favor of new.

Cathy readily admits that had she not had this ongoing support, she would still be trying creative but safe lessons as "enriching" supplements to her textbook curriculum.

Teachers can only teach powerful mathematics when they have had opportunities over time to develop their own mathematical understandings and to experience for themselves the usefulness and beauty of mathematics. This has clear implications for the professional development of mathematics teachers. Even for teachers, mathematical understandings are constructed over time as the result of numerous encounters with mathematical ideas in context. Such long-term support is rarely provided. Preservice and inservice courses must be redesigned to provide teachers ongoing opportunities to be active learners, constructing their own understanding of important mathematical ideas and of what it means to "do" mathematics as defined by the NCTM *Standards* and other reform documents. Teaching in ways that support the development of mathematical power necessitates a comprehensive restructuring of nearly every aspect of teaching: the content of the curriculum, the learning environment, the role of the teacher, and assessment practices. Successful restructuring is likely to occur only if teachers are given intensive and ongoing support within an environment that supports risk taking.

Efforts to date have not produced very many classrooms aligned with mathematics reform goals. We need programs that support the development of teachers' understanding of mathematics and that provide ongoing support as teachers work to change their instructional practices. We need clear recognition that the challenge teachers have been given is enormous and that real change will be messy, scary, and difficult as well as challenging and exciting. We need professional communities and school environments that support risk taking and encourage change—communities that consider being a learner an important part of being a teacher.

Teachers need access to new mathematics curriculum materials— materials that truly align with the goals of the NCTM *Standards*—as soon as those materials become available. Having quality curriculum units such as *Used Numbers* and *Seeing Fractions* available made it much easier for Cathy, a teacher lacking confidence in her own understanding of mathematics, to provide meaningful mathematics instruction for her students.

The research community needs to provide more case studies that give teachers, teacher educators, and staff developers a vision of what can be: of what it means and what it takes to provide powerful mathematics programs that work for all kids.

Conclusions

Mathematics classrooms that support the development of mathematical power for all children are possible. A clear vision for mathematics education has been presented by the NCTM *Standards* and other reform documents. To attain that vision everyone involved needs to be willing to reexamine current beliefs and practices and to take risks.

We have heard numerous reports about what children in this country are not able to do in mathematics. The evidence is quite dismal. The work on which this book is based suggests that the poor mathematics performance we are seeing throughout the country is the end result of a dead-end curriculum that teaches children that mathematics is about memorizing rules and procedures and about learning isolated skills removed from any meaningful or useful context.

As members of the professional mathematics community have worked to redefine mathematics education, they have identified important mathematical ideas and concepts that must form the core of mathematics programs. It was exciting to observe how children in a fifth-grade classroom interacted with these ideas. As we worked to open up our curriculum to include the investigation of mathematical ideas across the strands and as we worked to help children experience mathematics as a powerful tool for making sense of information and situations in their world, we were able to observe children as mathematicians. They rose to the challenges provided.

Cathy and I are quite certain that we only scratched the surface of these children's potential. They repeatedly surprised us with the sophistication of their thinking about mathematics. We are confident they were capable of much more than we knew how to offer. And although we still have unanswered questions about their mathematical potential, we know with certainty that children are powerful sense makers.

■ ■ ■ References

Akers, J., W. Finzer, J. Gutierrez, and D. Resek. 1989. "Sampling." *Journal of Mathematical Behavior* 6(2):149–56.

Atwell, N. 1987. *In the middle: Writing, reading, and learning with adolescents*. Portsmouth, NH: Boynton-Cook.

Ball, D. L. 1990. "Prospective elementary and secondary teachers' understanding of division." *Journal for Research in Mathematics Education* 21(2):132–44.

Ball, D. L., and G. W. McDiarmid. 1988. "Research on teacher learning: Studying how teachers' knowledge changes." *Action in Teacher Education* 10(2):14–21.

Biggs, E. 1987a. "The central problem: Establishing change." *Journal of Mathematical Behavior* 6(2):197–99.

———. 1987b. "Understanding area." *Journal of Mathematical Behavior* 6(2):183–90.

Brown, J. S., A. Collins, and P. Duguid. 1989. "Situated cognition and the culture of learning." *Educational Researcher* 18(1):32–42.

Bulmahn, B., and D. Young. 1982. "On the transmission of mathematics anxiety." *Arithmetic Teacher* 30(11):155–56.

Burns, M. *Math solutions*. In-service courses for K–12 teachers and administrators. Sausalito, CA: Marilyn Burns Education Associates.

———. 1987. *A classroom collection of math lessons from grades 3 through 6*. Sausalito, CA: Math Solutions Publications; distributed by Cuisenaire Company of America, Inc.

———. 1992. *About teaching mathematics*. Sausalito, CA: Math Solutions Publications; distributed by Cuisenaire Company of America, Inc.

Burton, L. 1984. "Mathematical thinking: The struggle for meaning." *Journal for Research in Mathematics Education* 15(1):35–49.

California Department of Education. 1987. *Mathematics model curriculum guide: Kindergarten through grade eight*. Sacramento, CA: California Department of Education.

————. 1989. *A question of thinking: A first look at students' performance on open-ended questions in mathematics*. Sacramento, CA: California Department of Education.

————. 1991. *Seeing fractions: A unit for the upper elementary grades*. Sacramento, CA: California Department of Education.

————. In press. *Mathematics framework for California public schools: Kindergarten through grade twelve*. Sacramento, CA: California Department of Education.

Calkins, L. M. 1985. *Lessons from a child: On the teaching and learning of writing*. Portsmouth, NH: Heinemann.

Carpenter, T. P. 1988. *Teaching as problem solving*. Reston, VA: National Council of Teachers of Mathematics.

Carpenter, T. P., M. K. Corbitt, H. S. Kepner, Jr., M. M. Lindquist, and R. Reys. 1981. *Results from the second mathematics assessment of the National Assessment of Educational Progress*. Reston, VA: National Council of Teachers of Mathematics.

Chaille, C., and L. Brittain. 1991. *The young child as scientist*. New York: HarperCollins.

Cobb, P. 1985. "Mathematical actions, mathematical objects, and mathematical symbols." *Journal of Mathematical Behavior* 4(2):127–34.

————. 1989. "Experiential, cognitive, and anthropological perspectives in mathematics education." *For the Learning of Mathematics* 9(2):32–42.

Cohen, E. G. 1986. *Designing groupwork*. New York: Teachers College Press.

Curwin, R. L., and A. N. Mendler. *Discipline with dignity*. Alexandria, VA: Association for Supervision and Curriculum Development.

Davis, R. B. 1986. *Conceptual and procedural knowledge in mathematics: Summary analysis*. Hillsdale, NJ: Erlbaum.

————. 1987. "Mathematics as a performing art." *Journal of Mathematical Behavior* 7(1):157–70.

————. 1989. "The culture of mathematics and the culture of schools." *Journal of Mathematical Behavior* 8(2):143–60.

Dennett, D. C. 1980. *Brainstorms: Philosophical essays on mind and psychology*. Cambridge, MA: Bradford.

Dienes, Z. P. 1987. "Lessons involving music, language, and mathematics." *Journal of Mathematical Behavior* 6(2):171–81.

Dossey, J., I. Mullis, M. Lindquist, and D. Chambers. 1988. *The mathematics report card: Are we measuring up? (Trends in Achievement Based on the 1986 National Assessment No. 17-M-01)*. Princeton, NJ: Educational Testing Service.

Dreikurs, R. R. 1953. *Fundamentals of Adlerian psychology*. Chicago: Alfred Adler Institute.

Dubinsky, E., and P. Lewin. 1986. "Reflective abstraction and mathematics education: The genetic decomposition of induction and compactness." *Journal of Mathematical Behavior* 5(1):55–92.

Duckworth, E. 1972. "The having of wonderful ideas." *Harvard Educational Review* 42(2):217–31.

Fennema, E., and J. Sherman. 1977. "Sex-related differences in mathematics achievement, spatial visualization and affective factors." *American Educational Research Journal* 14(1):51–71.

———. 1978. "Sex-related differences in mathematics achievement and related factors: A further study." *Journal for Research in Mathematics Education* 9(2):189–203.

Ferrini-Mundy, J. 1986. "Mathematics teachers' attitudes and beliefs: Implications for inservice education." Paper presented at the annual conference of the American Educational Research Association, San Francisco.

Fraser, S. *SPACES*. 1982. Palo Alto, CA: Dale Seymour.

Fullan, M. 1982. *The meaning of educational change*. New York: Teachers College Press.

Goldenberg, P. 1989. "Seeing beauty in mathematics: Using fractal geometry to build a spirit of mathematical inquiry." *Journal of Mathematical Behavior* 8(2):169–204.

Graeber, A., D. Tirosh, and R. Glover. 1989. "Preservice teachers' misconceptions in solving verbal problems in multiplication and division." *Journal for Research in Mathematics Education* 20(1):95–102.

Graves, D. 1983. *Writing: Teachers and children at work*. Portsmouth, NH: Heinemann.

Hillary, J. 1990. "Paradigm change: More magic than logic." *Connections: Journal for Outcome Based Schools* 9(4):30–38.

Hilton, P. ed. 1981. *Avoiding math avoidance*. Mathematics tomorrow. New York: Springer-Verlag.

Holdaway, D. 1979. *The foundations of literacy*. New York: Aston Scholastic.

Hunter, M. 1976. *Improved instruction*. El Segundo, CA: TIP Publications.

Johnson, D. W., and R. Johnson. 1986. *Circles of learning*. Edina, MN: Interaction.

Johnson, M. L., and J. Ferrini-Mundy. 1989. "The mathematics education of underserved and under-represented groups: A continuing challenge." *Journal for Research in Mathematical Behavior* 20(4):371–75.

Kamii, C. 1983a. "Autonomy." *Phi Delta Kappan* 65(6):410–15.

———. 1983b. *Children reinvent arithmetic*. New York: Teachers College Press.

Kline, M. 1985. *Mathematics and the search for knowledge*. New York: Oxford University Press.

Kohn, A. 1986. *No contest: The case against competition*. Boston: Houghton Mifflin.

Koretz, D. 1988. "Arriving in Lake Wobegon: Are standardized tests exaggerating achievement and distorting instruction?" *American Educator* 12(2):8–15, 46–51.

Kouba, V. L., C. A. Brown, T. P. Carpenter, M. M. Lindquist, E. A. Silver, and J. O. Swafford. 1988. "Results of the fourth NAEP assessment of mathematics: Number, operations, and word problems." *Arithmetic Teacher* 35(8):14–19.

Kuhs, T. 1980. "Elementary school teachers' conceptions of mathematics content as a potential influence on classroom instruction." Ph.D. dissertation, Michigan State University.

Kulm, G. 1990. *Assessing higher order mathematical thinking: What we need to know*. Washington, DC: American Association for the Advancement of Science.

Lampert, M. 1985. "How do teachers manage to teach? Perspectives on problems in practice." *Harvard Educational Review* 55(2):178–94.

———. 1986. "Knowing, doing, and teaching multiplication." *Cognition and Instruction* 3(4):305–42.

Lappan, G. T., and J. Ferrini-Mundy. 1992. "Knowing and doing mathematics: A new vision for middle school students." Paper presented at the annual meeting of the American Educational Research Association, Chicago.

Lefcort, H. M. 1982. *Locus of control*. Hillsdale, NJ: Erlbaum.

———, ed. 1989. *Results from the fourth mathematics assessment of the National Assessment of Educational Progress*. Reston, VA: National Council of Teachers of Mathematics.

National Assessment of Educational Progress. 1983. *The third national mathematics assessment: Results, trends, and issues*, no. 13-M-01. Princeton, NJ: Educational Commission of the United States.

National Council of Teachers of Mathematics. 1980. *An agenda for action: Recommendations for school mathematics in the 1980s*. Reston, VA: National Council of Teachers of Mathematics.

———. 1989. *Curriculum and evaluation standards for school mathematics*. Reston, VA: National Council of Teachers of Mathematics.

————. 1991a. *Calculators and the education of youth: A position paper*. Reston, VA: National Council of Teachers of Mathematics.

————. 1991b. *Mathematics assessment myths, models, good questions, and practical suggestions*. Reston, VA: National Council of Teachers of Mathematics.

————. 1991c. *Professional standards for teaching mathematics*. Reston, VA: National Council of Teachers of Mathematics.

National Research Council. 1989. *Everybody counts: A report to the nation on the future of mathematics education*. Washington, DC: National Academy Press.

————. 1990a. *On the shoulders of giants*. Washington, DC: National Academy Press.

————. 1990b. *Reshaping school mathematics*. Washington, DC: National Academy Press.

————. 1991. *Moving beyond myths: Revitalizing undergraduate mathematics*. Washington, DC: National Academy Press.

Nelson, J. 1987. *Positive discipline*. New York: Ballantine.

Oakes, J. 1985. *Keeping track: How schools structure inequality*. New Haven, CT: Yale University Press.

————. 1990. *Multiplying inequalities: The effects of race, social class, and tracking on opportunities to learn mathematics and science*. Santa Monica, CA: Rand Corporation.

Papert, S. 1980. *Mindstorms: Children, computers, and powerful ideas*. New York: Basic.

Parker, R. E. 1991. "Implementing the curriculum and evaluation standards: What will implementation take?" *Mathematics Teacher* 84(6):442–78.

Paulos, J. A. 1988. *Innumeracy*. New York: Hill & Wang.

Peterson, P., E. Fennema, T. Carpenter, and M. Loef. 1989. "Teachers' pedagogical content beliefs in mathematics." *Cognition and Instruction* 6(1):1–40.

Piaget, J. 1963. *The origins of intelligence in children*. New York: Basic.

Polya, G. 1965. *Mathematical discovery*. New York: John Wiley & Sons.

Resnick, L. B. 1987a. *Constructing knowledge in school*. Hillsdale, NJ: Erlbaum.

————. 1987b. *Education and learning to think*. Washington, DC: National Academy Press.

Resnick, L. B., and D. Resnick. 1991. "Assessing the thinking curriculum: New tools for educational reform." In *Changing assessments: Alternative views of aptitude achievement and instruction*, ed. B. R. Gifford and M. C. O'Connor, 38–75. Boston: Kluwer.

Richardson, K. 1984. *Developing number concepts using Unifix cubes*. Palo Alto, CA: Addison-Wesley.

Romberg, T., K. Zarinnia, and A. Collins. 1990. "A new world view of assessment in mathematics." In *Assessing higher order thinking in mathematics*, ed. K. G. Kulm, 21–38. Washington, DC: American Association for the Advancement of Science.

Russell, S. J., and R. B. Corwin. 1989. *Used numbers: The shape of the data*. Palo Alto, CA: Seymour.

Schoenfeld, A. H. 1983. *Episodes and executive decisions in mathematical problem solving*. New York: Academic Press.

———. 1988. "When good teaching leads to bad results: The disasters of 'well-taught' mathematics classes." *Educational Psychologist* 23(2):145–66.

———. 1989. "Explorations of students' mathematical beliefs and behavior." *Journal for Research in Mathematics Education* 20(4):338–55.

Scholastic News. 1991. 60(2)[September]:1–4.

Secada, W. G. 1988. *Diversity, equity, and cognitivist research*. Madison: Wisconsin Center for Educational Research.

Shulman, L. S. 1986. "Those who understand: Knowledge growth in teaching." *Educational Researcher* 15(2):4–14.

Slavin, R. 1983. *Cooperative learning*. New York: Longman.

Sowder, J. T. 1990. "Mental computation and number sense." *Arithmetic Teacher* 38(3):18–20.

Sowder, J. T., and M. M. Wheeler. 1989. "The development of concepts and strategies used in computational estimation." *Journal for Research in Mathematics Education* 20(2):130–46.

Stein, L. A. 1989. "Teaching mathematics for tomorrow's world." *Educational Leadership* 47(1):18–22.

Steinberg, R., J. Haymore, and R. Marks. 1985. "Teachers' knowledge and content structuring in mathematics." Paper presented at the annual meeting of the American Educational Research Association, Chicago.

Stenmark, J. K. 1989. *Assessment alternatives in mathematics: An overview of assessment techniques that promote learning*. Berkeley, CA: Lawrence Hall of Science.

Thompson, A. 1984. "The relationship of teachers' conceptions of mathematics and mathematics teaching to instructional practice." *Educational Studies in Mathematics* 15(1):105–27.

Tobias, S. 1978. *Overcoming math anxiety*. New York: W. W. Norton.

Trafton, P. R. 1086. *Teaching and computational estimation: Establishing an estimation mind-set*. Reston, VA: National Council of Teachers of Mathematics.

Walter, M., and S. Brown. 1983. *The art of problem posing*. Hillsdale, NJ: Erlbaum.

Wiggins, G. 1989a. "The futility of trying to teach everything of importance." *Educational Leadership* 47(3):44–49.

———. 1989b. "A true test: Toward authentic and equitable assessment." *Phi Delta Kappan* 70(9):703–13.

Willoughby, S. 1983. "Mathematics for the 21st century." *Educational Leadership* 41(4):45–50.